Deconstructing
Tyrone

DATE DUE

DATE DUE
08 10 09

DEMCO 128-8155

Deconstructing
Tyrone.

*A New Look at Black Masculinity
in the Hip-Hop Generation*

by NATALIE HOPKINSON
and NATALIE Y. MOORE

CLEIS
PRESS

305.38
HoP

Published in the United States by Cleis Press Inc., P.O. Box 14697, San Francisco, California 94114.

Printed in the United States.
Cover design: Scott Idleman
Cover photograph: Eric Glenn/Getty
Photograph of Natalie Y. Moore by Regina Boone
Photograph of Natalie Hopkinson by Marvin Joseph
Book design: Karen Quigg
Cleis Press logo art: Juana Alicia
First Edition.
10 9 8 7 6 5 4 3 2 1

Library of Congress Cataloging-in-Publication Data

Hopkinson, Natalie.
    Deconstructing Tyrone : a new look at black masculinity in the hip-hop generation / by Natalie Hopkinson and Natalie Y. Moore. — 1st ed.
         p. cm.
      ISBN-13: 978-1-57344-257-2 (pbk. : alk. paper)
      ISBN-10: 1-57344-257-7 (pbk. : alk. paper)
1. African American men—Psychology. 2. Sex role—United States. 3. Masculinity—United States. I. Moore, Natalie Y. II. Title.
E185.86.H748 2006
305.38'896073—dc22
                              2006018067

Acknowledgments

THANKS TO THE WHOLE HOPKINSON CLAN: Serena, Terrence, Michael, Denise and Nicole Rose, my grandmothers Christina Baird and Gertrude Henry Hopkinson. All of the McGanns, especially my mother-in-law, Beverley McGann, for taking such wonderful care of my children while we hashed out the manuscript, and Hal McGann, for the URL. The Ajabu family. Allison Brown and Derek Andrews. Ann and Angie Brown for the couch in Indy. The Moores of Chicago. The incomparable DJ Renegade, for your characteristically blunt editing suggestions, ditto Chana O. Garcia and Tina Beyene. Simba Sana and Sunny Sumter-Sana, Katrina Pratt, Kelli E. Daniels, Yolanda Young, Sam McLemore and James Braithwaite, Glynn Jackson, "Damon," Etan Thomas and Jessica Care Moore-Poole. My brother-in-love Ben Rose for the couch in ATL. All who came out for the Tyrone Happy Hour. Daniel Illori Cooper, Celo Gill, Lorenzo McCrae and Nancy Brown, Clint and Lauryl Jackson, Tonita Ross and Mustafa Dozier, Rhome Anderson, Reshma Sinanan, Autumn Saxton-Ross, Darrell and Pam Fogan. Ron Stodghill. My *Washington Post* colleagues and mentors: Lynn Medford, Kevin Merida, Lonnae O'Neal Parker, Deb Heard, Teresa Wiltz, Milton Coleman, Hamil Harris, DeNeen Brown, Marcia Davis, Jabari Asim, Tracey Reeves Lumpkin, Dorothy Gilliam, Lisa Frazier Page, Alexa Steele, Nicole Arthur, Gene Robinson, and Len Downie. My University of Maryland friends and colleagues, especially Chris Callahan and Tom Kunkel for the warm welcome to academia, and Dr. Carolina Robertson and Dr. Carol Rogers for their most timely introduction to social constructionism and the world of qualitative research. Dystel & Goderich Literary Management for advice on the first proposal. Cleis, for "getting" us and making it happen. Nat M.—thanks for inviting me on this incredible journey. Thanks to my children, Maverick and Maven, who motivate me to keep elevating my game. Last and the most, I would like to thank my husband, Rudy McGann, my partner in all things. — *Natalie Hopkinson*

THANKS TO MY PARENTS YVONNE AND JOE for putting up with my creative quirks and providing me the gift of exposure. Thanks to my siblings, Joey and Megan, for their humor and no-nonsense feedback on all matters. I thank my family for their enthusiasm and support: Norman, Aunt Martha, Aunt Joyce and Maya, Afi Scruggs, Tracey Austin, the Goodwins, the Moores and Kennebrew-Perkins. Thanks to my adopted Hopkinson/McGann extended family. Many thanks to people who read a draft, offered input, or helped somehow along this journey: Tamaria Dewdney (our wonderful intern), Ron Stodghill, Chana O. Garcia, E. Ethelbert Miller, Roz Bentley and Kristina Torres, Charese Woods, Aida Strom and Nancy Smith, the Women's Foundation of Minnesota, the National Association of Black Journalists, Ernie Suggs, my former journalism colleagues in the Twin Cities and Detroit, Chuck Laszewski, Darci McConnell, Nichole Christian, Chris Singer, Regina Boone, Terry Collins, Reggie Royston, Reginald Stuart, Portia Bruner, Aysha Somasundaram, Cepa Sparks, Candice Washington, Marlon Lord, Christian Hayes and the Tyrone Happy Hour participants, Lauryl and Clint Jackson, Rachel and Kenny Carroll, Brian Foster, Suzanne Griffith, Josh Bassett, Chris Alexander, Pam Smock, Sholnn Freeman, Nicole Rose, Dayo Kefentse, Vladimir Leveque, Ginger Wilson, Ayana Byrd, Tai Coleman, Nnedi Okorafor-Mbachu, Allison Brown, Yolanda Young, Donna Dillingham, Tina Beyene, Alexs Pate. Thanks to all the interview participants for their candor and time. To Cleis Press, especially Felice Newman and Frédérique Delacoste—thanks for believing in us. And here's to Natalie H., the best book partner a gal could have. — Natalie Y. Moore

In memory of my grandparents—Joseph and
Frances Moore and James and Nina Goodwin.
And to A.D. Harris, in honor of our friendship.
—*Natalie Y. Moore*

For Rudy.
—*Natalie Hopkinson*

Contents

Introduction

Tyrone is a county in Ireland. It also means "king" in Greek. The word traveled across the Atlantic, then had a slight change of plans. Tyrone is a larger-than-life politician. Tyrone is caught up in the criminal justice system. Tyrone is a cultural construction. Tyrone is the man Erykah Badu called out, in a 1998 song, a brother tainted by association. Recall, there Tyrone is not the trifling boyfriend, but an anonymous crony summoned to rescue his wayward pal.

Truth is, we don't know much about Tyrone. It's just a name that has come to speak to a unique form of black male identity, an archetype that was converted into a hit single. As an abstract idea, Tyrone tends to evoke a range of emotions, several of which we explore throughout the course of this book. On that level, he represents a mythical figure, just one prototype for black manhood, one flavored with a distinctly postsoul aesthetic. Simply put: Tyrone is our boy.

Deconstruction is a concept that caught on as an academic movement in the 1970s. The French philosopher Jacques Derrida questioned whether language, usage, and text can have a fixed meaning. He argued that language is a series of signs that can be interpreted in ways that are vague and open-ended. The idea is to take apart fake constructions to reach a greater understanding.

In our Tyrone, deconstructionists may never have found a better subject. Black males make up about 6 percent of the U.S. population, yet they loom colossal in their constructions as broadcast by media all over the world via sports, crime, and entertainment.[1] In mass media, stereotypical portrayals of ethnic groups have been a tried-and-true shortcut to character development. So misperceptions about Tyrone abound.

We don't pretend to correct these. (We haven't got that much time.) Nor can we provide the definitive stamp on black manhood. Before we can even get to the point of criticism, we need a balance of voices and perspectives. *Deconstructing Tyrone* represents the journey of two black women examining masculinity in our own lives, through the eyes of interview participants, and also through the lens we as professional journalists have come to know intimately: the media. We employ a range of lenses, from our own eyes to postmodernism to global media. Frankly, they all lie. There are no absolute "truths" to be found here, just honest reflections and impressions we've collected on this journey.

We present a range of speakers, most of them our peers in the Hip-Hop Generation—those born between 1965 and 1984, according to author Bakari Kitwana.[2] They include men and women, some in politics, others in the work world, sports, and entertainment, many from our own lives. This book reflects our hunger for a more evenhanded picture: feminine and masculine; theory and pop culture; perception and understanding; highbrow and lowbrow.

When it comes to Tyrone, there is a profound disconnection between perception and reality, but no C-O-N-spiracy. A lack of diversity in media ownership and control contributes to creating a consistent pattern of misrepresentation. A spiral of silence has enveloped black men

who fall outside the established narratives. This silence is perpetuated by cultural hegemony, with economics driving the bottom line.

Even as we have strived to cast a more nuanced, critical eye on
Tyrone and the mythology around him, many, inevitably, have questioned our intent. Were we nouveau Terry McMillan wannabes?
Conspiring against the black man? What could two black women
possibly say that isn't a verbal lynching of black men? The winning
question was whether this book was going to be "positive" or "negative." Even some of our closest male friends would explain to
others—in our defense, no doubt—that the book was sure to be "positive." Despite the kind intentions, we cringe at such a classification.
To reduce our efforts to a black/white, good/bad dichotomy wouldn't
be intellectually honest, or reflective of this new look. As feminists
who embrace and critique masculinity, our lens is complicated. Art
curator Thelma Golden says it best in chapter 2, "Tyroninity," which
discusses the evolution of media portrayals of black men: The positive–negative thing? We are *so* over that.

We got used to the "male-bashing" questions, smiled, and tried to
answer, understanding that gender relations can be so distorted in our
community that suspicions are second nature. Commercial success
aside, black female writers have been largely dismissed when it
comes to telling the "authentic" black story, as Patricia Hill Collins
and Calvin C. Hernton explained. In his book *The Sexual Mountain
and Black Women Writers*, Hernton points to the example of Zora
Neale Hurston. Before her legacy was rescued by Alice Walker, she
was derided as an " 'oddball' eccentric who wrote folktales and ran
around measuring Negroes' heads."[3] Meanwhile, Hurston's nemesis
Richard Wright was barely called out for his sexist and flawed portrayals of black women in *Native Son*. Conversely, Walker, Ntozake
Shange, and Michele Wallace have been deemed traitors to the race
for their depictions of black men. We regret that much of the Third

Wave feminist literature is of little relevance to us as black women. Much of the discourse does not speak to the unique issues black women face, especially as it relates to masculinity.

Throughout the course of this project, we've found the idea of legacy to be a controlling theme. There is wrangling over family legacies, cultural legacies, and legacies created by society at large. Chapter 1, "Boy Born Saturday," a profile of Detroit Mayor Kwame Kilpatrick, examines how the bombastic, charming, and larger-than-life "Hip-Hop Mayor" attempts to build on his parents' political legacies and the colorful tradition of Motown politics. At the same time, he has struggled to fend off increasingly nasty attacks from the news media—skirmishes we experienced with him firsthand.

In chapter 9, "Boy Born Friday," we revisit a childhood friend struggling with the legacy of being born the son of Indiana's most feared black man, the commander of the Black Panther militia in the birthplace of the Ku Klux Klan. When Kofi "Debo" Ajabu, a brainy, sensitive college student, was implicated in a brutal triple crime—a murder, kidnapping, and robbery—in 1994, it produced Indiana's racially charged Trial of the Century. When we visit him toward the beginning of his 180-year prison sentence, he discusses how a tradition of racism and patriarchy conspired to place him among the scores of young black men disproportionately represented in the U.S. prison system.

Creating a legacy of self-determination and wealth building was also on the minds of many of our interviewees in chapter 8, "Tyrone at Work." For some white-collar workers, this goal trumps individual riches, which explains why black men age 25–44 continue to be the group most likely to try to start their own businesses. In chapter 4, "Thomas, 36," we show how the poet, activist, and Washington Wizards basketball player Etan Thomas strives to present a new view of professional athletes, one that builds on the legacy of warrior-activists such as Muhammad Ali, John Carlos, Tommie Smith, and Jackie Robinson. This is a burden that Thomas could use some help bearing.

When we told friends we were writing chapter 3, "Visible Tyrone," which deals with gay black men, many of them questioned what in the world *that* had to do with black masculinity. Some of our male friends raised their hands to say, "Hey, I'm not on the DL"—the Down Low—as if anyone even asked. There is, of course, a whole lot to say about black gay men besides how they fit into the heterosexual dating sphere. Scores of men are living and loving each other with gay marriage far from their minds. They are adopting children. They work. Go to church. Renovate houses. Have love and heartbreak, make bad choices. Kind of like everyone else.

In the rest of the book, we intentionally allow women to journal their relationship with men and masculinity as a way to cut through the veneer of representations of men and gender relations. In chapter 6, "The Pole Test," we profile strippers and examine their relationships with their dads. In chapter 5, "Hip-Hop," we look at the contradictions inherent in the work lives of the seen but rarely heard women of rap: video stars, music executives, handlers, artists, and intellectuals—to examine the largely schizophrenic relationship between women and the industry.

In chapter 10, "Raising Tyrone," we write about Natalie H.'s personal experience as a mother, as well as review some of the latest literature on how to raise a happy, healthy black boy—one who can appreciate our beloved hip-hop while properly pronouncing the word *misogyny*. Similarly, in chapter 7, "Babydaddy," we talk to women about their bond with the father of their child—when he's not their husband. Here, we attempt a more meaningful look at the roots of this pop-culture term and social phenomenon that is directly tied to marriage as an evolving institution, at a time when 70 percent of black babies are born to single mothers.

In the final chapter, "Tyrones in Training," we asked teenage girls to talk about the boys in their lives. This is a roundtable discussion with two grous of girls, ages 12–15, from the Midwest flatlands. We realize that the future of genter relations ultimately lies with them. And hearing them talk candidly about everything from boys' hygiene to video hos to their own influences, we were refreshed. These girls are smart, funny, tender, and vulnerable. The future is in perfectly capable hands.

Finally, a note on our style of delivery. We have long admired folklorists and novelists who honor the idiom and rhythms of black language. Throughout the book, we set the scene, frame the picture, and then we tried to get out of the way. We refused to allow mainstream cultural norms and "good taste" function as straightjackets on the expression of ourselves or our speakers. Perhaps the inimitable Coleman A. Young, late mayor of Detroit, said it best: "Swearing is an art form. You can express yourself much more directly, much more exactly, much more succinctly, with properly used curse words."[4] We are having a conversation with you, and we hope to serve as a conduit for the various voices throughout the book. While we try to keep our cynicism in check, it certainly creeps out. We try to be witty, too, but appreciate that only our mothers may be entertained.

This is not the first discussion around black men and masculinity, and it won't be the last. In many ways, the American story stays the same regardless of the century; representations from Buck to Trickster are ever present, smudging the lines between shuffling and dancing. And perceptions sometimes surpass reality. To wit: One of the white journalism students we taught pitched a story comparing convicted felon and hip-hop businessman Suge Knight to Detroit Mayor Kwame Kilpatrick. Huh?

We feel fortunate to be among an increasing number of black cultural guardians who have the opportunity to produce and critique these images in the public sphere. We hope this book makes people think, and maybe makes them a little uncomfortable. There are few conclusions here, and definitely no easy moral lessons. Complicated tensions and dilemmas require complicated answers, and the lives we are looking at anew are often those that exist in the gray areas. These ambiguities are part and parcel of life in the Hip-Hop Generation.

Natalie Hopkinson and Natalie Y. Moore
May 2006

Chapter 1

Boy Born Saturday

The job was running me ragged. It was my day off, but my cell phone rang insistently. It was a female voice, a Detroit cop, uttering every newspaper reporter's favorite word: *whistleblower*. She had The Tape.

I (Natalie M.) was relatively new to town and to the Detroit political beat, but it was hard to avoid blather about The Tape, which was part of a nearly two-year-old rumor that had entered into the already abundant local lore. As the yarn goes, Mayor Kwame Kilpatrick, the political scion and former college football player elected at age 31 to lead the blackest big city in America, hosted a party at the mayoral residence, the Manoogian Mansion, months after he took office in 2002. The party got rowdy, the story goes, with strippers. Supposedly, Detroit's first lady came home early, and promptly beat a stripper's ass, sending her to the hospital. The local and national media chased the story like a lost winning lotto ticket. But there was no proof. The Michigan state attorney general, a Republican, investigated too, and eventually dismissed the party as urban legend.

Still, everyone in Metro Detroit boasted a theory about the party. They knew somebody who knew somebody who knew somebody who was there. Maybe it was a babydaddy's play cousin's sister's uncle. Or a neighbor's dentist's sister-in-law worked at the hospital where the stripper was treated. Once, out of state, I went out on a bad blind date with a guy who swore he was at that late-night soiree. I told him he had no proof; he corrected me by saying I had none.

But this cop on the cell phone informed me that she actually possessed video footage of two topless female strippers, at the Manoogian, lap-dancing for the mayor. Both strippers had since died. That there were two dead strippers—with zero evidence linking them to the mayor—was one of the wild fringes of the story that had actually been verified. The cop gave me her name and cell number and promised to fork over the tape to me only. Utterly rattled, I phoned Natalie H. Was the tape legit? If so, how should I handle the story? What if the tape was grainy, of the R. Kelly ilk? Despite the common perception of journalists, it was not my kind of chase. I'm into policy. I loved covering Detroit because it was the place where the heart of the post–civil rights struggle lay: intractable poverty and crumbling schools.

Plus, I was skeptical. How could they have kept it secret for so long? Why me? Why now? But being a newspaper writer also means always worrying about the next scoop. I had no time to waste. I agreed to meet the cop a few hours later in the parking lot of the restaurant known as the Anita Baker IHOP, after its former owner. I told the cop what kind of car I drove so she would recognize me. I called the newsroom to tell them my whereabouts in case some shit popped off. When I finally got through to the editors, I could hear the saliva dripping over the bad connection.

His nicknames, some bestowed by the local media during his first term, have run the gamut: "Big Diamond," "thug," "pimp," "player," "Kwame Soprano," "Swami," "his thugness," "ghetto," "gangsta," "inept club crawler," "hustler," "Puffy Kilpatrick."[1] Frequently, it's just plain ole Kwame—the reverent titles of "Mayor," "Mr. Mayor" or "Mr. Kilpatrick" chucked aside.

Outside Michigan, they've come to know him as the "Hip-Hop Mayor"—a title he didn't invent but has not rejected, either. He is imposing and magnetic, all eyes on him when descending upon a room. He's 6'4", shoulders broad enough to carry water jugs. His skin is roasted coffee, his beard manicured. His upper lip curls when he grins, flashing straight, white teeth. His wardrobe alone delivers a keynote address: There's the one-and-a-half-carat diamond earring that for years flashed from his ear and was mentioned within the first ten seconds of any news account of the wonder-boy mayor. He definitely oozes that Detroit flair, but he draws the line at colored suits. "If I wore a red suit, it'd be on the front page of the papers," he sarcastically explained once. Apparently this does not rule out purple ties, pink handkerchiefs, electric-blue stripes, or classic Detroit gators. He's been seen stepping out with his sons in matching black suits and gold ascots—his fraternity colors. An asterisk to his florid style is a mayoral fleet that includes a black Cadillac Escalade.

In other words, he hand-delivers chalk to caricature artists. Chris Rock has said he used Mayor Kilpatrick, in part, as a model for his role as the first black president in the movie *Head of State*. But during my short stint covering him for the *Detroit News,* while reporting on the Detroit City Council, I came to see other images: a father of three, former schoolteacher married to his college sweetheart. I found a self-described "citizen of the world" who loves to quote the Bible. A lawyer. A man of privilege who refused to turn his back on his hometown.

The mayor's manner is folksy. His vocabulary includes *ain't*, and he knows how to snake-charm a crowd. Kilpatrick is so affable that it's hard to walk away from him without a tingling feeling, or the gumption to pick up a trash bag and start sprucing up the city. Enemies concede that Kilpatrick's charisma is like poison ivy and his communication skills exhilarate a room.

Not that I was special to the mayor, or vice versa, but watching him sparkle on the political stage was like having your boy in office. We are both of the Hip-Hop Generation. We are both midwesterners from big cities who chose to attend historically black colleges—despite never knowing what it's like to drink out of colored water fountains. He loves tailored suits, I adore Diane von Furstenberg.

Some folks winced when he addressed his rival on the city council, an older black woman, as "Mama" during a showdown public meeting over funding pension obligation bonds. It was a rare, and dire, occasion that brought Kilpatrick to council chambers that day. I got that *Mama* was a term of endearment popular in the current rap lexicon and a throwback to his Pan-African upbringing. To the old heads, Kilpatrick's busy Al Wissam jacket, worn at the Detroit Thanksgiving Day Parade in 2004, was tacky. I recognized that the ostentatious outerwear, designed by a trendy, popular Arab designer, delivered a message directly to his young constituents: I'm one of you. To implore young people to register to vote, Kilpatrick made public service announcements on the hip-hop radio station over the beat to Usher's "Yeah." On the same station, he had a meet-the-mayor segment during drive time.

When it comes to Mayor Kilpatrick and black masculinity, perception and reality have met, and they ignore the middle ground. He is a symbol of both the coming generation of black leadership and the city of Detroit itself: postmodern, postindustrial, and so black it's postblack. A McDonald's in a city that sold sweet potato pie.

Like hip-hop, he's flashy, fresh, a finger-to-the-establishment. Like hip-hop, he is, at his worst, arrogant, unfocused, and undisciplined. He was the youngest big-city mayor in the U.S.; regardless of his administration's foibles, observing him from the sidelines was never dreary.

As for which image was false, I would have to see for myself.

"We Gonna Make It,"—JADAKISS

Kwame M. Kilpatrick was born on June 8, 1970. His name alone is ironically American: In Ghana his first name means "born on Saturday," and his surname is Irish. His father, Bernard Kilpatrick, was the chief of staff for a powerful county government executive. His mother, Carolyn Cheeks Kilpatrick, is a Detroit congresswoman, elected in 1996.

His mother drilled into him that he was the best and could go anywhere his heart desired. She taught him to be comfortable in any setting—Florida A & M University, his alma mater; Harvard University; General Motors; Frankfurt, Germany; and, no doubt, Linwood and The Boulevard, the neighborhood that reared him.

His parents instilled in him a sense of self-assuredness and empowerment as a black man. Young Kwame was known for his big personality as a child, singing Motown doo-wop and Troop's "All I Do Is Think of You" with his friends and cousins. Nine-year-old Kilpatrick visited Mayor Coleman Young to interview him for a school project and was inspired. High school friends recall Kilpatrick as hanging with a crew of jocks. In the yearbook, the future mayor and college football lineman predicted a career either in professional football or politics. The Kilpatrick family basement was a favorite hangout. Often friends would be recruited to work on his mother's state rep campaign, which Kilpatrick first managed at age 13.

Kilpatrick was the kid who always had folks laughing. He was also the consummate gentleman. One old-time friend, Saunteel Jenkins, recalled visiting him in college with her girlfriends and being left vulnerable to some frat boys after a night of drinking. Jenkins had first met Kilpatrick in tenth grade at the prestigious Cass Tech High School. (They graduated in 1988.) Her old high school friend came to their rescue on that evening. "Kwame literally saved our lives," she says.

Kilpatrick earned a degree in political science and a teaching certificate from Florida A & M in 1992. In 1998, he received a law degree from Detroit College of Law. For a while, he taught in a public middle school in Detroit. When his mother vacated her seat as a state representative, he decided to campaign for it. Jenkins served as his campaign treasurer. "Kwame's a very intelligent guy," Jenkins says. "I believed in him, and it was exciting to be a part of someone from my generation, my childhood."

Her friend won.

When he arrived at the Michigan legislature in 1997, Kilpatrick quickly got to work building relationships. There, he was chosen as leader of the Democratic Caucus, the first African American in Michigan history to lead any party in the state legislature. His personality shone as a Democratic leader with friends on the other side of the aisle, and he achieved celebrity status in other white quarters of the state. Working closely with him as a newly minted politician, Jenkins says he had a knack for getting other people to believe in him. It's easy to be intimidated by him, she says, but he quickly puts people at ease with his down-to-earth, everyday-guy persona.

When he began to set his sights on the mayor's office, he was barely into his thirties. Family connections and an existing political machine helped with fund-raising. Following the advice of political pollsters, Kilpatrick removed his diamond stud earring. He also ran a campaign that capitalized on the youth vote. His slogan was "Our Future...Right Here, Right Now." He promised a revival of Detroit's blighted core, more housing and commercial development, and lower property taxes. He had big plans for the city's $3 billion budget. His agenda included improving education, reorganizing the police department, cleaning up the streets, replacing broken street lights, and tearing down thousands of the city's abandoned homes. When folks derided him because of his age, Kilpatrick put forth campaign literature featuring Martin Luther King Jr. and John F. Kennedy, suggesting that those men had achieved prominence at an early age as well.

The primary election was held on September 11, 2001. Voter turnout was low. Two months later, in the general election on November 7, Kilpatrick won, with 55 percent.[2]

On his inaugural keepsake bookmark was a quote from Hebrews 11:16: "But now they desire a better country, that is a heavenly: wherefore God is not ashamed to be called their God: for he hath prepared for them a city."

"We have nowhere to go but up," he promised in his inauguration speech.

He and his wife, Carlita—also a FAMU alum and a stay-at-home mom pregnant with their third son, Jonas—moved into the Manoogian Mansion. Having a family political dynasty and bringing kids into the mansion gave them a black Kennedy aura.

Kilpatrick got to work—and promptly restored his diamond stud earring.

Eight Mile

For a while, I've believed that anyone looking to enact social change should descend upon careworn Detroit. Michigan's largest city has been fighting its image across the country and the globe, an image built on crime and frayed race relations. Memories of the 1967 riots haven't evaporated. Detroit (82 percent black) and suburban Livonia (96.5 percent white) are among the country's most racially segregated cities, according to the U.S. Census Bureau,[3] and they are just miles apart. The metro area is divided into little suburban fiefdoms, crippling the region. Mass transit is elusive, and the clogged arteries of the highways extend across the back of the urban core.

The famed 8 Mile Road that Eminem rapped about is the physical and social border that separates the Motor City from its suburban neighbors. Sprawl prevents smart growth.

An example of bad attitudes? People even talk shit on Martin Luther King Jr.'s birthday. If a high-profile crime happens in Detroit, the national and local media hand-wring about the city's "negative image." Driving along certain corridors of the metropolis presents a vivid picture of urban blight—deteriorated storefronts, vast swaths of empty land, and rampant economic disinvestment.

Detroit is at the forefront of many of the pressing problems facing the black community. Twenty-six percent of residents live in poverty.[4] Forty-seven percent of Detroiters are functionally illiterate.[5] Forty-three percent of residents earn under $25,000 a year.[6] In 2005, the city's financial quagmire expanded to a projected $300 million budget shortfall for the next fiscal year. Rumors abounded that the state might take over the city. Explanations for the red ink are manifold. Pension and health-care costs for city workers are soaring. In 1950, at its peak, Detroit had a population of nearly 2 million residents.[7] But the workforce didn't reflect a decline; at one point, in 1990, there were 18.5 city workers per 1,000 residents.[8]

White flight happened long ago; now it's the black middle class fleeing like embittered Cuban exiles because of lackluster public schools, a muted tax base, and crime. Property taxes tend to be the bread-and-butter revenue for municipalities big and small. In Detroit, property taxes account for 11 percent of income, while neighboring suburbs report 60 to 70 percent of their money from that source. The lack of a tax base, exacerbated by the exodus of people and businesses, has resulted in a city income tax. Because of the economic imbalance that impacts the housing stock, more expensive homes bear the tax brunt. I interviewed a couple who lived in one of the city's most elite sections. Their 6,000-square-foot house, with a built-in backyard pool, comes with a yearly property-tax price tag of $19,000 a year.

But, regardless of the challenges, the city feels that it's on the brink of something magnificent. The potential is awesome. For every burned-to-a-crisp, hollow Victorian house, one can see a couple applying their vision to make over a lovely dwelling. In some pockets of the rows of abandoned storefronts, inconspicuous structures are housing avant-garde art and clothing. Energetic neighborhood associations rival those of any suburban cul-de-sac. Cutting-edge house and techno music boom in the city. Amid black poverty, there are pockets of black wealth. Every year, companies in the city are ranked among *Black Enterprise* magazine's top 100 black businesses.[9] Here is the nation's hair capital. And cats in Detroit wore suits to go out before Jay-Z popularized the style. The city is delectably gritty, and its impact can be seen in the rebellious arts scene.

In the 1970s, as waves of black men were being elected to lead cities such as Atlanta and Los Angeles, Detroit was in the vanguard. Coleman "Don't-Nobody-Say-Anything-Bad-About" Young was the first African American to take office in the Motor City. He had brass, and he alienated many white suburbanites with his in-your-face language and ideas. "Aloha, muthafuckers," he once told a group of reporters via closed-circuit television during a trip to Hawaii.[10] Young opened up the previously locked doors of city hall to blacks and purged a group of police officers connected to killing young black men. Dennis Archer, a former Michigan Supreme Court justice, succeeded Young and served as mayor from 1993 to 2001, during the country's economic boom. President Clinton befriended Detroit, and millions of federal enterprise dollars fell upon the city. During Archer's term, downtown was rebuilt and new development—commercial and residential—rained on Detroit. Many suburbanites felt comfortable with the inroads he made, while many residents felt their neighborhoods were ignored.

Kilpatrick has inherited some of Archer's halo, reaping the benefits of ribbon-cutting projects initiated by the previous administration. At times it's hard to decipher which are Kilpatrick's accomplishments and which are Archer's.

The 2001 election, in which Kilpatrick defeated former Detroit Councilman Gil Hill (aka Eddie Murphy's cop boss in the *Beverly Hills Cop* franchise), placed Kilpatrick among a cadre of political leaders of the Hip-Hop Generation: all male, with professional degrees, middle-class upbringings, and dynastic political legacies. Harold Ford Jr. took over his father's seat in the U.S. Congress in 1996. Jesse Jackson Jr. parlayed his father's political connections to earn a congressional seat in Illinois in 1995. Ras Baraka, the son of the poet Amiri Baraka, is deputy mayor of Newark, New Jersey. Since 2003, Kendrick Meek has held the U.S. House seat for Florida formerly occupied by his mother.

Other than by their blood relations, by and large, the old guard of civil rights leaders has not handed the baton to the younger generation. For decades, we've seen the same faces on our television screens (Rev. Al, Jesse, Kweisi, et al.) planning the next boycott, protest, or march. As the post–civil rights Generation X hunts for definition, hip-hop has been applied in the political realm, almost by default.

Some are skeptical of the label. Farai Chideya, author of *Trust: Reaching the 100 Million Missing Voters* and a commentator on political trends among young African Americans, says, "The hip-hop generation has to have a more rigorous analysis. It helps to make that comparison when a group of people are united by similar struggles. But it hurts when equating something political with something cultural. This is what the hip-hop generation is dealing with."

"This generation does not have a single issue like the color line," she tells us. "The civil rights movement had the color line, and it was a unifying enemy. Hip-hop has...the harder task of figuring out how to move society. What is it we're going to change?"

The civil rights movement did not remove poverty or crime, she says, and generational comparisons—fair or not—are going to be made. Reflecting on economics for black people and the prison industry, she says, "One of the failures of the civil rights movement was that it didn't have a next stage of [the] game. We're going to end the color line, then it was okay. It's never over. Just be engaged. Be in the game."

Chideya believes the future lies in grassroots activists around the country, not the elected officials, doing community-based work. Yvonne Bynoe, author of *Stand & Deliver: Political Activism, Leadership, and Hip Hop Culture*, agrees that ceding the leadership positions to hip-hop is counterproductive. She notes that during the civil rights movement artists like Ruby Dee, Ossie Davis, and Harry Belafonte helped promote the cause, but they were neither in charge of it nor were they handed that responsibility. Our generation, which has never experienced the legal obstacles of segregation, does business in a technological global age. We've grown up seeing black mayors and black city council members. Yet, the current crop of new black leaders has not impressed Bynoe. "I'm not 100 percent sold yet that there are any politicians running with systemic change," she says. "If they are saying the same things as the old guard, we could have kept the old guard. They didn't get to where they are because of ideas, but because of their mother, father, legacy. Political operatives helped them with name value. It takes time to see if people stand on their own."

Newark is one city where the showdown between the civil rights generation and Hip-Hop Generation has been most acute. As a majority-black city with a black seat of power, facing a postindustrial economy, crime, blight, and high levels of unemployment, Newark mirrors Detroit in many ways. In the 2002 showdown, civil rights veteran Sharpe James, mayor since 1986, was challenged by Cory Booker, a young, Yale-trained lawyer. Booker was challenged for his black manhood, characterized as a tool for white political interests.

James ultimately held on to his seat in the mayor's office. (In spring 2006, Booker won the mayoral seat when James declined to seek another term.) However, James, after the 2002 race against Booker, attempted to neutralize the valid criticism that the civil rights generation is not getting out of the way by appointing Ras Baraka deputy mayor. Baraka holds close ties to hip-hop, and he has galvanized rappers and activists. He ran unsuccessfully for mayor in 1994. Initially hesitant about taking the seat, Baraka decided to use the opportunity to build on his political base. "It's been positive for us," Baraka says. "It was a good decision."

Baraka still sees a generational rift. The civil rights generation, he says, has failed to produce any viable young leadership. "Most young people who are political organizers that have potential to do different things are on their own outside or still serving those guys waiting for time to come.... The majority of young people my age still believe that we have a long way to go—the necessity for affirmative action, more education. We believe in it. That keeps us attached to the old guard. But the problem is some of these people themselves have abandoned it in practice. We've been struggling to remove these people. We see them becoming old and corrupt."

In college, Baraka says, he never dreamed he'd run for office. "I thought they were criminals and they were corrupt. I still believe that. The system is inherently a problem. My strategy in that is change.

Malcolm talked about the ballot or the bullet. That's real to me. People have real problems—housing, development, etc. Running for office became a way to organize people in the community around those issues, to provide a voice for people I didn't think had a voice when I came back to the city. It's about power."

Kilpatrick, the Media, and the Public

"This is Mayor Kwame Kilpatrick," the message on my voicemail said. The mayor had just read an article I had written in fall 2004 about a rash of layoffs to come the following year in order to balance Detroit's budget. It quoted his chief financial officer predicting up to 2,000 layoffs the following year, but Kilpatrick stopped short of saying he would carry out the plan. The piece pointed out that the mayor would be in a difficult campaign race during that time. In an effort to play nice with doubtful unions, Kilpatrick rehired thirty bus cleaners even though he had said the transportation department needed an overhaul.[11]

"That was a real interesting article that you had in today's paper," his message continued. "Hmmhmmm...I see what you're trying to do—make it political."

Huh?

At a press conference the next day, the mayor stood at the lectern dealing with an unrelated police matter. For the rest of the presser, he directed all of his answers to me, calling me out by name. His bass voice dripping with sarcasm, he said "We're going to give *Natalie* all the material she needs."

"That's why I asked," I snapped.

After the press conference, he told me, "Dang, you have an attitude."

"So did you," I shot back, and we laughed.

Our relationship over the short time I covered him was good-humored, given our antagonistic roles. "You eat pork?" he once asked incredulously during a breakfast interview, skinning his face as though I'd slaughtered the pig with my bare hands. This, after he'd ordered enough food for two starving people.

At the opening of the 2005 auto show, Kilpatrick held a black-tie after-party (not funded by taxpayers), and ribbed me about always being at events by myself. "What are you, a loner?" he asked. Wrinkling my nose, I said, "Mayor, I'm working." Gee, nothing like a mayor to remind you of your single status.

By definition, politicians are bound to have tension with the media that perform a watchdog role. But when it comes to black politicians, the relationship becomes more of a paradox. After being elected to positions of power, black politicians reflexively assume a beleaguered stance, which isn't unusual, given the historical representations of blacks in the media. But they seem to forget that the whole point of electing black leaders is for them not to be helpless actors, but to wield power and influence. As a whole, black politicians are surprisingly naive and often willfully ignorant of the way the media work. And they either don't care or don't realize that their ethical gaffes play right into the media's hands.

So it was when Kilpatrick breezed into office in 2002. At first, the local and national media descended, fawning over his youth and his vision for a new Detroit. An article in the *Christian Science Monitor* assessing his first six months in office was representative: " 'Hip-hop mayor' aims to rev Motor City engine," the headline read. The youngest big-city mayor was described as "bold, charming, direct, and determined to succeed.... He's taken on his job with all the vigor and—some would say—bravado expected of someone his age."[12]

There was a brief moment of optimism for reporters who were hungry to hear new political voices. But the honeymoon didn't last long. Besides, the national media are more interested in parachuting in to report the surface issues. Buttressing that dynamic is the media's attitude toward Detroit. The slogan "If it bleeds, it leads" is accurate. Suburban coverage is becoming increasingly important to newspapers as they provide dwindling coverage of urban centers like Detroit.

In 2003, the *Detroit News* reported that Kilpatrick hired at least seventeen people who were either relatives or longtime friends.[13] Some were cousins; some attended high school with him; others grew up with him. They had positions such as director of neighborhood city hall, director of the Detroit Building Authority, constituent relations, and executive assistants. One member of the mayor's security detail played high school football with Kilpatrick.

The story had legs, despite the low number cited, and it became a joke that never eluded him. Every politician must appoint people he trusts, or else gets screwed. And seventeen friends in office is little more than a speck of an 18,000-strong workforce. Still, the suggestions of cronyism and corruption have trailed the mayor throughout his time in office.

In other instances, Kilpatrick begged for this kind of treatment. Reporters swooned when he lied about leasing a Lincoln Navigator for his wife with $25,000 in city money in early 2005. It could have been a one-day story if the mayor hadn't lied about it. Everyone could have kept it moving to deal with the bigger issues, namely the city's finances. Instead, the stupidity carried on for more than a week and would continually resurface. No one could let it go, holding on to the cherry-red SUV as a symbol, though I'm not sure of what. By then, the chalk was filling in the caricature. By then, the mayor was "Kwame." By then, personality had trumped policy when it came to scrutinizing him.

The *Detroit Free Press*'s driving columnist got ridiculously giddy with the story. He wrote a column asking readers to suggest what the first family should drive. The next day, the reporter printed the comments—unsurprisingly, mostly from suburbanites.[14] Kilpatrick's denial and handling of the mess gave respectability to an obnoxious television "reporter" for the local ABC affiliate, a Michael Moore knockoff who stalked the mayor like a one-night stand who didn't get the hint. "Oh, my *goodness,*" the mayor said under his breath after being confronted by the reporter in a stealth ambush in Washington. "I'd be happy to give an interview," Kilpatrick told his plump nemesis as a camera rolled. "We can go liiiiive, anytime," Kilpatrick taunted, eight times, jabbing his finger in the air. Watching their pissing match escalate into a series of television reports in which the reporter was shoved into a wall by a member of the mayoral security detail, you're thinking, this can't be good for democracy. Eventually it dissolved into farce. "Quit hiring prostitutes," the mayor told the ABC guy as cameras chased him through the streets of Detroit. Then, maybe in homage to his idol, former mayor Coleman Young, Kilpatrick added for measure: "Fat-ass."

And Kilpatrick continued to hand ammunition to his critics on the mostly black Detroit City Council—albeit a questionable bunch—by keeping them out of the loop on projects and legislation.

He used taxpayer money to pay for limos, nightclubs, and lavish meals for supposedly drumming up business for the city. When the *Detroit News* reported the dalliances in 2003, little noise was made.[15] When the *Detroit Free Press* reported the same story two years later, a hullabaloo broke out, dovetailing with the rising anti-Kilpatrick sentiment in an election year. The collective media salivated as if the information was totally new.

It was also news when a police officer was transferred out of the executive protection unit amid criminal allegations and cover-ups of timesheets.

In a 2003 interview with the *New York Times,* Kilpatrick played the role of the media victim. "If I was sixty years old, if I came from the 'country club community,' if I came out of an established private firm or something like that, none of these would get the lift that they have," he told the reporter. "I guess it's believable that a thirty-two-year-old black man with an earring in his ear has parties like that. It's so unfortunate. I'm here to fight that stigma."[16]

He's right, there is a double standard, but savvy politicians accept, even cherish, that paradigm and proceed accordingly. At times, Kilpatrick pouts like Kobe Bryant or a kid on the playground who got his ice cream money stolen. Belly-aching won't change the tenor of the media.

In a 2004 speech about the state of black boys, he took another swipe at the media, earning him a standing ovation: "We believe the traditional things said about African American men: philanderer, thug, hang with drug dealers."

The mayor did try to exert some damage control over the scandals. He convened a press conference in spring 2003 outside the Manoogian to refute rumors about "the party" and defend the firing of a deputy police chief in the Detroit Police Department. The deputy chief, Gary Brown, sued the mayor and the city for wrongful termination under the Whistleblower Act. As head of internal affairs, Brown was investigating allegations of wrongdoings by the mayor, his family, and his inner circle. This included "the party." Kilpatrick said that Brown was untrustworthy to lead the unit. The civil lawsuit was brought for $14 million.

A series of depositions related to the case, which inflicted embarrassment on Kilpatrick, provided material that would make the erotic writer Zane envious. I wrote stories about it, along with the rest of the Detroit press corps.

Police Officer Walt Harris, a former member of the mayor's security detail, also filed a lawsuit against Kilpatrick and the former police chief, alleging that they fabricated citizen complaints against him. In his testimony, Harris accused the mayor of conducting trysts with the help of his twenty-four-hour security detail during late-night outings. Harris said that the mayor asked him one night to drive to meet a woman at an apartment building in Detroit. The woman was outside, naked under a flapping mink coat, and Kilpatrick entered the apartment and stayed with her for forty-five minutes. Harris also said that members of the detail suspected "inappropriate" meetings with Kilpatrick's married pal and chief of staff, Christine Beatty, the aide who recommended firing the other police officer, Brown.[17]

During his deposition in the Brown lawsuit, Kilpatrick put on a show. The plaintiff's attorney, Mike Stefani, noted that Kilpatrick was chewing on an apple while giving his testimony.[18] The mayor continued to deny having extramarital affairs. In his second deposition, taken in October 2004, he reasserted his reason for firing Brown and his authority to do so. "I'm the CEO of the tenth-largest city in America. I'm the CEO of the thirty-seventh-largest economy in the world. I didn't need the chief to sign off," he said.[19]

Once the depositions went public, the whole town had a field day—the transcripts were a hot topic everywhere: newspapers, talk radio, television. On one morning show, radio personalities did a dramatic interpretation, using the deposition as a script.

But Kilpatrick has exhibited some rubberlike qualities. He has never been charged with a crime, and the whistleblower lawsuit, originally scheduled to go to trial in 2005, smack in the middle of the reelection cycle, was postponed.

In a rare self-deprecating moment, Kilpatrick flexed his damage control for another set of constituents. When hometown hero Eminem brought his tour to Detroit in 2003, a prelude video comedy skit played on a big screen for the concertgoers. The mayor called the rapper, asking him about doing a concert in Detroit. At the end of the conversation, Eminem quipped to the mayor that the concert after-party should be at the Manoogian. Kilpatrick looked at the phone in joking disbelief. The audience laughed. It's rare to publicly see the mayor laugh at himself. It's also unlikely that political observers and adversaries caught the moment.

Yet, in some ways, the publication of the depositions only invigorated his base. After writing a string of stories about the depositions, I got a message from an elderly woman on my voicemail. "Just leave him alone! Let that boy alone! Just let the man be!" Click. A man, tripping on his own words, left this message: "I can't stand that ole be-bop mayor. That's right. That ole be-bop." Click. Everyone had something to say about the media's coverage of the depositions, which made national news when it was reported that Kilpatrick had taken his security detail into Dream, a Washington, D.C., nightclub. My younger sister Megan, who is a former Michigan politico, scoffed. "You *like* writing about this?!" My brother Joey signified, "I heard you're like the *National Enquirer*."

Around the city, residents have mixed feelings about the mayor and how he has handled the job. I've heard young blacks say—casually, on the street, in the club—that the brother hasn't been given a fair shake; he deserves a chance under tough circumstances. Everyone who lives in Metro Detroit is a stakeholder to the city's future, but most of the armchair observers don't live in Detroit proper (myself included), underscoring a detachment they have with the populace.

Many people rightly believe Kilpatrick has become a media magnet because he reinforces certain stereotypes. "Here's this big, black guy out here who's in a position of power," Detroiter Kwame Woodard, 32, says. Woodard feels that Kilpatrick has been scrutinized more than his white counterparts for playing a political game he didn't invent. But he says people in the hood empathize. "My grandparents look at him as a strong black leader," he says. "They like his style. It's like relating to themselves."

Others aren't so enamored. Once, a newspaper reader e-mailed me: "Let's face it, Detroit politicians and the city council couldn't run a lemonade stand." Another frequent letter writer suggested renaming Detroit the "New Nigeria" because "then the city can apply for dollars from the United Nations and the International Monetary Fund." Who knows if the onlooker was racist or cheeky? I had to admit, watching city government was sometimes like watching the deckchairs being rearranged on the Titanic. The political climate can be icky and pedestrian in its squabbles, pettiness, and delusions of grandeur. The focus on personalities and goofy squabbles debases the pressing problems threatening Detroit's livelihood: the population drain and business drain are creating a city full of poor black people with no means of amping up the city's tax base. Detroit can only wish for the gentrification that is choking cities like Washington, D.C.

Public policy suffers because the media and politicians pay far more attention to personal peccadilloes than to good government. And many citizens seem happy to watch Detroit spin down the toilet. Once, a retired Detroit cop, presumably white, scribbled on the margins of a news story I had written about incentives to get youth to move back in the city, and mailed it to me. "Where black folks go, nothing grows," he wrote. "Curse the day the white man set foot on the continent of Africa. You have a legacy, Coleman A. Young."

Maybe Kilpatrick was mimicking his hero. Young, known for his cussing, had an overwrought relationship with the mainstream media, but he was in office about two decades. Young felt the FBI encouraged negative media reports. A famed memo from the *Detroit News* during the 1970s was leaked.[20] It was from an editor who said he wanted Detroit coverage to spark conversations at suburban cocktail parties. That memo is still talked about in the city. But while Young has had his share of media run-ins, he was in office long enough to secure mass popularity among residents and build alliances.

Although Kilpatrick's relations with the media were strained, he bounced back, snatching some upbeat coverage during the 2004 Democratic National Convention in Boston. The media is starved for young voices with real political power, and Michigan was one of the battleground states in the 2004 election, with Detroit playing a key role. The party chose Kilpatrick to share the stage with Senator John Kerry on national television after the presidential candidate's speech.

Democratic strategist Donna Brazile has said that Kilpatrick has been a source of inspiration to the party, that he is viewed as understanding urban issues.[21] In 2005, the Initiative for a Competitive Inner City, founded by a Harvard University professor, awarded Kilpatrick and Detroit the Top City award, based on the number of business ventures initiated in the urban core.

Jamaine Dickens is an executive assistant to Kilpatrick, and his former press secretary. He says one of the biggest misconceptions about Kilpatrick is that he is not experienced enough to run the city. "Who is?" he says. "No one has been mayor before. Whatever your background, nothing compares. There is no prototype for being mayor." Aesthetically, what's the big deal if Kilpatrick wears nice suits and gators? After all, Dickens says, Coleman Young wore leisure suits. He offers one word for the media coverage of his boss: horrible. "There aren't many stories about government.... It's horrible the media ran buck wild with the Manoogian party. How could anyone believe that? The media did an investigation. If there were a party, the media would have had it before Mike Cox [Michigan's state attorney general]."

Kilpatrick initially agreed to do a sit-down interview with me for this book, but time elapsed, schedules got filled, and a dirty election was underway. It never happened. When I told him I was leaving the newspaper following a presser on city finances, he called me into his office, zooming past his aides. Kilpatrick asked what I was going to do for money while writing this book. Get on food stamps, I joked. He responded, "Naw. For real?" I said yes, laughing. I wasn't serious. He wished me luck.

Much of assessing Kilpatrick boils down to style versus substance. Detroit, the town that produced Motown legends and a sound track for the latter part of the twentieth century, also birthed a so-called hip-hop mayor, a representative of a new generation of music.

But is he a hip-hop interlude—riffing on a dope beat, but a lackluster album? Kinship to the hip-hop genre has heralded and haunted him. Without providing details, in one speech Kilpatrick admitted he had been an imperfect servant. Given the buffet of hip-hop on rotation—bitches, hos in different area codes, cash, magic sticks, dick whispering—it was getting hard to defend the music. It was also getting harder for people to defend Kilpatrick.

His image—partly his fault, partly the fault of external forces— has overshadowed his reign. The list of first-term allegations against Kilpatrick is arguably longer than his accomplishments. Media distractions, lawsuits, and staff members have run rampant. Many people think he should dump Christine Beatty, whom they consider the chink in his armor for her role in the police lawsuits and the heavy-handedness in police matters (as described by Mike Cox).

So these were the questions for Detroit voters in 2005: Is life better for residents pre- or post-Kilpatrick? What does his tenure say about black leadership? Has he given us new ideas to build on? Has he helped or hurt the image of the black man?

The race wasn't about Kilpatrick's challenger; it was a referendum on an incumbent (who by that time had snatched the earring out of his ear permanently). After having trailed by nearly twenty points in the polls months earlier, the mayor won reelection. In November 2005, he was referred to as "scandal-plagued" and his success in the election as "the ultimate comeback." The media collectively wiped the egg off its face. His win was hardly a mandate—it was a tight race—but voters listened when Kilpatrick pleaded for another chance and told them he had grown.[22]

Kilpatrick has kept the momentum for development in the city, which is experiencing a renaissance in entertainment, buppie housing, restaurants, and antiestablishment artist venues. The city says it has made progress in housing. From 2002 to 2003, the number of housing permits jumped 53 percent.[23] The surge encompasses a range from major developments to infill homes on traditional blocks to airy lofts. Roads are being repaved, and the grass is being cut more reliably in the parks, many boasting new equipment and facilities. Kilpatrick has slashed overtime abuse and is attempting to reengineer city government as well as the police department, which is under monitoring by the U.S. Justice Department for abuse against detainees.

Kilpatrick started a network of after-school programs, and he has been lauded for his preparations for homeland security, which helped the city during a massive blackout in 2003. He created a Department of Administrative Hearings to target the property-blight violators who are marring the face of the city—instead of allowing those offenders to clog the overworked criminal court. Despite some high-profile killings, city officials insist that violent crime is down. Kilpatrick convinced voters to pass bonds totaling $215 million that will upgrade police, recreation facilities, transportation, and the beleaguered public lighting. Construction of new police precincts is underway.

Kilpatrick is also dealing with some issues that his predecessors did not. The economy overall is much less bubbly than during Archer's reign, and the Bush administration has cut funding to cities. Unemployment in Michigan has ranked among the worst in the U.S.

The city is still searching for an identity that is not tied to the auto industry.

Many have noted Kilpatrick's stubbornness, a refusal to listen— even to his mama and daddy; arrogance jams his view, they say. He has an amen corner who constantly tell their boss what he wants to hear. He refuses to let go of those in his inner circle, even as their missteps create political liabilities. His childhood friend Saunteel Jenkins said she was accused of drinking the Kool-Aid for pointing out problems before the mayoral race. "It was taken as me not believing [in him]. But I also believe in the reality of the system."

Jenkins believes Kilpatrick succumbed to his image. For his first inauguration, Kilpatrick engaged in a celebratory club crawl. Jenkins said she watched him groove to AMG's "Bitch Betta Have My Money," which did little to dissuade critics who called him inexperienced for the mayor's office. "He helped to create the atmosphere.... When people don't know what's between the lines, they fill them in.... People are fascinated and curious. His personality is bigger than life. There was not the same fascination with Archer, so he [Kilpatrick] is watched more."

Others say it is impossible to overestimate the high profile Kilpatrick has given to the city. "What he's given to Detroit that they haven't had in so long is a spirit," Onitara Nelson says. Her family started the same church Kilpatrick was raised in, The Shrine of the Black Madonna, a Pan-African Orthodox Christian Church. "It looks so desolate now. But when Kwame became mayor, the spirit and energy of Detroit has come to life. Detroit produces a lot of people. They graduate and leave the city. He shows a new generation of young people they can be there and have a sense of empowerment. They can actually make a difference from their hard work."

Political consultant Kamau Marable, who is in his early thirties, disagrees. He gives the mayor a "D." He says Kilpatrick has exploited and maximized his youth but doesn't believe it's his job to represent our generation. Marable feels that youth is now inextricably linked to inexperience in public service because of Kilpatrick's blunders. Great speeches haven't translated into sound public policy, he says. In the 2001 race Marable backed Kilpatrick's opponent, Gil Hill. He feels the scandals have eroded Kilpatrick's credibility. As for the truth of the allegations against Kilpatrick: "How could this guy have this kind of luck? How much bad luck could you have? There's a real lack of confidence in his leadership.... I feel he's not maximized his potential."

Kilpatrick himself doesn't judge his tenure in terms of development, but according to something deeper. "We can't economic-develop our way out," he said at the forum on black boys. "We need some spiritual revolution. We need people to change on the inside...[to] have the community God intended us to have."

Perhaps if Kilpatrick had executed one big-ticket item—say, a new police headquarters—or landed a big-name department store downtown, or put a dent in a problem like the demolition of abandoned buildings, his standing with observers would be better. He failed to get voters to approve his plan for a desperately needed new form of public school governance; and the number of demolished abandoned buildings actually decreased under his watch. His administration has made its accomplishments, but the antagonistic environment festering among the vested parties—the media, city council, unions, Kilpatrick appointees—has kept Detroit from glowing in its full potential. The strong-form mayor of government in Detroit is poles apart from the quid pro quo world of state legislation, which is all about the votes. (As an aside, those state capital relationships haven't benefited Detroit; for example, by lowering property taxes.)

To me, an apt emblem of Kilpatrick's first-term tenure is the Michigan Central Depot on the outskirts of downtown Detroit. If there was ever a monument to urban decay, this is it. The eighteen-story Italianate structure was built in 1913 and has been unoccupied since the 1980s. This formerly grand train station, now a target of vandalism, has the eeriness of a Wes Craven movie. The ship-wrecked depot is a cloud hovering over southwest Detroit; residents recoil at its emptiness, broken glass, and crumbling facade.

Kilpatrick, who has known this incredible, hulking structure since his youth, proposed converting it into a spanking-new head-quarters for the Detroit Police Department. The area is one of the fastest growing in the city, and developers and community leaders hoped this advertisement for blight would shepherd more momentum for renewing the surrounding neighborhood.

In March 2004, Kilpatrick held a press conference in front of the depot, flanked by the police chief and other cabinet officials, to announce a deal to the buy the building. But it was an empty statement—there were no terms to the transaction, no principals to an agreement. For all practical purposes, it was a blue-sky vision, an ambitious one, but bereft of details or a conversion plan for the cash-strapped city to foot the bill.

"Grow Detroit" was a Kilpatrick mantra. To him, Detroit is "dynamic" and a "world-class city." Dreams are admirable—Kilpatrick adores them, the bigger the better. But, in this case, his execution fails, in contrast to his earnest wish. Sure, no money was dumped to prepare for the depot's conversion, but vision needs more than a showy press conference—it needs details.

In his 2005 state of the city address, Kilpatrick spoke of moving forward with selflessness and imagination. "The world needs to see a Detroit that loves itself, because no one will love you if you don't love yourself." His words were true, and inspiring. Months later, no plans for the depot had yet moved forward. Months after that, the plans were officially scrapped.

Holding my breath, I arrived at the IHOP to meet the cop on that late-spring afternoon in 2004. I had butterflies in my stomach, and my mind raced with ideas about what might happen if I got The Tape. I felt sleazy yet dutiful, excited and curious. Natalie H. had told me to be careful and promised to check in later. My nerves and my cynicism battled to see which could kick me the hardest in the stomach. Would I be sitting at the roundtable in the newsroom conference room, among bosses, viewing soft porn? The rumors about the mayor were so out of control that a man I know, after reading my stories and the depositions posted online, warned me about writing such salacious drivel. Remember, there are two dead strippers, he said. I rolled my eyes.

After fifteen minutes, still no cop. I hit "Redial" several times to reach her. Hang-ups.

I had a reporter colleague call the cop shop. Turns out the name and rank the cop gave me were false. Another cop I called for advice tongue-lashed me for arranging to meet with the person. "There is no tape!" he shouted over the phone. Don't go straight home, he advised.

You've been set up.

Chapter 2

Tyroninity

So who *is* this Tyrone fellow? How has he been viewed histori- cally? How has he been interpreted? How does he see himself? Some of us yearn for sunnier, more upbeat views of Tyrone as reparations from mass media that have given him a bad rap. Others are resigned to the trade in the usual tacky stereotypes—a throwback to the days before the Kerner Commission Report linked sensation- alist news media to the 1960s race riots.[1] Some of us are artists just trying to make a dollar out of 15 cents.[2] For others the bottom-line question is: This Tyrone—is he good for the race?

What is often overlooked in contemporary discussions about the images of black masculinity is that while mass media are all-power- ful, seditious messages do sneak out. Clever cultural producers ride established communication channels to snatch their own power. They put out their ideas like an inside joke or an internal memo cir- culating in the black community. Here, we look to three cultural flashpoints since the mid-1990s: art curator Thelma Golden's Black Male show at the Whitney Museum, the Million Man March in Washington, D.C., and comedian Dave Chappelle's high-profile retreat from show business in 2005. Each of these moments recog- nized the symbolism in the Tyrone narrative but recast his image in a way that at a minimum provoked a much-needed discourse and at a maximum shone a brand-new light.

Black males are one of the greatest inventions of the 20th century. —NEW YORK ART CURATOR THELMA GOLDEN[3]

In 1994, curator Thelma Golden put on a show called Black Male: Representations of Masculinity in Contemporary Art at New York's Whitney Museum. To date, few aesthetic treatments of black masculinity have been as comprehensive, challenging, thoughtful, and straight-up ballsy as this exhibition. Mind you, this was a year before the Million Man March, years before both Biggie and Tupac would be slaughtered in the streets. A decade before the rise of neogangster rapper 50 Cent and Dave Chappelle made comic history by signing a $50 million cable TV contract. Before Sean Combs had another name change and Bobby Brown got a reality show. In 1994, a twentysomething junior curator at the Whitney took on black masculinity, assembling images created by a cross section of artists who approached the subject with ironic distance and a whole lot of cheek.

Needless to say, the show kicked up a shitstorm.

Hated by reviewers, it was received even worse by the black establishment, which declared it degrading, demeaning, stereotypical, and pornographic. "Filtered through their eyes, the way America looks at the Black Male hasn't changed since the day they sold us cutrate and cutthroat on those slave cruise ships," the black New York newspaper the *Amsterdam News* wrote. "...nobody sees the Black man as a monumental figure who can conquer, love and rule."[4]

Some reactions took longer to percolate. The next year, two outraged black LA artists created a response show titled African American Representations of Masculinity, which the organizers said would project the images that reflect the "depth, the courage and strength of the black male."[5] It took even longer for other reactions to fully gel. Four years later, the noted writer Carl Hancock Rux completed a poem, "Hell No Won't Be No Black Male Show Shown Today," and in three more years, he staged his poem as a four-person play in Baltimore.[6]

The catalog for Black Male presented a visual history of five major evolutions of the black male aesthetic that took place from the 1960s to the 1990s. In the introduction, Golden described black males as "one of the greatest inventions of the twentieth century," an amalgam of fears and projections that don't begin to describe the way black men actually live.[7] The first of Golden's five "historical signposts" was the transition from the civil rights movement to the Black Power era. Then the images charted the rise of the blaxploitation film. Next was the statistically endangered black male of the 1980s. Then she examined the decline of R & B and the rise of hip-hop. Finally, she included iconic images of black men who played or were played by American politics during the 1980s and 1990s: Rodney King, Willie Horton, Clarence Thomas, Magic Johnson, O. J. Simpson, Colin Powell, Colin Ferguson, Bill Cosby, Richard Pryor, David Dinkins, and Marion Barry.

Some images were more historical than artistic, drawn from documentaries and old newspaper photographs, reading like a history of the black man in the media. There was a 1964 black-and-white photo of Martin Luther King Jr. and Malcolm X performing a visual truce for the cameras in their conservative suits and ties, hands gripped and faces grim. A 1968 news photograph showed Memphis sanitation workers holding hundreds of signs that read "I AM A MAN." The leather-and-beret-clad Black Panthers held "Free Huey" signs. More contemporary news events included a photo of Magic Johnson at his press conference announcing that he had HIV, his beautiful wife, Cookie, at his side. O. J. Simpson was pictured during his murder trial. And there was footage of Rodney King being beaten by Los Angeles police officers, later acquitted, the verdict sparking urban riots more than two decades after the cities burned for Martin Luther King Jr.

There was a photograph of hip-hop artist Tupac Shakur, carved and shirtless, wearing a gun in his waistband, waving one middle finger as the other fondles a blunt—a pose that would be recreated by rappers for the next decade. Ditto for neopimp rapper Snoop Dogg in his brim hat, oversized sunglasses, and fur-trimmed coat; the frowning Geto Boys; Biggie Smalls scowling before an urban backdrop; and Ice Cube, looking angry and lost at the same time. Lovable Cliff Huxtable from *The Cosby Show*, stuffed into in his college football gear. A procession of film stills: *Demolition Man*'s Wesley Snipes in a platinum 'fro. The girls from *Paris Is Burning*. Spike Lee and Giancarlo Esposito facing off in *School Daze*. Gregory Hines dancing in Francis Ford Coppola's *The Cotton Club*.

The works by contemporary artists pushed the debate around black masculinity even further. Some of the more political pieces used text to make literal statements, such as Robert Arneson's "Special Assistant to the President," which featured a sketch of the felon Willie Horton, whose recidivism was blamed on Democratic presidential nominee Michael Dukakis and contributed to his loss to the first President Bush in 1988. David Hammons's 1970 "Injustice Case" showed a black man sitting on a chair, bound and gagged and grimacing; the image was presented with an X-ray quality.

Adrian Piper created several striking sketches, including "Vanilla Nightmares," a Bloomingdale's ad of a milky white woman being fondled and bitten by five black apparitions, one of whom sinks his fangs into her neck as the others look on with pupilless eyes. Above it, the inscription reads "Poison: The Silent Potion exclusively ours for you." Perhaps most striking were nude black male figures by the celebrated gay white photographer Robert Mapplethorpe. His 1980 photograph "Man in Polyester Suit" showed a black-and-white image of a well-fitted three-piece gray suit, cut off just above the knees and below the shoulders of a black man. The photograph's focal point was a big, uncircumcised penis poking out right below the vest, with a wisp of a white button-down shirt hanging around it.

In the catalog's introductory essay, Golden acknowledged the challenges inherent in representing black folk. She realized from the outset the problems an establishment museum like the Whitney faced by projecting images of black men, even for a black woman to spearhead it when the black art world had been historically slighted by mainstream institutions. "There is no question that representation is central to power," she wrote. "Much of the debate around negative imagery is rooted in a dialogue about who holds the power to create and disseminate images."[8]

The show aimed to examine the black male body as an American icon, a metaphor in Western culture. Aware of the media fascination with black men and masculinity, Golden was trying to nudge viewers into considering a new look while subversively countering the messages these images were supposed to convey. It may have been too conceptually abstract on the one hand, and too humiliating on the other, for black men to see themselves on open display like a Hottentot Venus with a penis.

But after going toe to toe with her critics on radio and television to defend the show, Golden grew less understanding of the power struggle over the image of the black male body. She rightly declared the debate over "positive" versus "negative" images bankrupt. Fixed ideas about what is good and bad cannot accurately characterize the complexities attached to images. "I'm *so* finished with that, the positive/negative thing? I'm done with that," she said in a 1995 *Los Angeles Times* interview. "I can't even go there anymore.... Work that is branded homoerotic in content is branded negative, and implicit in that statement is that that is *wrong*—so therefore the work is negative. You can't even talk about an entry into a certain feminist dialogue, because *feminism* is wrong!"[9]

Golden was at times flippant in the *Los Angeles Times* interview, incorrectly reducing the critical motivations to mere homophobia: "The black people are the ones who are doing it, which is what really flips me out—they can't get with the Mapplethorpe because he's gay, but I'm like, these are some of the most beautiful photographs of black men ever taken, who cares?" But even the *New York Times* art critic wondered if Golden was critiquing or celebrating imagery that was dehumanizing and objectifying.[10] We agree that certain elements of the contemporary fine art representations, by contemporary artists who should know better, were a setback. Mapplethorpe's images are passé, played out. Black male humiliation is a standard trope: tried and true—and tired.

Overall, though, Black Male was a triumph. As then Whitney director David Ross pointed out in the catalog, this show was among the first wave of high-art museums devoting considerable space for the "media arts," allowing such trifles as film stills and news photographs to invade their hallowed halls. Golden deserves enormous credit for the role she played in learning the game, ascending to influential perches from which to push the black (and postblack) art worlds forward. Most important, she opened the door to a space in which contemporary black representations can stare down convention—and laugh.

What does it feel like to be a myth? —CLYDE TAYLOR[11]

In the months following Black Male, the plight of the black man continued to be an evening news staple, splashed across newspaper headlines, the topic of roundtable debates, films about the hood, and talk-radio discussions, and of course, shouted in rap lyrics. October 1995 represented the apex of the crisis-talk, which reached full pitch with the publication of several reports. The news was dire. More black men were in prison than in college. A third of black men were under the supervision of the criminal justice system. Big, black O. J. Simpson had been acquitted of murdering his white wife before a media freak show. Former U.S. Speaker of the House Newt Gingrich was masterminding a neoconservative revolution designed, in part, to force black men to replace the role of government in black households. And perhaps the biggest sign that Armageddon was near: Nation of Islam minister Louis Farrakhan had invited one million black men to march on the U.S. Capitol on October 16, 1995.

Street closings and traffic gridlock were expected. A lot of city workers decided to stay home—and not to meditate per Farrakhan's orders, either. Some of the more conspiracy minded wondered if the whole thing was a setup, a chance for the powers that be to take out a whole bunch of black men in one fell swoop. At his television anchor desk, Dan Rather tried to make sense of it all. "Then there's the matter of the one man, a man with an anti-Semitic record, who's the driving force behind the march," he intoned. A reporter from *NBC Nightly News* wondered aloud, "Will a march designed to bring black men together pull the nation apart?"[12]

From the beginning, the Million Man March/Day of Atonement was designed as a media event, as scholar S. Craig Watkins pointed out in his study of the network coverage of the march. It was planned nearly a year in advance, announced during a press conference, and famous spokespeople were recruited to endorse and vouch for it. Thousands of marches and demonstrations take place on the Mall each year but are not nearly as successful in getting coverage. All the networks plus CNN and C-SPAN carried large swaths of live footage of the Million Man March. According to Watkins's analysis, the duo of O. J. (declared not guilty a couple of weeks earlier) and Farrakhan helped it command the unusually large amount of coverage, both before and after the march.

Watkins examined several network news reports and found that much of the coverage highlighted racial and gender polarization. He found that 71 percent of black women interviewed about their views of the march said they were against it, while 29 percent of black men told television reporters in sound bites that they didn't support the march. "Deviance is what constitutes the essence of their newsworthiness, it is what enables them to move onto the otherwise impenetrable space of network news," Watkins wrote. On CBS News, for example, he noted that the most persistent claim made by journalists covering the Million Man March was that "the message of the march could not be separated from the messenger."

Farrakhan was a factor, but also beside the point. The event drew its real power from the fear, the headlines, the studies, the reports, the music, the madness circulating around black men. As march leaders stated later in their remembrances, the event came off *in spite* of the disorganization of its leadership.[13] Farrakhan had the stature, public profile, and street cred to allow this call to be heard. He masterfully tuned the pitch to hit the sweet spot. After that, the exercise took on a spiritual life of its own. The "million" became a fetish, a magical, mystical threshold the men hoped to cross in order to overcome misperceptions both to the world and to themselves. That is why to this day the marchers take so personally the media's suggestion, later retracted, that fewer than a million men arrived in Washington to meet this challenge.

Although the press coverage of the march was filled with the usual red herrings and misunderstandings, a million men bought into the idea of traveling to Washington, pulling off a media coup that was unprecedented. The genius of the Million Man March was that it showed how the tools of American capitalism—in this case the mass media—can be co-opted. All around the world, men have organized violent and destructive uprisings against a paternalistic world order that strips men of their humanity. On October 16, 1995, a million black men commandeered the spotlight to reinvent their collective aesthetic. History books and media had projected black men one way. This was the remix of black masculinity, not sanitized but humbled and chastened with an eight-point pledge for atonement.

Almost twenty years earlier, Michele Wallace had concluded that "a big Afro, a rifle, and a penis in good working order were not enough to lick the white man's world after all."[14] The question in 1995 was: What could the *symbol* of the big black penis do? At the time, and since then, there have been powerful criticisms from feminists such as bell hooks, who argued that excluding black women from the march perpetuated patriarchy.[15] Black theorists have rightly argued that the time has long passed when women's interests should be held subordinate to those of men for the good of the race. This truth does not address nuances in the crisis of black media misrepresentation, which fall along clear gender lines. In her own 1994 essay "Feminism Inside: Toward a Black Body Politic," hooks suggested that the black male body has been emasculated and feminized by hegemonic forces. To break with the oppressive images, she recommended that "a revolutionary visual aesthetic must emerge that reappropriates, revises, and invents, that gives everyone something new to look at."[16]

The Million Man March/Day of Atonement was exactly such a revolutionary aesthetic. Ultimately, this was a visual and spiritual insurgency that had to be an all-male affair because it was countering specific attacks against black men. Black women, of course, face their own misrepresentations, but these challenges are parallel—not the same. If the purpose of the march was for the black race to eat, that would absolutely entitle black women a seat at the table. But the marchers never pretended to thrust out a cup. There was a whole lot of speechifying to wade through that day, but what did the men really have to say? To each other, it was: *We need to get our shit together.* A million black men had essentially traveled by foot, bus, train, plane, and automobile to the seat of political power to bear a profoundly postmodern message: *We don't want nothing.*

Years after the march, phantom notions of an old-school political agenda continued to be used to reduce the march to mere patriarchal chest-thumping. It was deeply political, but not in the traditional sense. Under the model of the 1963 March on Washington, success was gauged by new government policies or budget line items. The Million Man March launched a new front in black politics in which battles are waged in the realm of perception. This message was delivered just as the first stirrings of the Internet revolution showed that real power can take the form of ideas, rhetoric, and symbols. The Million Man March sampled the methods of the civil rights movement in tribute, while at the same time shelving the idea of marching as a traditional political strategy. Ultimately, the march would usher in an era of post–civil rights movement political action, which led to a copycat franchise of Million Marches featuring women, families, and moms, all of which chose symbolism over spoils.

On a human level, we understand the longing behind and for such symbolism. It's that warm, fuzzy feeling that wrongs will be rectified, short and long term. There, for the world to see, were myriad images of black men in America gathered together without violence or strife. Men returned from the daylong session relieved and reveling in the fact that brothers didn't trip if some accidentally stepped on a sneaker. The photographs, footage, and aerials took the paintbrush to fill in the images black men themselves created.

Yes, the moment was fleeting. Yes, the feeling was ephemeral, but that's mass media. It flashes in an instant, but imprints a message on the brain that can last a lifetime. Ten years after the historic gathering, anniversaries and reflections hit the media again. No one forgot. The Million Man March was one of those moments when an impression is set, new possibilities are opened up. In the best of worlds, this is the place where Tyrone lives.

> *Through the guise and masks of the trickster, the game has always produced black performers who mimic once meaningful survival strategies for their personal profit.*
> —CLYDE TAYLOR[17]

> *Don't let people kill your spirit or create this inferiority complex, trying to accommodate or apologize for who you are.*
> —DAVE CHAPPELLE[18]

More than a decade has passed since the mid-1990s peak of the academic and journalistic discourse around the statistically endangered black man. Over the past decade, the market share devoted to the black male aesthetic has multiplied in professional sports, music, entertainment, and in the news media. In the early 2000s, the rap industry saw a revival of images created at the height of the Crack Era: the big, black man, often with a sculpted body, flaunting diamonds and guns. Statistically speaking, writers like our friend Ta-Nehisi Coates have argued that images of rappers such as 50 Cent reflect an outdated description of the state of black masculinity. With crime and murder rates falling, the crack "crisis" has ebbed. Instead of reflecting that evolution, these images play into hackneyed stereotypes, abandoning hip-hop's traditional role of journaling the fever and pitch of the streets. Coates calls for the industry to observe the ghetto through a more honest lens that is reflective of where black America stands. In other words, he says, it's time to retire an old friend, Bigger Thomas.[19]

Retiring Bigger would mean moving away from a long tradition of black male characters—including media constructions—playing the role of the trickster, titillating and entertaining white audiences while secretly lampooning them and the society they have created. He's been called Esu, the Yoruba deity who stands at the crossroads between the spiritual and material worlds.[20] He is a blues performer like Robert Johnson making deals with the devil. He is Flava Flav. He is Tupac. The trickster has no allegiances, least of all to "truth." And perhaps it's time we accepted the evolution of the role of hip-hop: from art/ghetto barometer into an international commodity and postmodern joke. As our friend Clint likes to say in rabid defense of 50 Cent, "He's not an artist; he's a criminal!"

Even if the streets don't smolder at the level they did in the 1980s, they still deserve attention. The carcasses of the Crack Era are littered throughout the black landscape in the form of violence, incarceration rates, and life expectancy, crumbling schools, and infrastructure, and on the psyche of survivors who've lived through King Crack. Since it hit the streets, few things have inspired black artists of our generation as much as crack: making it, selling it, using it, and even going to jail for it. The rapper 50 Cent may be marketing an image on the wane, but some research has shown that the decline has been overstated by journalists, according to *Freakonomics* authors and *New York Times Magazine* columnists Stephen J. Dubner and Steven D. Levitt. Because of declining prices and profits, it is the crack-related violence that has taken a dive. "And it is that violence that made crack most relevant to the middle class," they write. Far from being played out, crack use remains steady.[21]

And so it is for the crackhead Tyrone Biggums, the creation of comic Dave Chappelle, whose name is an inspired coincidence with our own book title. On the show, we see snapshots of his character: speaking against the evils of drugs to a school classroom audience, or appearing in a spoof of *Fear Factor*, eating and sleeping in slimy bugs all too happily. In another sketch, he's peddling "Red Balls," which gives him superhuman strength, allowing him to lift buses off the ground to get change to support his habit. Tyrone can also be seen resisting the interventions of kindly white people and black women alike. He's the one onstage during a Snoop performance, scratching himself and hyping the crowd like Flava Flav circa 1989 hypeman.

Tyrone Biggums is just part of a large repertoire that helped Chappelle pull off the trickster's biggest heist: a $50 million payday. Chappelle's timely pop-culture spoofs of everyone from P. Diddy to Lil Jon to President George W. Bush to Prince catapulted Chappelle to black man of the hour. He had the streets singing in call and response "Yeah!" "Okay!" because of a successful Lil Jon hit. He also made "I'm Rick James, Bitch!" a crossracial rallying cry—and revival of the funkster's career—months before James's death. Chappelle's first two seasons drew some of the largest audiences in the history of the Comedy Central network.

When *Chappelle's Show* debuted, in 2003, Chappelle seemed secure in the direction he wanted to take the show, a cult classic for the underground cultural heads. "This is the best job I've ever had in my life. I don't have to be Urkel or none of this crazy stuff," he told Africana.com in 2003.[22] "These are the types of characters"—a crackhead who does drug education with kids, a blind white supremacist who doesn't realize he's black—"that a black dude will never do. For a black dude to play this point of view you have to think, you've really got to stretch. We're in this holding pattern of political correctness, which is not gonna get anything done for anybody.... Before I do it, I pre-think it out: is this a disservice? And I don't think I'm doing a disservice to anybody."[23]

But by spring 2005, with several deadlines for delivering the third season blown, he saw some holes in his own personal system of accountability. So, for a while, Chappelle disappeared from the set. Rumors of drug abuse, writer's block, a crisis of conscience/confidence abounded, as hundreds of thousands of copies of the DVD of *Chappelle's Show*, season two, flew off the shelves. The public didn't quite know what to make of a young black man—especially one who liked to proclaim "I'm rich, Beeyatch!" during commercial breaks—not cashing a $50 million check as fast as humanly possible. Internet message boards exploded with debate over Chappelle's sanity, often covering the same old themes.

Some saw the crisis as a front for the old trickster once again, gittin ovah on The Man.[24] "Trust me ol' Dave got yawl fooled ol boy bout to come back out and wear yawl out," "thatlilboy" wrote, in a post to the Electronic Urban Report website. He added that Chappelle's respite in Africa was all part of a plan to build intrigue and hype—and ratings. "When his season drops everyone and there [sic] mother will be watching too [sic] see what he is going to do.... Just watch and see...this is all a part of the plan...all the way to the bank...."[25]

Others wondered about the need for the pause at all. "He signed a contract to do a job," Good Doctor wrote. "He should be a man, step up, and just do his job. I'm tired of him and his foolishness now. He gets no sympathy from me. Dave, do your job and shut up. NEXT."

On www.keithboykin.com another poster wrote, "He is a modern-day minstrel or jester, the job of which is to tell us the uncomfortable truths about ourselves. It's the stuff we CAN'T talk about or make fun of that cause the most damage to our society. The first step is to ADMIT that you have a problem, even if it is in the context of humor." A poster named "Che" spat back, "We need new images."[26]

After the debate over the fate of *Chappelle's Show* traveled all over the world, Chappelle sat down with *Time* magazine to explain his absence and crush rumors of drug addiction and rehab. He said he had begun to question the quality of the show and whether he could defend it. "Everyone around me says, 'You're a genius!'; 'You're great!'; 'That's your voice!' But I'm not sure that they're right."[27]

Whether Chappelle was getting black masculinity right is a fair question when reading the sketch of the crackhead Tyrone Biggums. We are not fans of crackheads, or of making light of their addictions—that's so *In Living Color* passé. Besides AIDS, crack may be the most devastating epidemic to face our generation. Biggums is our least favorite skit—it's painful to watch. Who wants to see a man defecate in public, or get flushed down a toilet? Like a real crackhead, Tyrone Biggums is not fun to look at.

Of course, by one measure, that we flinch to look at him is a sign that he has struck a nerve. During his May 2005 respite in South Africa, Chappelle realized that he needed to check his intentions. "Whatever decisions I make right now I'm going to have to live with. Your soul is priceless," Chappelle told *Time*. Our stylist Paunice in Detroit told us she appreciated Chappelle's timeout. Her theory is that some of his kinfolk down South called him up to chastise him for going too far, especially in his prevalent use of the "n" word. The argument here is that Chappelle gets plenty of laughs that ring true for black people and our existence, but why are white people really laughing, for example, at the character on the show who finally gets a job but smells like French fries? Paunice said she was curious why white people slapped their knees at some of Chappelle's skits, and the comedian later told Oprah in an interview that it bothered him too. It's like, it's okay for white people to laugh, but not that hard. Even when Jay-Z performs his song "Nigga What, Nigga Who," the rapper has been known to instruct the white people in the audience not to say the "n" word.

With Chappelle's "priceless soul" statement, he is essentially making the same argument as Thelma Golden a decade before: He's ironizing stereotypes and flipping them back at the viewer. Mass media is all-powerful, but individuals have the agency to seize their own power.

The black man and his role in society are evolving, and so should the imagery that depicts him. Watching Tyrone Biggums produces a sinking feeling, the sensation of staying suspended in the wrong place. We're stuck either "correcting" old images of black masculinity or remaking them for profit. We are looking for the new images of Tyrone, images that reflect the growth and evolution of the black man. We admire Chappelle's introspective stance and his ability, unlike many rap artists, to appreciate the ironies and ambiguities. But we must keep moving forward—or become stuck. As Chappelle told *Time* magazine, "I want to make sure I'm dancing and not shuffling." If we are stopping to ask that question, we're halfway there.

Chapter 3

Visible Tyrone

N ormally, the house, nestled among nineteenth-century brownstones in Washington, D.C.'s, Bloomingdale section, is the picture of contemporary Victorian style. The town home's décor is a mixture of antique furniture pieces, massive oriental rugs, original oil pieces collected from all over the world, and contemporary accents like deep-canary-yellow walls.

On this day, though, the house is a mess. The kids have been shipped off to "one of the better" summer camps in Pennsylvania. The 5,000-square-foot house resembles an airport runway, a maze of contractors zooming in and out. There's the crew installing central air for the third and fourth floors. The carpenters are finishing up the basement, which is being transformed into a movie theater, a stone-covered shower room, a kitchen with wall tiles imported from Italy, and a home office with floors made of glazed concrete.

The workers breeze in and out, seeking advice and approval from the home's owners, Sam McLemore and James Brathwaite. If the black workers have any qualms about taking orders from the two men of the house, they don't let on. They appear at ease even when Sam thanks each of them with a man-hug. The workers may be more progressive than most when it comes to "alternative" lifestyles. Or, it could be that, like many people who meet Sam and James, they find it hard to put their minds around two deep-chocolate, masculine men making a home. Forget about the family portrait of Daddy, Papa, daughter, and son visible on the mantel as soon as you walk through the double doors at the main entrance. Why not just call them brothers? Cousins? Roommates, possibly? Definitely not gay.

Questions about Sam and James's sexuality evaporate soon after we pop in a DVD press promo of *Noah's Arc*, a new cable television drama that was just picked up by the new all-gay network, Logo. We sit around an antique wood dining table watching a flat-screen monitor to check out the series that marked a milestone in media representation of gayness. For the first time in history, any unsuspecting channel surfer might stumble across the story of four upwardly mobile and gorgeous black gay men, living and loving in Los Angeles.

We watch the opening episode. The show's obligatory queen character is shocked to discover the online name his boyfriend has used to post a sex ad.

"*Pussy*bottom!?!?"

The word rings out from Sam's speakers as if in slow motion, echoing throughout the old house, doing pirouettes, swinging around the golden wood banister and hanging pregnant in the air, smack into the AC guy, now paralyzed at the steps. The worker descends the steps in stunned silence, and Sam leans back in his chair to face him.

"You know, this is...a documentary," Sam says.

On the DVD, the boyfriend's sex ad is read: "Amazing bubble-butt here. Love to be fucked all up inside my gut. Love to drink piss and deep-throat long dicks—"

Sam hits the pause button.

"It's a...documentary on the practices of the...tribes of Africa," Sam continues, a wink in his voice. "Only practiced by the native pygmies of that region."

The four of us laugh, slightly awkwardly. After the AC guy leaves, we finish watching the show, which culminates in the main character, Noah, convincing a "confused straight boy" named Wade to make love.

Sitting at the wood table, James looks on knowingly at Wade, the curious-straight-guy character. He "calls himself straight and acts straight, but something isn't quite clicking right. He's on this journey that he doesn't want to go on."

James predicts a tough road ahead for openly gay Noah if he continues to pursue a relationship with Wade. "If you are someone's first who is just coming into the lifestyle, there is no way you can be the last," James says. "He's in for some serious aspirins."

Same-gender lovin' has ancient roots, but it's only relatively recently that the word *homosexual* has appeared in our language as a noun rather than an adjective. This means that it is now possible to talk about a "homosexual" who is a person, rather than "homosexual practices," which are something a person *does,* as scholar Vivien Burr points out.[1] Burr is a psychologist whose work in social constructionist theory is particularly well suited for a discussion of the media discourse around gay black men. With this linguistic trick— the shift of *homosexual* from an adjective to a noun—Burr notes that we have created a certain kind of person. And with a new kind of person coming into being, the laws of mass media dictate that eventually there will be a new way to portray them. Throw race into the mix, and you've got a heady, potent brew of stereotypes.

For a sampling, start with Damon Wayans and David Alan Grier's early-1990s limp-wristed "Men on Film" characters on *In Living Color,* who brought the finger snaps to Middle America. RuPaul made history by becoming the first drag queen turned MAC cosmetics spokesmodel. And novelist E. Lynn Harris ruled the world of black gay male representations during the mid-1990s; his sexually ambiguous characters titillated and captured a generation of black women readers, opening their minds to an alternative reality sharing their space. In relating the tale of Raymond Tyler Jr.—an all-American, second-generation attorney who never had a homosexual thought until a football player seduced him during his senior year in college—Harris took readers into a subculture where professional athletes and married-with-children executives shattered the stereotype of the flamboyantly effeminate gay male.

In the early 2000s, with the worsening of the AIDS crisis among black women, the mainstream news media began to catch on to the reality of a black male gay world. News stories and even network television began to explore the "down low" or "DL" phenomenon, an "outbreak" of black men infecting black women with viruses caught during secret trysts with male lovers. The phrase was used initially, in the mid-1990s, by R & B artists: TLC had the song "Creep," Brian McKnight had "On the Down Low," and R. Kelly made the song "Down Low (Nobody Has to Know)." Those artists were talking about a secret, illicit romance, but the phrase came to be adopted by the news media to describe a "subculture" of black men living in the closet.

Author Keith Boykin charts the evolution of the coverage in his smart 2005 book *Beyond the Down Low*.[2] It all started in February 2001, when the Centers for Disease Control and Prevention released an alarming report about the penetration of AIDS among gay black men in six major cities. When the AIDS rates among black women began climbing, public health experts began to speak of the black male "bisexual bridge" to AIDS. Everyone in the news media wanted a piece of the story: the *Los Angeles Times, USA Today,* the *New York Times,* then *Ebony, Jet, Vibe,* the *San Diego Union Tribune.* In 2002, there was an episode about the down low on *ER.* In August of

2003, a *New York Times Magazine* cover story explored the world of black men on the down low. In 2004, the television program *Law and Order: SVU* did an episode on the DL. Then, in early 2004, Oprah devoted an episode to the down low, plugging author J. L. King's blockbuster book *On the Down Low*.[3]

When it comes down to it, the hubbub is really the story of the lies that men *and women* tell themselves about their relationships, according to Boykin, a Harvard-trained lawyer who served as White House aide to President Clinton. It's not necessarily about sexuality, but about less sexy, old-fashioned notions like integrity, honesty, and trust. Boykin believes the hysteria around the down low is also "a story about the lies that we tell the media, which the media in turn tell back to us about who we are."

Male infidelity is nothing new. Closeted homosexuality is nothing new. But combining the two with black masculinity has scared a whole lot of women and sold a bunch of books. DL is not a "trend" at all—just a snazzy new construction that has allowed us to talk about things that used to be rude to say out loud.

The person whose story should be by far the highest-profile DL story is former New Jersey Gov. Jim McGreevy, who announced that he was a "gay American" and that his marriage to his wife was a lie. There was a crucial difference: He was white.

Essentially, a new Black Male Menace has come to town, casing the innocent like wolves in the fields. But the discussion echoes beyond the issue of sexuality. It has forced us to grapple with a post-modern reality with porous boundaries. Nothing is what it seems. Seeing is not believing. Somewhere between these constructions are black men, trying to live their lives.

D.C. Black Pride started in 1991 as a modest AIDS prevention fundraiser at a local high school field in Washington, D.C. Fifteen years later, it had grown to become the premier black gay celebration, replicated in dozens of cities around the world. D.C.'s version of Black Pride had been upstaged by trendier locales such as Miami and Puerto Rico, but it still drew thousands from around the country when I (Natalie H.) checked it out for the first time in the summer of 2005. At the Memorial Day Weekend event, Washington's black gay, lesbian, and transgender community recognized folks in the arts, politics, and the corporate world. Conventiongoers could attend workshops such as "That's Not Love, That's Stupid," "Internet Dating: You've Got Male," and "Black and Out at an HBCU." But the real action was the parties, picnics, and other see-and-be-seen events like the one taking place at D.C.'s convention center.

I walk into the convention center exhibit hall with my friend Glynn Jackson, a radio personality, hair and fashion show producer extraordinaire, and black culture maven. Glynn rarely comes to events like this, but today he's playing tour guide for my benefit. As usual, he's also seized the moment as another marketing opportunity. He passes out flyers for LaPink, his latest hair and fashion extravaganza, an event that will celebrate his twenty-five years as an event producer. His 6'2" frame is covered with a pink linen suit, off-white gaiters, and shiny silver belt buckle. It will take me days to realize how perfectly Glynn's outfit plays off the LaPink theme: "Synergy!"

Inside the convention hall, the theme is "Taste the Chocolate." It could easily be mistaken for the largest music-video set ever assembled. Hundreds of beautiful black men mill around the convention site, some freshly scrubbed, baby-faced, many with shiny bald heads. Muslim-style scruffy goatees are abundant, along with other street-corner staples like black do-rags and white wave caps tucked under baseball caps. Plump triceps and biceps burst through wifebeaters, brimmed hats are pulled low over the eyes. Collars are popped on polo shirts and Jay-Z-inspired stripes. I see a few cuties wearing tight T-shirts with slogans like "Dickies," "Hung," and "I Would Do Me."

It pretty much looks like any mainstream black event, where everyone performs a carefully orchestrated ruse. Outfits are meticulously constructed to appear casually thrown together. It is impossible not to be awed by such a dazzling array of black beauty, yet everyone looks bored, ambling through the convention hall, screwing up their faces as if something stinks. And although their sexuality is what has drawn them here, aside from a handful of amorous lesbians tangling tongues, all signs of sexuality are carefully tucked away. As a whole, the black men here look cut-up, well-rested, and exfoliated—and ready to knock heads if necessary. Their extreme masculinity and conspicuous good health is a powerful visual antidote to a community devastated by HIV and AIDS.

Every five minutes, Glynn stops to chat with somebody. It's unclear who actually knows him from his work in the community, from his radio show *Changing Gears* on XM satellite radio, or *Tangles and Locks*, a documentary about his hair show, which has been airing repeatedly on the black cable station TV One.

"Oh my God, you're Glynn Jackson!" a woman from New York tells him. "You're the reason why I wear a wig now!" Glynn chats her up as if he's known her all his life. Then he plucks off a few glossy LaPink flyers from his stack, and tells her to call him. Every time he stops to talk, I stand awkwardly, positive that my earth-toned frilly skirt and jacket ensemble don't pass muster as eyes scan from Glynn to me.

It was like that the first time I met Glynn, in 2001, when I was writing a profile of him for the *Washington Post*.[4] I was halfway to the suburban Maryland radio studio where he recorded segments for his fashion commentary, *Fashion Faux Pas*. My hands on the steering wheel, I looked down at my outfit—scuffed-up leather Mary Jane shoes, a long gray skirt that was the shape of a paper bag, and a vinyl jacket with multiple buttons missing. I briefly considered making a U-turn back to my wardrobe, but I was already late for the taping.

Glynn had sparked fear in the hearts of millions of listeners on the nationally syndicated *Russ Parr Morning Show*. During his fashion segments, he would snap on big girls in tube dresses, bunion-toes in sandals, nasty acrylic fingernails, and the like. So I strolled into the studio mentally preparing myself for a live, on-air slaughter. But when I made a self-deprecating comment, he stopped me with a raised hand. "Child, please," he said. He was wearing a shiny, chocolate-brown button-down shirt. He lifted up one leg of his tan, tailored slacks. "Do you see my white socks?" Sure enough, there they were. Not trouser socks, mind you, but thick running socks, bunched at the ankle.

It was the beginning of a beautiful friendship.

I consider Glynn one of the true guardians of black culture. He started producing shows when he was a high school student in rural New Roads, Louisiana, in the 1980s. He began organizing talent and fashion shows in high school, where he spent four years unchallenged as class president, with the motto "Action Jackson Makes It Happen." Indeed, he began showing a knack for making the impossible come to life. As a parting gift to his school, he managed to have a monumental shrine to his class made of marble and brick.

Coming to accept his sexuality was a long process. An uncle, noting that Rock Hudson had died of AIDS, told Glynn he would be next; he got scared. For two years, his mother took 17-year-old Glynn from doctor to doctor, testing his HIV status. Each time, it came up negative, but each time, he wanted another opinion. One day, his mother had had enough. Glynn likes to give a dramatic interpretation of his conversation with his mom:

"There is nothing wrong with your ass, Glynn. The doctors say there is *nothing fucking wrong!*"

"But Ma," Glynn replies, "when I cough, blood comes up."

"Glynn, your ass just had a glass of fucking Kool-Aid!"

He wasn't convinced that he wasn't going to die until after high school, when he passed the physical test to get into the navy. Hearing his name called out as having passed the battery of physical assessments, he was finally satisfied. If Uncle Sam says he's HIV-negative, it must be so. As he walked out the door of the training center, the recruiter promptly asked him where he was going.

"Home" was the reply. "I ain't going in no goddamned navy!"

"So why are you here?"

"It's a long-ass story."

He ended up toughing it out in the navy, where he soon found a familiar niche. For the decade he was in the service, he was a radioman by trade, but he spent most of his time producing talent shows. When he left the service in the mid-1990s, he continued producing shows in D.C., where he quickly became an integral cog in the city's black culture industry. Glynn spends his days pounding the pavement, hustling up sponsors and recruiting talent for his next production. As a cultural entrepreneur, his niche is helping black women of all shapes and sizes believe in themselves, and showcasing the unique vitality that is black culture, from gravity-defying hair to high couture on a low budget.

His life's work reflects a bond with black women. In this he is similar to the gay black male writer Hilton Als, who in his book *The Women* describes his propensity for identifying with the "Negress," a long-suffering line of black women, as the dramatic center of his life.[5] Take the show Glynn was plugging, LaPink. Originally it was supposed to celebrate his twenty-five years in the business. But instead he turned the event into a celebration of breast cancer survivors—a nod to his key constituency, black women. Like the ill-fated Negress, Glynn has taken many knocks in love. He's struggled to find a partner and a sense of peace. During more somber moments, he wonders if being gay means never—ever—finding true happiness.

Despite his over-the-top emcee style at his events, Glynn says he tries to stay away from overtly gay representations in his productions, especially with male models. He says the black community—and his sponsors, comprising mostly black mom-and-pop stores—wouldn't feel comfortable. This is odd, because his own sexuality is as transparent as Saran Wrap. In a weird way, you could call him postgay. It was years into our friendship before we actually had a conversation about his sexuality. He doesn't talk about it, but he appears to be constantly performing his identity, whether it's giving a theatrical pep talk to beauty students or threatening to send his grandmother to pick up the writer from *Essence* to come see his show. Regardless of how he makes others feel, there is no denying that Glynn is part of the cultural architecture of black Washington. Everyone in the black community—from hard-core roughnecks to church folk—loves, accepts, and supports him. That's just Glynn.

And that was just Glynn at the 2005 D.C. Black Pride festival. As Glynn strides by, shoulders erect in his pink linen suit, the other men survey him. Eyeballs scan him up and down, none too pleased. Smug in their Timberlands, do-rags, and wifebeaters, the men look at Glynn with mild distaste, as they might regard an uncle who tunes his station to classic R & B when everyone wants to hear hip-hop. When Glynn catches these attitudinous vibes, he preempts them with friendly greetings. Where are you from? How are you doing? I like your look, have you ever done any modeling?

As we stand outside, ready to leave the convention hall, the extent to which things have changed has Glynn shaking his head. He eventually falls in with a group of older gentleman who have been in the life much longer than Glynn. They are all bewildered by the forceful show of testosterone around them. Partly as a result of the

AIDS crisis, black gay men underwent an evolution in the way they performed their sexuality in public—even in safe places like Pride. Glynn sighs and looks around. "Ain't too many of us dinosaurs left," he says.

It is hard to overstate the impact that author E. Lynn Harris has had on our generation. Like any good literature, his work goes beyond storytelling. For a generation of black women, his books represent nothing less than a paradigm shift in the way we view ourselves, the way we view our men, and the way we view reality. My freshman year in college, a friend enthusiastically endorsed reading Harris's 1991 novel *Invisible Life*,[6] the title a clever play on Ralph Ellison's *Invisible Man*. "After you read this, you will never look at black men the same again," she warned.

We devoured Harris's books the way we devoured Judy Blume. Even after the novelty of Harris's gender-bending characters wore off and we outgrew the pedestrian quality of the writing, black women have remained loyal, delivering Harris best seller after best seller. The kinship between the black gay man and the Negress was on full display.

I remember going with my girlfriend Yolanda to a fund-raiser for the black literature organization the Hurston/Wright Foundation in 2003, where Harris, a formidable patron of black letters, was a main attraction. Karibu Books in Bowie, Maryland, the well-to-do black suburb of Washington in Prince George's County, was filled with well-groomed black women who had gathered to contribute to the foundation for black writers, and no doubt, to see Harris, the literary superstar. Harris spoke of his just-released memoir *What Becomes of the Brokenhearted*, about his lifelong struggle for love and understanding from black men.[7] When he took questions, women from the audience piped in with their own heartaches and insecurities. It was like one long therapy session, Harris and the black women commiserating about the heartache they suffered in love—and at the hands of black men.

The foundation auctioned off a weekend and dinner with Harris in Fayetteville, Arkansas, where he was a visiting professor of English at the University of Arkansas. Bidding grew intense. When it was all over, an attractive thirtyish woman in a business suit won the prize; she paid more than $1,000 for the privilege. Yolanda and I sat a few chairs away from her when she whipped out her cell phone to tell her husband the good news. I bet he was thrilled.

Naturally, both of the us have written our share of DL stories for newspapers. Natalie M. wrote a piece in the *Detroit News* about a black woman who contracted AIDS from a man to increase awareness of the alarmingly high rates of infection among black women. In 2001, I (Natalie H.) interviewed Harris for a piece in the *Washington Post,* tied to the release of one of his novels.[8] In a way, Harris was successful, in that he forced us to increase our consciousness of alternative realities and changed the way we date. We are more cautious. No free love for this generation.

The mania about author J. L. King sort of took us by surprise. We thought we'd been there, done that. Thanks to a 2004 episode of *Oprah*, his life's story has now become legend: King was 27, happily married, with the house, two dogs, two kids, two cars. Then an older man from his church turned him out. The "perfect wife" caught them in the act and promptly threw him out.

Years later, King, having just left his job at a black publishing company, decided to help put together a brochure, "Secrets of the African American Bisexual Man." The pamphlet caught the eye of a few state health departments looking for new ways to increase awareness of AIDS. In early 2001, the Centers for Disease Control began releasing a series of increasingly startling reports on black people with

AIDS. Journalists and health policymakers alike hunted for the silver bullet.

Weeks later, King addressed the African American AIDS Conference in Washington, D.C., speaking openly about living on the down low. "He started exciting people about this whole theory," Keith Boykin explained to me. "This was his explanation about why AIDS is prominent in the black community. These men on the down low are HIV-positive and they are spreading it to black women."

When King was preparing to write the book, he was looking for a ghostwriter. He asked Boykin, whose first book, *One More River to Cross: Black & Gay in America,* with an introduction written by Harris, helped launch Boykin's career and placed him among the premier voices articulating black sexuality.[9] Boykin had heard King's message, delivered to anyone with a notepad or microphone, and he couldn't get with it. He saw it as alarmist and demonizing to black men. "J. L. King goes out of his way to scare people about AIDS," Boykin told me. It's as if King is saying, " 'Not only do you have to be concerned about that man, but you need to be concerned that that man will kill you.' And black women have to be afraid and concerned about AIDS because of the down low.' That's bullshit. They shouldn't just be concerned about the down low. They need to be concerned about any [dishonest behavior.] It's irresponsible and outrageous."

Needless to say, Boykin decided against joining the project.

But the media storm kept brewing around the issue of black male sexuality. King was a key bridge that took the down low phenomenon out of the world of fiction and into the evening news: He was among the few willing to be tagged and photographed as a real, live specimen. He swiftly became the "official" face of down low men, despite, as Boykin points out, having no credentials as an expert on sex other than his own experience. Judging from the book, his research appeared to consist mainly of finding interviews by trolling the Internet—not exactly a place known for its forthrightness and honesty. But a fun time was had by all.

Before J. L. King's book even hits bookstores, Oprah gave it the full treatment: *It's a shocker. It's called living on the "Down Low." Men with wives and girlfriends secretly having sex with other men. One man blows the lid.*[10]

Oprah spent the night before the taping reading an advance copy of the book. "I couldn't put it down," she said before her studio audience. "Best-Friend-of-Staff Gayle read it, too, and she's terrified."

"She *should* be scared," King replied.

The book describes a force stronger than men. No time for condoms, because that "stops it from being a thoughtless, lustful act that they have no control over," King writes. "If you wear a condom, it couldn't be the liquor that made you have sex with a man."[11]

Later, he writes: "What's really scary about this thing, at least for me, is that the desire to be with other men has such a strong pull that it feels like you can't resist it. It's like something overtakes you. It's insanity. I discussed this with a minister friend, who describes the lust, the drive as akin to being possessed."[12]

King describes an animal lust, akin to dogs in heat. It is as if he is saying, *It was only a matter of time, America. The black man's penis has gone mad! It's loaded. It's lethal. And it's coming to your towwwwn!*

King was all business, sitting in Oprah's studio. Staring down from nerdy-chic glasses, wearing a nice suit and peacock-blue shirt, he dispensed the facts with the toughness of a scare-'em-straight drill sergeant. Their secret is all in the eyes, he instructed. "Get nosy," he advised suspicious wives and girlfriends. Real DL brothers don't go to the gay clubs. They cruise for guys at church, a gym, a grocery store.

"Anywhere, because we are everywhere," he said. The camera panned to young, nubile white and black women in the audience, their wide eyes barely blinking.

Boykin passed on ghostwriting King's first book. Instead, in his own 2005 book, *Beyond the Down Low*, he sought to neutralize the hysteria around the phenomenon. "My objective was to desensationalize the issue, and educating the public so that we could create the conditions where men didn't have to be on the down low."

But even for more thoughtful representations like Boykin's, the "down low" in the title soon became a sort of marketing joke. In 2005, King's former wife, Brenda Stone Browder, came out with her own book, *On the Up and Up: A Survival Guide for Women Living with Men on the Down Low.*[13] King and his ex-wife announced that they were staging a joint book tour plugging her book and his sequel, *Coming Up from the Down Low: The Journey to Acceptance, Healing, and Honest Love.*[14] The tour was called "A Conversation of Reconciliation."

The news of the joint tour, along with the revelation that author Terry McMillan's husband, the young Jamaican who at 20 years old had helped her get her groove back and inspired a major motion picture, was also living on the DL, had flaps yakking. The Internet message boards were howling. "So it's come to this. We now have a down low tour," wailed a poster named "B00TANEB00TUS" on the Entertainment Urban Report website. "This ain't no Hallmark card moment."[15]

"Mayday" agreed. "I can't believe that his ex-wife is going to be out pimping their books together, we have poverty pimps and now DL pimps what the hell?"

When it comes down to it, we are left with two dueling media representations of gay black men: the flaming guy we feel comfortable around, like the sassy stylists on *Girlfriends*, or the lurking black man on the down low.

We're having lunch on a summer afternoon in Baltimore's trendy Mount Vernon district, at the type of shop where you can get a $7

Bailey's latte. Glynn settles into his seat next to Damon, whom I first met three months ago, after he'd delivered a thundering Baptist eulogy.

"Glynn, are you going to give me a bracelet like that so I can bling?" Damon says, pointing to Glynn's fake platinum and diamond links, held together by a white twisty tie.

"Yes," Glynn replies. "I'll give it to you so when you have that meeting with your boss, she'll know you like mon-ney."

Damon (not his real name) is brown, about 5'9", and a little plump. He's wearing brown rectangular Dolce & Gabbana glasses. His shirt cuffs are blue. His whole outfit is a web of subtle lime green, purple, and yellow stripes. Think architect; Wesley Snipes in *Jungle Fever*, but with a paunch.

I compliment him on the smart outfit. "Everywhere he works, he's the fashion plate of the organization," Glynn explains.

"I'm an icon," Damon proclaims. For the rest of the afternoon, that's how it goes, Glynn and Damon trading gossip and taunts like the Olsen twins. Sometimes, Glynn refers to Damon as "my soror over here." Other times it's just "the bitch"—as in "the bitch done gave up her lip gloss and everything."

Sitting back in his chair, wearing a Burberryesque black T-shirt with the plaid "42" tucked into black slacks, Glynn tells the story of how the two friends met. More than a decade ago, Damon's older sister was in the navy with Glynn while Damon was in college studying business. She arranged for the two men to meet because she wanted to find out if her brother was gay. Soon, word got back to their parents in the Midwest. Emergency family meetings were called, and the Tylenol-popping commenced.

Damon is now a 32-year-old real estate executive and an associate minister at a Baltimore church. He describes his lifestyle not as being in the closet, but rather as choosing not to project his sexuality on the world. "People don't see you," Damon explains. "All they see is what you are labeled as. People are mean. It kind of forces you to be discreet about who you are." He used to "fake the funk" at work, bragging about his sexual conquests with women. "I don't know if I want to be the guy that's just flaming in the office. I think there is a time and place for that."

But in his off-time, he likes to let loose. "That's part of the fun of going out. You escape yourself." Like the time on a road trip, when the song "Mr. Love" came on the radio and Damon and Glynn pulled over and got out to do the coochie-pop dance.

When I ask Damon if he's ever been with a woman, he says no, at which point Glynn makes a big show of dropping his fork. Damon counters that Glynn is the one who took a trip on the dark side. "You had sex with a *giiiirl!*" Damon taunts. Glynn screws up his face as if he's realized too late that he's eaten a moldy pork chop.

Sometimes, Glynn says, it gets hard to pursue same-sex relationships. Many men are freeloading divas. Others are criminal, and shady. "It gets pretty tiring after a while," he says. "You keep trying and trying."

One episode made him want to give up altogether. Glynn was driving through D.C. when the "check engine" light began blinking on his dashboard. "Are you having car trouble?" a man asked from the side of the road. "Um, ye-e-e-s," Glynn recalls replying. "And it was downhill from there."

Damon smiles at the memory of this man, Rico. "After Glynn had a visit from Rico, he was in *such* a good mood."

The good feelings disintegrated when Glynn and Damon found out Rico had stolen all the furniture and electronics out of the apartment they shared. The neighbors spotted Rico driving his girlfriend's white van off with their stuff. Police didn't have enough evidence to charge him. So the two roommates waited until he was on trial for something else.

Glynn showed up in court, wearing a butterscotch knit-and-leather number, knotted above his belly button, with yellow snakeskin cowboy boots. "I hunted his ass down like a dog," Glynn says. When that didn't work, they put together a sting operation. They went to where Rico's girlfriend worked, flashed a fake police badge, and informed her, "We have reason to believe your car was involved in a robbery."

Ultimately, Glynn and Damon had to eat the loss.

Later, Glynn ran into Rico at the post office. Glynn took the opportunity to thank him for putting him through all of that drama, which he said ultimately made him a stronger person.

"You know what he said?" Glynn asks. "Okay."

"You know you love you some Rico," Damon says, and Glynn rolls his eyes.

At the Baptist church where Damon is an associate minister, he is not out to the congregation. "Them babies ain't ready for that," he says. He loves the church for the sense of tradition, and the opportunity to serve his fellow man. He hopes to start his own, nondenominational, church sometime soon.

Damon hasn't been in a relationship for a long time. He says that though he has not found happiness in a same-sex relationship, he finds satisfaction in other parts of his life. He doesn't see his single status as any different from the situation of his single girlfriends and his sister who are getting older. The man shortage doesn't know gender boundaries. "The choices out here are slim. You don't want someone with their hand out. I'm concerned about my image. And being respected means being a positive person. People have so many negative stereotypes about gay people. So that makes things tough."

He says that once he's been on his new job for a while, he might consider telling people at his office. But right now, there's too much at stake. He doesn't even do taxicab confessions anymore.

"No matter where you are, people wanna know," Damon says. "So I keep 'em guessing."

By the middle of the 2000s, big strides were being made in the media representation of black male homosexuality. The HBO series *Oz* (1997–2002) presented a prison drama that sexually titillated audiences with its boy-on-boy play and myriad gratuitous ass and penis shots. Then there was Keith, the sexy, black, übermasculine cop on the HBO series *Six Feet Under*, who, inexplicably, is in a relationship with a pasty white male mortician.

In 2005, *Noah's Arc* creator Patrik-Ian Polk had seen the unprecedented in-your-face representations of gay and feminine sexuality in *Sex and the City* and *Queer as Folk*, and as an alumnus of the production staff of *Soul Food*, he brought with him a similar aesthetic: vibrant, freshly styled characters that glow under the cameras. *Noah's Arc* was also in some ways a public service announcement about AIDS awareness, supported by the Human Rights Campaign and the Black AIDS Institute.

With its deliciously subversive biblical title, *Noah's Arc* was designed as a fable representing the diversity of the black gay experience. There's the luscious title character Noah, an aspiring young screenwriter, who is played by actor Darryl Stephens. His arms are bulky and buff, his waist curves down to a taut onion. He's vulnerable and hard, neck-tied ascots and crunched-up abs. He's both beautifully feminine and masculine. The primary plot line follows Noah as he pursues Wade, who also loves women.

The supporting characters have their own lusty subplots. Ricky, a straight-haired, buff, light-skinned sexual marauder aka "The Ho," has a fling with a precocious employee of his hip-clothing shop in LA. Then there's Alex, "The Diva," who is an HIV counselor navigating the vagaries of interactive porn with his boyfriend, who is a hot anesthesiologist. And then there's Chance, an Ivy-league-educated college professor, a straight arrow who fends off advances from an amorous male teaching assistant. Chance is married and has adopted his husband's daughter. In this sexually charged milieu, he's a committed family man whose mantra is "resist temptation."

Noah hooks up with Wade, ignoring his friends' advice. "Those straight-but-curious boys come with way too much emotional baggage," Chance tells him. But Noah thinks Wade might be The One.

Some of the acting is campy, as is the tongue-in-cheek dialogue. In a scene where they trade screenplays in a coffee shop, Wade asks Noah what he wants to order. "Mocha ice, blended," Noah says, "hold the cream." Leering, Wade shoots back: "I'd love to."

As beautifully shot as the series is, it still broadcasts images that America has never seen before: black men kissing and engaged in oral and anal sex. Polk must know that it will take a while to normalize such graphic depictions for straight audiences, but he doesn't seem to care. He's gotten his chance and he's going for it.

In the climax (pun intended), set to a Janet Jackson standard, Noah stays in the bathroom on his cell phone, getting advice from his three otherwise, uh, engaged friends. Ricky is on the phone while trading oral favors with his newest store clerk. Alex and his doctor boyfriend are learning to embrace cyberporn. Chance is preparing a rose-petal-filled bubble bath, waiting for his husband to come home.

Finally, Noah gently coaches Wade in the art of lovemaking: "You gotta go slow at first," he says, as he rides Wade face-to-face in missionary position. "It's not like with a woman."

But of course, Noah wouldn't know.

Sam and James laugh heartily throughout *Noah's Arc*. After it is over, Sam jokes that he wishes I hadn't been there, so they could really relax and enjoy it. Naturally, they identify with Chance, the married-with-child gay professor. Sam and James think the love scenes are tastefully done. (In the scene at the gay nightclub, James points out author Keith Boykin, making a cameo appearance on the dance floor.)

Sam regrets that the characters fall into stereotypes, and in the end, all their interactions revolve around sex. But he likes that the professor resists temptation. "That's the kind of positive image I'd like to see. It was very entertaining to me as a black gay man," he says. "In their own way they are all attractive characters. They are all people you could relate to. Even the slut. We all know people who are like that."

James says, "That's going to be a hit. And it will be interesting to see if a white audience accepts it."

I met Sam and James soon after I moved to D.C.'s Bloomingdale neighborhood in 2000. They had a reception for me after I published an article about the coming gentrification in our community of brownstones near Howard University.[16] At the time, they were active in the Bloomingdale Boys Club, a social club for black gays living in the neighborhood.

They moved to the community a year before we did, making a huge statement by buying one of the largest houses in the neighborhood at a time when it was just beginning to rebound from the ravages of white and black flight. We immediately connected about the need to maintain a black presence in the neighborhood. I was touched by their gesture to invite me, my husband, and our then infant son into their home to talk about the article. And being new homeowners, it was hard not to be inspired by the elegant stakes they put down.

We would see them occasionally, as our kids went to the same public school for a while. But they are a very busy team. When I finally tracked them down over the summer of 2005 to interview them, I learned the whole story of how they became a couple. Sam and James take turns telling the story of how they met eight years ago, at the mostly straight party of a mutual friend. Both had been burned in relationships; Sam from a marriage to a woman, and James by a roller-coaster three-year romance with a man.

"Can I speak to you for a minute?" Sam asked James at the party. "I have a question for you. Would you mind having dinner?"

James agreed to dinner but wondered why this straight boy was asking. They talked most of the night. It wasn't until Sam asked James if he was seeing anyone, because he "didn't want to be a home-wrecker," that the light flashed on.

Later that night, alone together in Sam's apartment, Sam asked if he could kiss James. Hours later, they fell asleep fully clothed. They spent the first night in a chaste spoon. Months later, they were intimate for the first time. They have spoken to each other every day since the day they met.

James is a 41-year-old computer programmer, about 6'3"; he moves with a calm grace. A native of Trinidad, he accepted himself as gay when he was 27. He grew up middle class, but left the island to study at Howard University. He has a master's degree in marketing but works as a computer programmer.

Sam, a 37-year-old Web designer, born in Alabama, was raised in a housing project in Boston, where his brother was stabbed and killed over his sneakers. As a kid he studied the dictionary, which shows in his flawless diction. He attended Morehouse as a 19-year-old, but he had to leave when his mom and brother had to move into the dorm with him.

He eventually moved on his own to Washington, and took a job as a manager at a high-end department store. Sam had known since he was 17 that he was attracted to men. For a while in his 20s, he was married to a woman. "At the time, even though I was gay, I was really afraid of being that old man in the club," Sam says. "That was my path to a white picket fence."

His former wife married Sam knowing he was gay. Sam was faithful to her, but he says things didn't work out for reasons other than his sexuality.

Since connecting with James, Sam's life has grown more fulfilling. They have an enviable level of commitment and support in their relationship. Sam says he enjoys sharing a life "with someone I know, love, and respect."

Although they are not effeminate or flamboyantly gay, they don't knock gay men who are. "From a very young age, I admired the courage it took every day to be effeminate," James says. "I admired that because they are fighting the battle for me every day, to have to deal with the taunts and the threats."

There is nothing unnatural or forced about their personas, which they describe as "regular guys." Neither of them acts the role of the man or the woman, neither leads the household as the "top" nor follows as the "bottom," as the way King describes in his book. They are both men. "I don't dress up in an apron when no one is around," Sam says. "And he's not wearing heels when no one is around. We are both men. We are both men who are in a committed relationship whose roles are not gender-related."

"Men have fragile egos. It's important to be right, important to be in control. We allow each other to be that.... Eight years later, we probably have it down to a science."

Two years ago, James gently coaxed Sam into agreeing to adopt. They became the parents of two siblings who had been in foster care, an eight-year-old boy and a seven-year-old girl. They went to therapy to prepare for the challenges that lay ahead.

Sometimes they think their son has doubts about whether they are really gay. "His concern is fun," Sam explains. The boy was excited because he had two men to play video games and do athletics with. Where they do try to compensate is in providing female role models for their daughter, which they do by arranging for her to hang out, go shopping, and have spa days with straight and lesbian female friends.

When I ask them if they would choose to be gay, they pause to think about it. Given the choice, Sam says he'd choose to be gay. "I'm proud of the man I am without apology. It's hard enough to grow up in a place that's racist, but to be gay on top of that. It requires a fortitude that I *may* have had if I were straight but that I *know* I have as a gay man."

They eschew the romance and mystique that has been constructed around the DL lifestyle—the subterfuge, cloak-and-dagger trysts, and secret love nests. "We seldom do things that are that exciting," Sam says. They like art shows, movies, concerts. They go to a lot of private parties and dinners, and give quite a few themselves.

The couple long ago gave up on the idea of looking outward for role models. "I think of our struggles on a minuscule level," Sam says. "We have to be our own role models."

James agrees. "Because I live in my black body, a large part of my idea of what it means to be a black man is my seeing myself in the mirror."

They also make a stunning picture for anyone walking past their beautiful home. Both literally and figuratively, they live their lives without curtains. At dusk, the house lights up like a museum, aglow in soft pastels and burnished wood. In the middle of Washington, a family is inside, walking across walnut-stained floors. Daughter, son, Daddy, and Papa.

Chapter 4

Thomas, 36

When the Congressional black Caucus called, he was there. Ditto for when John Kerry's people tapped him for the campaign. When the NAACP, ACLU, and Campaign to End the Death Penalty needed a celebrity endorser, they called him. In September 2005, the United for Peace and Justice and the ANSWER Coalition helped organize a rally to protest the war in Iraq. Would Etan Thomas read one of his poems?

This is how the Washington Wizards forward came to be here on this bright fall day, commanding the microphone like a seasoned emcee, on the Mall in Washington, D.C. The NBA dress code police have nothing to say about the 27-year-old's look today, which is more granola than Big Man: The goatee is scruffy, wireless glasses sensitive, the clay button-down shirt matches the Rasta hat cupping the dreadlocks that snake down his back.

Hundreds of thousands of bodies spread before him in the largest national display of anger since the beginning of the war in Iraq. He performs before thousands of fans, but his voice has never been heard live by this many people at once. Their homemade signs bear more urgent messages than Thomas is used to seeing while pursuing his first love, basketball, at the palatial Verizon Center blocks away, but their collective presence energizes him in a way that the buzzer never could. The ballplayer gently taps his heart as he thanks the audience for listening, then gestures heavenward in honor and praise.

"I wanna take some cats on a field trip," he tells the crowd, before launching into a verse he recently published in his first book of poems, *More Than an Athlete*.[1] The words tumble out; slow at first, then in a surge, ebbing and flowing in the cadence of a slam contender, the conviction of a high school debate team champion, the diction of the son of a schoolteacher.

"I wanna get one of those big yellow buses with no air-conditioning and no seat belts. Round up Bill O'Reilly, Pat Buchanan, Trent Lott, Sean Hannity, Ann Coulter, Karl Rove, Dick Cheney, Jeb Bush, Bush Jr. and Bush Sr., John McCain, John Ashcroft, Giuliani, Arnold, Katherine Harris, Ed Gillespie, that little bow-tied Tucker Carlson, and any other right-wing, conservative Republicans I can think of, and take them on a trip to the hood."

The crowd roars. Thomas goes on to narrate his fantasy tour through the horrors of America: jacked-up education system facing even worse solutions, no health care, pro-life zealotry, death penalty hypocrisy, police brutality, and of course, a war based on a lie.

"Corporate MERGERS...Undercover DEALINGS with ENRON and HALIBURTON..."

The giant hands slash the air behind the dais nonstop and his knees occasionally dip for emphasis, morphing his finely sculpted frame into a 6'10" exclamation point. "Take money out of THEIR schools, then call THEM inferior..."

"...The BIRD of democracy flew the COOP in Florida."

In just seven minutes, Thomas will conclude this bus trip with an exhortation of the crowd to vote, and a warning to the White House that "numbered are their days," his two fingers jabbing toward the Bush residence nearby.

Thomas will make several unplanned stops along the way, paus-
ing patiently at each stanza to allow the crowd's hoots and applause
to die down. He makes sure not a single word is lost in the commo-
tion and allows the sheer novelty of the occasion to marinate: Yes, this
very tall, chestnut-skinned, very well paid professional athlete just
called out the president of the United States, the media, and the political power structure in the town where he plies his trade. The audience
will need each pause for his words to register. It has been so long
since an athlete has spoken up like this; they have almost forgotten
such wonders are possible.

In the 1950s, Jackie Robinson showed that stealing home plate can
be the quintessential political statement. In the 1960s, Muhammad
Ali wrote in an *Esquire* magazine column that black athletes should
"take all this fame the white man gave to us because we fought for
his entertainment, and we can turn it around...we will use our fame
for freedom."[2] Olympians Tommie Smith and John Carlos, fist-
pumping track stars of the 1968 games in Mexico City, found that
their platform built on sweat and brawn could transcend the physical. "I didn't do what I did as an athlete," John Carlos told Zirin. "I
raised my voice in protest as a man."[3] As scholar bell hooks has
noted, sports figures such as boxers Jack Johnson and Joe Louis,
though sexualized and eroticized by women and men of all races,
transformed their bodies into political symbols.

Today's political and economic landscape has changed radi-
cally—as have the implications for the black male athlete of the
Hip-Hop Generation. The success of the black pioneers in athletics
and politics have created more opportunities for more black men to
become college educated, created more black male millionaires, and
created more arenas where black talents are celebrated and wor-
shipped on an international stage.

Still, some things haven't changed. Arenas are largely filled with white faces, casting their gaze on largely black contenders. One pro athlete was likened to "a monkey in a cage," Dave Zirin writes in his fascinating book *What's My Name, Fool? Sports and Resistance in the United States.* An integrated sports media workforce continues to depict white athletes as "intelligent" and black athletes as "natural." The advertising, sports, and entertainment industries trade and profit heavily on the perpetuation of stereotypes of black physical brawn at the expense of black players' intellectual capabilities.

We see many of the same attitudes expressed since the European and African first made contacts centuries ago: Bred, born, and then prized and enriched for their physical gifts; to the powers that be, the black male body is best seen and not heard.

Some have convincingly argued that images of young black success in sports alone represent a victory in the battle over perceptions about black men. Young, rich, black, and successful, these athletes provide a compelling picture of the world outside poor neighborhoods and a clear view of a ticket that can take young men there. But the reality remains that for the vast majority of young kids, the idea that they have the opportunities and physical gifts to become millionaires is a bit of a cruel joke. As Zirin points out, for "the overwhelming majority, [sports is] a ticket on a broken-down bus going absolutely nowhere."[4]

For the would-be athlete activist, another basic question is: So what, exactly, is a young black athlete to fight for? Today's political landscape is rife with ambiguities. The fight for dignity now takes place on a variety of different fronts. The post–civil rights era makes the struggle for black people in this country a lot less sexy and seemingly intangible: Legal segregation is over, but disparities remain in education, housing, and opportunities. The percentage of black children growing up in poverty today is the same as it was a half-century ago. Just like the "wars" that generation witnessed being waged against communism, drugs, and terrorism, the battle for black equality and justice is pitted against a faceless enemy. Do you boycott the public housing commission? Stage sit-ins at local school board meetings? Wage a rally against builders who underdevelop black neighborhoods? Would-be activists are forced to decode the nuances, deciphering right and wrong buried in the grays.

Even as challenges proliferate, today's professional athletes must go out of their way to engage in the world outside their privileged reality. While writers such as Zirin have argued that Etan Thomas's high-profile political stance signals a flowering of a new generation of athlete/activists, others aren't so sure. Gregory Lee Jr., a thirtyish sports editor in Boston who also heads the National Association of Black Journalists Sports Task Force, says Thomas is the exception rather than the rule among his peers. "Not this generation," he says. "Being a ballplayer is a laissez faire attitude. The hard work thing, it's not a part of this generation. They want it now."

If more athletes were active in politics, it would take the pressure off a single person, according to Drew Watkins, a 29-year-old basketball writer and producer for Turner Sports. "It probably would be a lot more prevalent and much cooler. Unfortunately, a lot of these guys, their primary personal influences are driven by people who want to see them maximize their earning potential."

Racial attitudes "will always take their cues from society," Watkins says. "I don't think sports are going to be on that leading edge of changing perceptions or diminishing stereotypes. At the end of the day, the whole point of sports is an athletic competition. The bigger, stronger guy is going to win, and nine times out of ten the stronger, faster guy is a black guy."

That black guy also happens to be a dominant source of perceptions about black men; sports is one of the most prevalent articulations of black masculinity worldwide. The scope and reach of what young black athletes do on and off the court is so vast that it creates a heavy burden. Whether or not they choose to accept the responsibility, each move they make on and off the court impacts the way society views all young black men.

Even if Etan Thomas does not motivate an entire league, he's refreshing enough to swallow. The NBA is undergoing a public divorce with hip-hop, but Thomas, too, is part of the culture. He is also defining his own brand of masculinity in a sport that is riddled with irony and contradictions. Um, even golden boys like Kobe Bryant get arrested. Thomas is like underground hip-hop: part of the culture, under the radar, and overshadowed by elements that are either ignorant or sensationalist. And of course, we all know that commercialism sells.

"Basketball is something I love to do, but it isn't all that I am," Thomas writes in the introduction to *More Than an Athlete*. "...Too many times in society, we allow others to dictate what box we are supposed to be in.... Well I refuse to allow anyone to put me in a box. I have many interests, and poetry is high on that list."

He goes on to describe how a young boy once asked him why he didn't wear any jewelry, why he wasn't flossing like Jay-Z with pink ice and a watch, and why in the world a multimillionaire was wearing beads. "From the time when I was little, I always wanted to be different," he explains. "For many young people, it's just not cool to be interested in poetry. Now, sports, hip-hop, cars, ice, those are well accepted interests, but poetry?"

The book is achingly earnest, vulnerable, and passionate. It reads more like a diary or collection of essays than like poetry. Like the title, the book is clear and direct. Thomas bemoans teen pregnancy in "Babies Having Babies," rampant anti-intellectualism in

"Thuggenometry." He praises the stands taken by his hero in "Brotha Malcolm." He explores his Caribbean roots and his reasons for growing dreadlocks in "My Heritage" and preaches racial uplift in "Return of the Warrior." His sincerity seems almost out of place in our cynical generation, but his idealism is admirable.

Often it appears that the Wizards player just picked up a pen in a fit of rage. In his poem "The 'N' Word," he rails against rappers and academics who embrace the word *nigger*, deriding Harvard legal scholar Randall Kennedy, for instance, as "an educated fool." There is no question how he really feels about, say, black Republicans. J. C. Watts is "that sell out Negro" and a "cockroach," while anti-affirmative-action activist Ward Connerly is "doing the devil's work."

In another poem he describes the mixed emotions he feels when a childhood friend reveals he is gay. He also takes on the voice of various characters, from children who are disadvantaged to a woman being abused to "Moses," a homeless man he met on the streets. In "Haters (Dedicated to Doug Collins, the coach who told me I'd never make it in the NBA)" he writes about an experience common to most adults: an abusive boss's "verbal beatdown." "Your desires for me to fail / will never stop me," he vows.

Finally, in "Poemslhaven'tgottenachancetowriteyet," he gives a list of topics he hopes to tackle in the future: The Palestinian/Israeli conflict, the Patriot Act, Virginia, and the NRA. In the poem, he lists other future topics: "The Fans. First they love you, then they hate you, then they love you again," "What Can Happen When You Drive Drunk," and "A Message to Colin Powell (It's time for you to speak the truth)."

It's disarming to see a high-profile figure making such impassioned arguments in his own book, where he can't hide behind the old standards "they misquoted me" or "that was taken out of context." Considering the millions of dollars in endorsements at stake, it's remarkable, actually. There he is, in this book, letting it all hang out, immortalized forever in black and white for all the maybe-would-but-probably-won't-now corporate sponsors and the rest of the world to see.

There were many challenges in Thomas's fifth season as a professional player. He enjoyed some financial security; he signed what was reported to be a six-year, $37 million contract extension with the Wizards in 2004. But he still struggled on the court in the 2005–06 season. At one point he averaged 4.1 points and 3.7 rebounds and 13.2 minutes of playing time. He was recovering from an abdominal muscle strain which had forced him to sit out most of the previous season. He couldn't even practice over the summer. Training camp was like walking a minefield, as he tried to avoid aggravating his injury.

His career off-court as a writer and activist, though, was thriving. Thomas has been quietly making a name as a poet around D.C., but with the publication of his first book, many other opportunities popped up. He visited Capitol Hill to speak at a news conference at the behest of the Congressional Black Caucus. He performed at various coffee houses and open mikes around the city's historic black U Street corridor; volunteered for writer's groups for teenagers and in classrooms. Thomas's speech during the historic protest of the Iraq war capped off the year.

The speech was widely circulated and debated on the Internet. Representative John Conyers, a Democrat from Michigan, raved in his blog that it was the best speech he'd heard in a long time. Another, less high profile, blogger gushed that Thomas was "as good a candidate as any for my generation's Muhammad Ali." On the message boards of lefty websites such as the Daily Kos blog, praise of Etan's speech was universal. But even there, the speech sparked a debate when one poster praised him as "articulate." Another poster snapped back that it is condescending to call African Americans "articulate," as if they normally express themselves in grunts. Other posters piped up in defense of using the word. "I didn't read it as Wow! He's really articulate for a black person. I read it as Wow! He's really articulate [for a basketball player].... Big difference."

Right...

A few weeks later, Thomas's stand was quickly overshadowed by another battle involving young black men who play pro basketball. In October 2005, NBA Commissioner David Stern announced that a new dress code would take effect off the court. To be banned: chains, pendants, and medallions worn outside clothes; do-rags, hats, and sunglasses; and sleeveless shirts, shorts, T-shirts. Also banned were stereo headphones. The men would be required to wear suits and ties, "corporate casual"—blazers, collared shirts, dress slacks, and dress shoes at all league functions and activities. Apparently the baggy, "hip-hop" look embraced by many players was getting to be too much.

Thomas, a team cocaptain and union rep for the Wizards, participated in the negotiations for the new contract that carried the dress code provisions. He took the announcement in stride. "It could have been a lot worse," he said, shrugging, to a reporter at the time. "They want us to look professional and I have no problems with that."[5]

It has been a long journey to that moment. During each successive decade, the NBA has evolved into an increasingly forceful articulation of the black male aesthetic. In the 1970s and 1980s, Kareem Abdul-Jabbar rarely smiled or outwardly celebrated. Magic Johnson's high-watt smile made him a crowd-pleasing showman, presenting a genial presence with crossover appeal. In the late 1980s and early 1990s, a bald and baggy-short-wearing Michael Jordan became an international icon at a time when it was seen as political to get paid off your image of being rich and black, according to author Todd Boyd.[6]

The University of Michigan Fab Five basketball players got permission to wear their shorts longer in the early 1990s. Their bald heads, aggressive playing, and short black socks made their jerseys popular gear across the country. As the Hip-Hop Generation began to take over professional basketball in the 1990s, a harder, more aggressive antihero began to emerge, one clearly linked to hip-hop. Allen Iverson was the poster boy for this trend. The former Hoya Iverson of Georgetown University, he was known to blow off practice but led the league in scoring, and once famously rejected Jordan as a hero because "none of my heroes wear suits."[7]

Right up to the announcement of the league's new dress code, signs indicated that the marriage between hoops and hip-hop was functional, if not harmonious. The hip-hop group the Black Eyed Peas was tapped to create the NBA's theme song, "Let's Get It Started." Basketball jerseys were ubiquitous in urban and suburban neighborhoods where in many cases no one had set foot in a sports arena. The rapper Jay-Z became part owner of the New Jersey Nets, and Nelly bought into BET founder Robert Johnson's Charlotte Bobcats. Players often made grand entrances onto the court to hip-hop tunes, and team cheerleaders danced to hit rap records. Jay-Z coproduced a playoffs song for the Nets. Bow Wow was on the NBA website. For crying out loud, the Philly 76ers named their mascot "Hip Hop."

The NBA embraced hip-hop as a marketing tool, just as corporate America has snuggled up to the culture to peddle everything from beverages to cars. Even as the league tries to distance itself from its overtly black aspects, the ironies abound. Black people aren't the ones who make hip-hop records cross over. That would be the young white demographic, which tramples into NBA fan territory.

Watkins, the Turner Sports producer, could see the shift in attitude during news meetings and planning discussions. There, the battle over perceptions of black masculinity played out in two ways: On the one hand, the mostly white top managers made a big (quite possibly satiric) show of avoiding anything that could be construed as stereotypical, deferring to the black males on staff for advice on how to avoid stereotypes. On the other hand, the sports division avoided storylines that emphasized the urban experience in basketball. If there was a choice between profiling an up-from-the-hood baller and a European implant, they would go with the latter every time, Watkins says.

When NBA Commissioner Stern handed down the dress code edict, which took effect in November 2005, it became clear that the marriage was a sham. The money people in advertising and the corporate sponsors wanted a more corporate image and more traditional heroes for their children to emulate. Many middle-aged sports commentators could barely contain their glee. They loudly ridiculed players such as Stephen Jackson, Marcus Camby, Tim Duncan, Allen Iverson, and Greg Ostertag who objected to the racial subtext underlying the new regulations, dismissing them as "whimpering rebels" and spoiled brats. An October 2005 column in the *New York Post* by Peter Vecsey was fairly representative of the level of discourse:

LIKE, woe. NBA players are still staggering around slurring speeches worse than their shots from the direct hit they took earlier this week.... David Stern, the devil incarnate, rocked their round of "chronic" privilege with the two nastiest words imaginable. No, not "paternity test." Though, judging by the resulting hysterics, you would have thought the commissioner had told them how many kids they were limited to each season out of wedlock. Seems the phrase he had the unprofessional impudence to utter was "dress code," a demand that his citizenry "Dress for Success, not Dress to Confess."[8]

Vecsey quipped that the commissioner has divided the new "business casual" standard "into a player's four most popular social settings—arrest, arraignment, trial and sentencing."

In November 2005, the *Washington Post* published an article by Etan Thomas in which he expounded on the subtext behind the dress code.[9] Thomas described his ongoing struggles with misperceptions about who he is as a young black man—especially as a baller. He described white women clutching their purses and making him uncomfortable, getting stopped by police in his car just because he is black, the humiliation of having to ask a white passerby to hail a cab for him. Thomas still had no problems with the more professional look for players. But he challenged the rationale behind the change. The new dress code, he said, in effect sanctions attitudes and assumptions about the type of person he is, based on what he looks like—misconceptions that prevail outside the basketball arena.

"It's almost as though [Commissioner Stern] is playing to society ignorance that has overtaken the mind frame of the masses for generations," Thomas wrote. "Does he think that fans are afraid of us?"

"Sometimes my mother and my brother will be like, Why do you have to be the person who speaks out?" Thomas told an interviewer from a Syracuse newspaper. "And my philosophy has always been, If not me, then who?"[10]

In an interview with us, he recalls how it was his mother who first encouraged him to speak up. Deborah Thomas was a schoolteacher by trade, but raising the Harlem-born Thomas in Oklahoma, she did as much teaching at home as she did at work. It was she who gave him *The Autobiography of Malcolm X*, which, as it did to many black people in his generation, radicalized him instantly. Malcolm X's story also fostered an interest in rhetoric.

Thomas remembers going to the Million Man March with his father and his brother Julian, now a Los Angeles actor, when he was in high school. "Just hearing all the things that brother Farrakhan was talking about," Thomas tells us, speaking on the phone from an away game in Los Angeles, "it was basically not that much different than Bill Cosby was saying, and ain't nobody gon' call out Mr. Farrakhan for being an Uncle Tom. What he's saying is 'take responsibility,' and that's the main thing. That's why I have so much respect for the Nation of Islam. They encourage the black man to walk upright."

Thomas joined the NAACP youth chapter in Tulsa and competed on the debate team. Even back then, giving speeches was not something that his coaches necessarily encouraged. "They were like, It's cool, but you're kind of doing it a lot," Thomas recalls. He kept doing it a lot, even as he became a star basketball player at Syracuse University, where he was an entrepreneurship major. His experiences touring with the team gave him plenty of inspiration. After a trip to South Carolina, for instance, he wrote a poem about a protest over displaying the Confederate flag.

Thomas won awards for his community service in the black communities around Syracuse. Even when he was trying to be low key, volunteering at a community center and identifying himself as a student and writer, word tended to get out he was also a basketball player. So he tried to make it work. For instance, he agreed to do an autograph signing for Black History Month at the community center, but kids could only participate if they agreed to write an essay about their black hero. He received more than a hundred essays.

When we tell him that some commentators have said that, with his speech on the Mall, he has entered the stratosphere of

Muhammad Ali, et al., he demurs. "I don't know about all *that*," he says. "Those are people that I admire, the way they are standing up and not afraid to speak out. I want to follow in their footsteps."

Thomas has not experienced any backlash against his stand (aside from some sportswriters sniping that he doesn't score enough points to have a real platform). When asked if he's afraid of repercussions for speaking out, the answer is no. "There is simply too much going on for me to keep silent," he told the Syracuse writer. "I have a voice, and I have to use it."

So we ask him: How does a multimillionaire doing his dream job and living a charmed life keep connected to the struggle outside his privileged world? "It's kind of easy to stay connected. It's just a mentality. You don't get caught up. You don't get lost."

Sometimes he gets inspiration from watching cable news channels. Fox media personality Bill O'Reilly is a favorite muse. "My wife will be, like, "Why are you watching that? That's something that Malcolm always said: You have to know the ways of your enemies. You have to know the issues."

Although he doesn't agree with everything the political action groups do, he says he enjoys his work with the American Civil Liberties Union, the Congressional Black Caucus, and anti–death penalty groups tremendously. He is not totally wedded to a single cause or group and occasionally crosses swords with some he is publicly aligned with. For instance, he says that by mutual agreement he and the NAACP parted ways. "Put it like this: They wanted to be a little more middle-of-the-road than I was."

He says that, contrary to commonly held perceptions about them, athletes are not apolitical as a group. "I don't feel alone. We'll have discussions. Guys couldn't stop talking about what happened with [executed former gang leader] Tookie Williams. They are aware; they are just not trying to speak out. That's *my* thing. People think [all basketball players] do one thing and that's it, they don't have a mind and opinions about anything. Guys are definitely aware, a lot more than people think. That's the whole thing with perceptions."

In the Verizon Center arena, the Washington Wizards family lounge is filled with game-night chatter. The decor is '80s retro. There is a massive red leather sectional sofa, navy-blue velvet couches. There are cookies and refreshments on the counter next to the fridge. A colorful corner filled with children's toys sits empty. Several señoras rock and soothe wailing babies. On one couch, wives and girlfriends watch a big-screen closed-circuit television broadcast as the Washington Wizards finish off the New Jersey Nets. The room fills with girl talk as they wait for players to emerge from the locker room.

Outside, in the arena, Etan Thomas is giving interviews about his good night. The team trounced the Nets, 94 to 74. Thomas scored 12 points. The *Washington Post* will write for the next day's paper that "Etan Thomas ended the quarter by snagging an offensive rebound, laying the ball in and drawing a foul on Lamond Murray. Thomas made the free throw, giving Washington a 73–52 lead heading into the fourth quarter."[11] *USA Today* will report that the Wizards managed to pull off the victory without their superstar guard, Gilbert Arenas, who was out with an injury but watched the teams on the sidelines in a snazzy dark suit.[12]

All-star Gilbert Arenas walks into the family lounge. He has traded his regulation dress-code suit for jeans and a T-Shirt. He chats with Etan Thomas's wife, Nichole, while the couple's five-month-old son, Malcolm, lies next to them, snug in a stroller.

When Etan Thomas enters the family lounge, Arenas starts playfully ribbing his cocaptain. Arenas's eyes bulge theatrically toward the Thomas infant, the baby boy named after a black revolutionary. "What? He's wearing a *white* hat!"

Nichole Thomas, an activist, middle-school teacher, and former Syracuse basketball player, giggles.

"We are not antiwhite…" Etan Thomas starts to explain, with a weary sigh.

"Does he know that a white man writes our checks?" Arenas says, laughing.

Thomas ignores this, and leans in to enjoy the best part of his day. He embraces his wife and together they coo at the mild-mannered baby Nichole tells us emerged from the womb with a grin on his face and a fist in the air. Malcolm Thomas gurgles and grins at his daddy.

Chances are we have not heard the last from Etan Thomas. There will certainly be plenty of opportunities to see him. That night, after the Wizards' beatdown of the Nets, thousands of television viewers saw Etan Thomas, No. 36, stuffing the ball down the hoop, bent knees hanging midair, his dreadlocks still in motion.

Chapter 5

Hip-Hop

It's 3 A.M. on a Saturday night, supposedly well after the weary have gone to bed. Flick on Black Entertainment Television, and a precoital-sounding female voiceover warns that the content for *BET: Uncut* may be unsuitable for those under 17. A procession of curvy bodies floats across the screen like a nude Miss America parade. Federation sings its ode to booty, "Donkey," while women compete to see who can best make it "bankhead bounce." In the "Shake It Like a Pit Bull" feature, dancers growl, wobbling in cages. Ladies soap each other in showers, chocolate and champagne pouring over their contours. Titties jingle, barely blurred out. Asses rattle, thongs barely covering the cracks. Pap smears offer more modesty. *Uncut* lasts an hour, followed by the gospel program *BET Inspiration*.

Uncut had been mostly under the radar until a 2003 video by the rapper Nelly went into the rotation. In "Tip Drill," a song about a girl with an ugly face but a dope body, throngs of women in bikinis swiveled their hips orgylike by a swimming pool among fully dressed men. Grinning, the rapper capped off the video by swiping a credit card down the derriere of a comely woman.

Turns out at least one woman was tuned in at 3 A.M. That was all it took to spark a shitstorm—launching yet another chapter in the long, complicated, and tortured relationship between women and hip-hop.

As commercial hip-hop has evolved over the past three decades, it has become an increasingly accurate mirror for American values. In the past decade, many of the most successful hip-hoppers have been enthralled with the persona of the pimp—the perfect metaphor for American capitalism. In the commercial hip-hop lyrics themselves, women enjoy a largely schizophrenic existence, primarily falling to the extremes of the age-old Madonna/whore split: Either "My mama is the best in the whole wide world" or "Bitch, eat my balls." If rappers are modern-day blues singers "telling it like 'tis" from the streets, then it's fair to conclude that in the hood you'll find a deep hatred toward women. Considering the international popularity of hip-hop, make that a widespread hatred toward black women around the world.

Black women have developed various coping strategies. Since black culture has enjoyed a long relationship with irony, some say that hip-hop is all about hyperbole and fantasy: "They just playin', y'all." Some of us take hip-hoppers' words literally, pointing out that there *are* bitches and hos inhabiting the world; others obey the sexist commands on the club dance floor and sing along, justifying it with a smug, internal common refrain: "*I'm* not a bitch or a ho." Well, then, who is?

For black women trying to get their slice of the billion-dollar pie, there are even more quandaries. With few exceptions, female emcees have been placed on the back burner, their voices muted or sexualized by male ghostwriters. Often, penetrating the genre visually has been the way to go. *BET: Uncut* is just a small sliver of a subculture that has been created around women who appear in videos. *Vibe* magazine gives out "Sexiest Video Vixen" awards. Video dancers like Ki Toy and Esther Baxter have graced the covers of *Smooth* and *King* magazines.

Far from new, the gender frictions that are apparent in hip-hop can be traced throughout history, in black scholarship, politics, and literature, where black men and women have been bickering. Our mothers seethed while black patriarchy raged during the civil rights movement. Women were expected to deal with such hostility in the name of racial solidarity, or else risk being deemed traitors to the race, "dykes," or conspirators with whites to undermine the brothers. Many black women and men chose to fight white racism while ignoring precarious black gender relations.

The Hip-Hop Generation is experiencing a new, updated battle. The Sapphires, Jezebels, and Mammies of old have given way to Lil' Kim, Melyssa Ford, and Whyte Chocolate. So what is the self-respecting black woman to do? How can you love your culture, hip-hop—but love yourself, too? We see how this layered, angst-ridden relationship plays out. Some women try to create their own brands of hip-hop. Others become critics and commentators of hip-hop, searching for solutions in the academy, in fine art galleries, and in film. Some join the industry behind the scenes, working as spin doctors and executives. And of course, others say fuck it, accept the "video ho" label, and wear it as a badge of pride—might as well get paid, too.

It's Friday night, and I (Natalie M.) am making a run with Melyssa Ford, aka Jessica Rabbit, the patron saint of video girls. We just met at a hip-hop feminism conference. I am driving her to Target at 87th and Cottage Grove on Chicago's South Side to buy a last-minute pair of shoes. As we walk in, customers point and whisper, wondering what in the world Melyssa Ford is doing at Target. On my cell phone, my younger brother Joey is begging to talk to her in person.

She is pleasant and indulges him in light conversation and flirtation. Meanwhile, some customers ask for autographs—including gawking young women. Along the way she explains how she tripped into hip-hop.

Ford is among the pioneers who parlayed the three-minute video prototype into their own piece of fame, a video star who negotiates her space. A cadre of these women have become nearly as recognizable as the rappers stroking them—maybe more so. Now they have websites, publicists, tell-all memoirs, and a devoted corps of fans.

Ford made her name dancing in videos for the likes of Jay-Z ("Big Pimpin"), Ghostface ("Cherchez La Ghost"), and Jadakiss ("Knock Yourself Out"). She has transitioned out of the video rotations and now writes a sex column for *Smooth* magazine and hosts a television show on BET. She's much prettier in person, sans makeup on her high, honey-colored cheekbones. Her long ponytail sways gently like spring leaves on a maple tree.

When Melyssa was growing up, in Canada, rap was as foreign to her as black urban life in the United States. She grew up listening to Def Leppard, Duke Ellington, Sting. She studied psychology in college for two years. She is articulate and self-aware, and owns a hint of elitism. While still in her teens, the ingenue was "discovered" by a video director and later moved to New York.

Ford, now in her mid-twenties, disdains the title "video girl." She explains the hierarchy on the sets as follows, starting at the top: A) video models—professionals who are sought out by the director; B) video chicks—they come out for the casting call and get hired, but are immature and mostly on the set for fun/partying; and C) video hos—down for whatever, including fucking, just to be included. Ford considers herself in the video model category and she takes the demarcations seriously, but she is quick to say that she does not represent the majority of video girls. She has her share of regrets about certain videos. "Shake It Fast" had terrible lyrical content. Now that she's learned the trade and has become a commodity in her own right, Ford has become more selective. But it wasn't always the case. One time, she says, a rapper, incensed by the perceived lackluster surroundings of the set, repeatedly cussed out all the "bitches" on standby. Meanwhile, his band of hangers-on stared at Ford in the break room with lustful intimidation, making her uncomfortable. Given the chance, she recalls, they would've attacked her. A crew member diffused the situation.

Ford says she usually kept to herself on location, asking myriad questions about the video production and photography. By soaking up her surroundings and the details of the videos she participated in—earning up to $5,000 a day—she began seriously considering when to say yes and when to say no. Video sets are actually boring, she says. Most rappers don't have any game, and their masculinity is exaggerated for the camera, just as much a part of the fantasy as the swarm of women dancing adoringly around them.

Hip-hop has been Ford's launchpad, and she is busy branding herself, just as rappers market themselves. Her last video appearance was in 2004. Since then she has appeared on the television shows *Soul Food*, *Platinum*, and *Playmakers*. She has hosted shows on MTV2 and BET and has had parts in independent films. She is trying to break into acting, and she sells her calendar on her website.

"What's the difference between me putting on booty shorts in a video and a girl walking down the street with booty shorts? You've got to be smart. I'm not afraid of what I look like."

But Ford is also critical of hip-hop and believes lyrics and videos can go too far. She believes that women should take responsibility for their part in the way black women are depicted.

"Why are video girls getting notoriety? Somebody could argue successfully that Melyssa was a part of the negative depiction of black women in videos. Usually [I was] scantily clad. But if I didn't want to do something, I didn't. You can take control of your career. You don't need men behind you holding strings."

Eventually, this is exactly what she began to do as her own conscience began to speak to her.

"Girls come up to me and say, 'Melyssa, I want to be a video girl.' They can't see past [my fame]. I understand I have a responsibility to young girls because I know they watch me closely. I let them know it's not about the almighty dollar; keep a sense of integrity by saying no to requests."

The word *no* didn't cross the mind of the bikini-clad model Whyte Chocolate on the set of Nelly's infamous "Tip Drill" video. With a ballerina's pride, she says she was the principal girl in the video. In an unscripted scene, hers is the ass swiped with a credit card. It netted her $1,500 for a day's work.

"It didn't bother me one way or another. It was a video. It was what it was. Mind you, we're in the entertainment industry," Whyte Chocolate says. "Nobody has to agree, nobody has to approve."

Whyte Chocolate has been one of the women following Ford's example, branding herself via a website, calendars, and posters. But she disagrees with Ford about the hierarchy. Call her a "video ho" if you like, she says. Just call her "paid," too.

She pushes a Jaguar, shops at Louis Vuitton, eats at Justin's, and lives in a five-bedroom house on the outskirts of Atlanta. "I think people are way too sensitive," she says. "People need to learn how to separate the entertainment side of things."

The "Tip Drill" controversy was good for business. She went on a nationwide "Tip Drill" tour flanked by an entourage of bodyguards, assistants, and stylists. She hawked ancillary "W.C." posters and calendars on her website, with the slogan "always sexy, never slutty." The *Atlanta Journal-Constitution* and *XXL* magazine have done feature articles on her.

Whyte Chocolate is a twentysomething fair-skinned woman with cascading hair, her body better than that of most *Jet* magazine Beauties of the Week. She grew up in Atlanta with two parents, who remain supportive of her chosen profession. She is a doting single mom of a nine-year-old boy whom she doesn't let watch videos. She loves Enya and rarely listens to rap.

"It's a supply-and-demand industry," she says of the hip-hop industry of videos and songs. "Harvard does not represent me. Nine-to-five does not represent me. I'm not saying society shouldn't have role models. I am representative in my industry."

It's a stark contrast to her life several years ago, when the feds nabbed her husband and the father of her son and sent him packing to prison. She worked a low-paying customer service job and eventually went on public assistance. She started stripping out of necessity.

"Either I was going to get up and do something or we were going to starve. We were almost at nothing.... I was down to four dollars and some change in my pocket. I knew quite a few people who had been dancing. It wasn't get-rich-and-get-famous. Nobody was celebrating the strong dancer."

Video directors often scout at strip clubs. Eventually W.C., as she is also known, graduated to doing videos, standing near rappers, leaning on cars, and lounging poolside. She has appeared in twenty-five rap videos from Petey Pablo and Nas to Master P. She has enough offers now that she doesn't always have to say yes.

In Melyssa Ford's hierarchy, Karrine Steffans would stand on the bottom rung. Still, she managed to shake up the hip-hop industry with her summer 2005 *New York Times* best-seller *Confessions of a*

Video Vixen, a tell-all by a woman who has trademarked her nick-name, "Superhead." She climbed the best-seller lists and made the urban radio rounds, feeding the celebrity fetishes of consumers. Steffans angered rappers' wives, infuriated hip-hop royalty, and had to hire a bodyguard. She details fucking Jay-Z, Ja Rule, Damon Dash, DMX, Dr. Dre, Irv Gotti, P. Diddy, Ice-T, et. al. The then-26-year-old single mother billed her story as a cautionary tale for the sumptuous lifestyle that weaved in and out of hip-hop inner circles during the early 2000s.

Truthfully, her narrative really isn't all that juicy—or shocking. Her talents inspired Shaq to fork over $10,000. She and Ja Rule indulged in Remy-and-XTC marathons. And gee, rappers like their dicks sucked early and often. Steffans writes as if she is holding a Chanel compact and reciting, "Mirror, mirror, on the wall, who's the fairest video chick of all?" She brags about being Gotti's favorite, and he was the lover who passed her around like a bottle of cognac.

But there is more to her than the drama. Steffans is relevant because women like her are usually just eye candy: scrutinized and deconstructed—but voiceless.

Her back story is what one would imagine: growing up poor, abusive mother, absent father, raped at 13, stripper, turning the occasional trick. She had a common-law relationship with rap pioneer Kool G Rap, who, she writes, made her perform oral sex until her nose bled. The couple have a son. A wayward Steffans moved to Los Angeles, uneducated and unskilled. She cavorted in the fast hip-hop world and practiced a sex-equals-power motto. Addicted to substances and the perks, she savored the moments all while being depressed and seeking unattainable love.

Aside from her sexual escapades, in her memoir Steffans spends little time actually chronicling the video-set environment. But that may be the book's biggest contribution because it sums up the current climate in hip-hop culture. Her first video was Jay-Z's "Hey Papi." A day's work ended with giving him a blow job near a beach. Steffan's second video, Ja Rule's "Between Me and You," began with her begging Gotti to let her stay on the set. She gave quite a convincing blow job.

To slice through the video competition, Steffans became the girl who wore what others wouldn't and pulled the most outlandish stunts to be cast. It paid off sometimes, because she learned to bypass the auditions. As she'd done most of her life to get by, Steffans thought she had to prove her worthiness via sex, showing that she was grateful.

Steffans introduces her book with the statement, "Where young girls once aspired to be models and ballerinas, they now aspire to be the hip-hop video girls, the next hot girl in the hottest artist's video. Having lived that life, I can say it's not everything it's cracked up to be."[1]

But it's unclear whether she truly learned any lessons. Steffans is not unlike current or former celebrities and ex–reality stars hankering to extend their pirouette in the limelight. She says her mission is to counsel young girls, yet after her ordeals—including being snubbed by former lovers when she asked for money after sinking into alcoholism and homelessness—Steffans trademarked her "Superhead" moniker. In an interview with the online entertainment magazine Panache-Report.com, Steffans explains the reasoning behind the trademark:

"This keeps anyone from using it without my written consent, especially in a derogatory manner. Or better yet, from some other girl, who sucks a good dick to adopt the name and make money off the legend that I created with my blood, sweat and tears...and spit."[2]

Another of the many ironies in the relationship between women and hip-hop is the women who play prominent roles behind the scenes. Often the most thugged-out rappers turn to sharp, educated women to market their images. Scores of black women coordinate media interviews, design publicity campaigns, cross *t*'s, dot *i*'s, and style video shoots. Steady paychecks keep them in the game as they ruminate over gender issues.

Zuhariah Khaldun is one such power broker. She has worked for the record companies Loud, Interscope, Tommy Boy, and Island Def Jam, and her own publicity firm, now defunct, represented artists such as De La Soul, Capone-N-Noreaga, Prince Paul, Memphis Bleek, Redman, Method Man, DMX, and Ludacris.

Initially, Khaldun saw hip-hop as a way to change the world for the better, but she now considers that attitude naive. She says sexuality is used in videos the same way it's used in advertising, reality television, and Hollywood: aimed to grab the wandering eye in an overstimulated market.

"I am not proud of hip-hop's exploitation of women in order to sell records. It's sad to see my young neighbors in Harlem sing 'from the windows to the walls...' despite the fact that I was screaming it the night before in the club."

Eventually, Khaldun abandoned her hip-hop career because the music became uninteresting to her. She now lives in The Hague, where she is working on a master's degree in cultural analysis at the University of Amsterdam.

"Looking back, I wonder what I could have done. Most were aware of my personal views on the exploitation of women in the videos. But to tell you the truth, that battle wasn't the reason I entered the music industry. Perhaps that will be part of this new journey.

"The industry has shifted from product- to market-driven. The music video is a marketing tool—give the people what they want. And let me tell you, it was often sad to be on the sets of these videos where girls walked around in bikinis, most from professional talent and modeling agencies, who really see this as a step toward the silver screen. Maybe that's how black girls have to do it.... Girls would show up uninvited and suck dick to have their fifteen seconds of fame in the video."

Other female hip-hop executives have tried to do their part to exert damage control. Since June 2002, Elon Johnson has been the senior writer/producer for the BET countdown show *106th & Park*. Once, the Atlanta crunk trio Trillville (definition: keeping it true *and* real) was scheduled for a show appearance. "Some Cut" was their popular song, and the show planned to play a game with the lyrics. Staffers had trouble deciphering the lyrics from the Southern-drawling rappers and the catchy hook eclipsed the words. When Johnson printed out the lyrics, she thought, "I have to quit this business." She killed the segment. "It was so ridiculously misogynistic!"

To summarize "Some Cut," the rap is about—surprise!—sex. The group instructs a woman how to catch a nut. An emcee says he'll bring her home so she can jiggle his balls and afterward he can tear down her—presumably vaginal—walls. This woman is also a certified "head doctor," taking dick in the ass and sucking said dick from behind.

"It's a very homosocial act," Johnson says of male rap camaraderie. "It's a sport for men to enjoy. They have fun caressing their egos while objectifying women. I've heard a lot of men say, 'If a woman is in the video shaking her ass, that justifies me calling her a ho.'"

Johnson has thought about what can be done to combat the worst parts of rap. "It's a tough thing; it's such a monster moneymaker. If Martin Luther King could change America...then certainly this could be changed. It may take a strong leader or it may not."

Nonetheless, Johnson, a former MTV News journalist and freelancer for numerous hip-hop publications, is accustomed to the eyebrow raising when people learn BET is her employer. "The first thing I always have to preface is my last name is not BET—it's Johnson. I do a certain type of work that's not *Uncut* videos."

As a writer, she's interviewed hundreds of rappers, and says she has never been disrespected. Sometimes the rappers themselves make the distinctions among types of women. During an interview with a rapper known for anger management problems, Johnson asked him about an antic that involved throwing champagne on a groupie. She recalls that he told her, "I prefer women like you with a career who are not hanging around."

New York public relations guru Tresa Sanders agrees that rappers are on their best behavior when dealing with female hip-hop executives. She's a former vice president at Loud Records. In 1994, Sanders started Tremedia. Clients have included Jay-Z, Jermaine Dupri, D12, Mike Jones, and David Banner.

"I find that rappers are some of the nicest people you could ever meet. People are so surprised when they sit down. Society has this opinion of what rappers represent. True, music put out is misogynistic and cursing," Sanders says. But even though David Banner, a former homeless man, raps "like a pimp," she says he is almost finished with a master's degree. RZA is one of the smartest men she's met, and he has no high school diploma. Jay-Z is wiser than you think.

The majority of rappers are trying to live the American Dream, Sanders says. It's hackneyed but true: Hip-hop has become a ticket out of poverty. When she visited some rappers in Tennessee and saw the squalor of the low-rise projects from which they hailed, Sanders had a better understanding of why people were "sippin' on syzzurp." She argues that the general public is wrapped up in the one-dimensional image of rappers, focusing only on the "bitch" and "ho" rhetoric. Until the black community gets straight, these guys will continue to talk about what's happening in the community, Sanders says. In entertainment, there is room for both the so-called thug and the Afrocentric, kufi-wearing brother. Besides, she says, radio is the culprit, playing the same record fifty times a day.

Sanders compares hip-hop to the raunchiness of blues music. "I don't agree with everything these guys do. But it's been around. It's been that way since the beginning of music. It's risqué for our time. You can't point your fingers at these guys.... I'm not that bitch or ho. We have to police ourselves as human beings and they wouldn't have anything to talk about."

She knows that rappers are considered role models and believes they can make a change. Sanders advocates forums where rappers can teach and elaborate on their upbringing and outlook to young people. Her moral compass tells her to stop at pornography. When pal Luther Campbell asked for her help publicizing his adult film, she declined.

Commercial rap is narrow, but the space for black women emcees is narrower than an airplane aisle. Luminaries like Queen Latifah, Monie Love, Salt-n-Pepa, and Roxanne Shante had something to say and legitimized the female emcee during the 1980s. Lauryn Hill and Eve at different junctures have promoted womanhood in their rhymes. But for the most part, creative space for female rappers is relegated to hooking up with a male crew for entrée into the industry. The current climate has caused MC Lyte to pause and join the ranks of other rappers-turned-actors, as she explained to a 2005 panel discussion at Spelman College about women and hip-hop.

"Women are at best a commodity and at worst expendable and feckless if one were to listen to hip-hop lyrics or watch videos," filmmaker Chana Garcia says. She is working with her cousin Calida Garcia on a documentary about women and hip-hop. In their film, *Treat Her Like a Prostitute*, they examine how sex and violence play out, what this says about relationships between black men and women, and its effect on young listeners.

Chana Garcia says women have bought into the prevailing notions of black femininity. "First there are the women who just can't relate to hip-hop music so they look at it as outsiders, if and when they pay attention to it. I think they can't relate because at its core, hip-hop largely appeals to adolescent men or men with an adolescent mentality."

Many prominent intellectuals and feminists have taken up the issue, including writers like Tricia Rose, Joan Morgan, and Imani Perry. They speak candidly about growing up loving hip-hop, and they feel degraded by the music blasting on contemporary airwaves. Many remain optimistic, though, about the possibility of hip-hop culture being a starting point for a conversation about gender relations.

"Rap music and Hip-Hop culture more generally, along with black feminism as an activist project, can be a part of the solution," Gwendolyn Pough writes in *Check It While I Wreck It: Black Womanhood, Hip-Hop Culture, and the Public Sphere*. "It is not just about counting the 'bitches' and 'hos' in each rap song. It is about exploring the nature of black male and female relationships."[3]

Writer Yvonne Bynoe agrees that black women have, again, let race outweigh gender on the matter of malfeasant content in hip-hop. Bynoe, author of *Stand and Deliver: Political Activism, Leadership, and Hip Hop Culture* and past president of the Urban Think Tank Institute, says, "I don't believe in censorship. Every community has to decide what is good for them, their airwaves, television. What's good in New York is not good in Atlanta. Artists, perhaps if there is a groundswell of incidents, will have to be mindful of what they put out there. The record companies and those ancillary industries...are not looking [to blacks] for sales. They're not looking to us. When you're thinking about putting together music, you're thinking about a young man. Even a young white man."

Some women have used hip-hop imagery and transformed it into cultural commentary. While students at Howard University in 2002, Jessica Lima and Megan Moore (Natalie M.'s sister) produced a homecoming fashion show entitled "Pimp Harder." Although the duo were lambasted for celebrating pimp imagery, they were trying to transform those images into a commentary about the power to make over old baggage into empowerment.

There is also an innate defense mechanism erected when outsiders critique the sometimes contradictory relationship between women and hip-hop, especially if the criticism originates from white quarters. Hip-hop is certainly not the sole form of popular music or artistry that is debasing to women. But it is the music du jour, wide open for global consumption. Racial suspicions arise when right-wingers seize the hip-hop cause. Tricia Rose, chair and professor of American studies at the University of California at Santa Cruz, has publicly said that the conservative Fox News Channel called her to appear on conservative Bill O'Reilly's show to lambaste hip-hop. Rose, author of *Black Noise: Rap Music and Black Culture in Contemporary America*, declined, sensitive to the possibility that her views would be co-opted.

Ayanah Moor, a visual artist and assistant art professor at Carnegie Mellon University, believes hip-hop is a reflection of changing values in society. In one of her performance pieces, she adopts a male persona, reciting Sir Mix-A-Lot's "Baby Got Back" a cappella and in a hyperbolic masculine cadence. The hit song, an ode to butt cheeks, encourages black women to embrace their non-European, shapely beauty.

Moor says the point of the piece is that she wants viewers to see the absurdities in the song. Judging from their reactions, most people in the audience get the joke. "People laugh," Moor says of viewers. "Then they start to say the lyrics also. Guys feel weird because it's a female. Some guys like it. We also have to include the voices of women in order to have dialogue. They shouldn't be ignored."

More than that, Moor's womanly perspective shapes her ideas on the industry and where females fall in the rap music paradigm. "We should help young women get into the studio. This is more about access than trying to police people. Misogyny shouldn't be limited to right or wrong. We have to argue for a broader representation [in hip-hop]."

Watching TV in the wee hours one night during her Christmas break, a Spelman College junior named Moya Bailey stumbled across BET's *Uncut*. She gaped as a cheesing Nelly slid a credit card down the behind of Whyte Chocolate. Enough is enough, Bailey thought.

She returned to the elite, all-woman, historically black campus the next semester and raised the subject of the video's content among members of the Feminist Majority Leadership Alliance—a student group led by Bailey that is the only collegiate chapter of the national Feminist Majority Foundation. The group talked about "Tip Drill" and the fact that Nelly was planning to visit the campus for a bone-marrow cancer fund-raising drive. Nelly started his foundation to raise awareness of the need for bone marrow donors among minorities after his (now deceased) sister was diagnosed with leukemia.

The alliance decided to post flyers around campus and worked to plan a forum with the St. Louis rapper, dubbing him "Misogynist of the Month." They figured, if he's coming to campus, he's not leaving without hearing objections to that gross video. They were in discussions with Nelly to appear at the forum, but at the last minute Nelly's 4Sho4Kids Foundation canceled the bone marrow drive and the visit altogether.

Bailey, a Fayetteville, Arkansas, native who aspires to a career in women's health, says, "It was never about Nelly being a scapegoat. We never lost sight about the industry as a whole."

The national media swarmed onto the campus to see what was billed as essentially another skirmish in the black gender wars. The national spotlight on the Spelman women inspired *Essence* magazine's "Take Back the Music" campaign—a response to the growth of violence against black women in rap lyrics.[4] The magazine's editors invited hip-hop artists, historians, activists, and label executives to a town hall meeting at Spelman in February 2005.

Nelly's defenders felt his cause was more important than the tits-and-ass romping in the video, and they chastised the college feminists and called them misguided. After the campus drive was canceled, a group of Spelmanites held their own blood drive at a local mall. They registered 400 people.

"We were black women painted as black women angry at black men. We're upset with Nelly's lyrics, but we come from a place of love of music," Bailey says.

Contrary to common belief, the whole campus did not rise up. Bailey and her peers were the campus squeaky wheels. However, a surge of support in the form of phone calls, letters, and e-mails did flood the organization's office. Second-wave black feminists supported Bailey's group, and esteemed professor Beverly Guy-Sheftall helped guide her student charges into making effective decisions.

"When we go out, we're very conscious of what we're listening to," Bailey says. "I'll leave the dance floor or stop dancing."

Spelmanites engaged in discussions about the effects of the music with students at the all-male Morehouse College, across the street. They talked about the vulgar exploitation of women, white capitalism, and the limited economic options facing black women who heed the video casting calls. Some men and women agreed. But the usual insults were hurled at the Spelmanites: You're keeping the black man down. You're airing dirty laundry.

"Before, I used to get upset; now I understand people's reluctance to weigh in. A lot of people feel we're harping on things unimportant," Bailey, who graduated in May 2005, says. On the other hand, it is hard for her to understand her peers' outright dismissal of their cause. "What has Nelly done for you that makes you want to protect him more so than the women who are in your immediate space?"

Many on *Essence*'s "Take Back the Music" panel hungered for a solution. The town hall meeting didn't solve anything—nor was that an expectation—but it did produce some frank, long overdue discussions. The flare-up at Spelman continues a tradition of black feminist activism in that it has resulted in a larger public debate. Long after the Nelly v. Spelman bout died down, some have called on Bailey and her peers to answer the question "What next?" Unfortunately, there is no easy resolution to a crisis that has been decades in the making.

Whether or not we choose to engage in these discussions, the tensions are thick. Sometimes, they rear their head when you least expect it. Last winter, on a visit to Memphis, some friends and I were invited to a free Ja Rule concert. I don't usually visit clubs advertised on the radio. The crowd was young—early twenties at most—and ready to kick it. A guy tried to get my attention by constantly touching me; I wasn't interested. When I walked away I told him, "You really shouldn't touch people you don't know."

That rankled him, because he spat back, "Bitch, why are you so mean? Fuck you," and proceeded to follow me through the club, cussing me out from here to kingdom come. My response was not exactly my finest moment. But his attitude and interaction with me appeared to reflect the extent to which black male-female relationships have become crippled. I'm not a bitch, or a ho, either, but that did not matter to this guy. So what can you do?

"Fuck you," I told him. "What the fuck are you going to do, muthafucker?"

Chapter 6

The Pole Test

I look into my daughter's eyes
And realize that I'ma learn through her.

—COMMON, "BE"

C omedian Chris Rock prowls the stage, bright lights blazing arou nd him, his mouth running at a clip. He cuts an impressive figure in his black-and-wine-colored striped suit as he surveys the audience at historic Constitution Hall in Washington, D.C. He's taping an HBO stand-up special called *Never Scared*, but as soon as the talk turns to fatherhood, it's clear that the man is *shook*.[1] Black male comedians have given us a variety of takes on black fatherhood. There are the late Robin Harris, Bernie Mac, D. L. Hughley, who describe the anguish of fathering bad-ass kids, also known as *Bebe*. Others, like Bill Cosby and Eddie Murphy, play the role of sober moralists.

Chris Rock takes the high road when the talk turns to his beloved baby girl. Worry lines crease his face, his visage full of angst. His eyes, always wild, appear to flash with genuine fear. He worries aloud about how what he does now will shape his daughter's future relationships. He does not want to send yet another woman out into the dating world with "daddy issues." After much thought and consideration, Rock says he's figured out his responsibility as a father to a little girl.

"My only job in life is to keep her off the pole," Rock says soberly. "They don't grade fathers, but if your daughter's a stripper, you fucked up!"

The idiom of fathers, daughters, and the stripper's pole has pierced black lexicon like memorable lines from *Def Comedy Jam* or *In Living Color*. By Rock's estimation, a whole lot of men are fucking up in America. Somebody produced the sperm that spawned all those booties grinding on BET's soft-porn video show *Uncut*. Someone helped populate the cult-hit documentaries *Pimps Up Ho's Down* and *American Pimp*. Someone sired the stripper-turned-emcee-turned-fashion-star Eve. What rapper hasn't included rhymes about strippers, from Ludacris to the Ying Yang Twins to the Notorious B.I.G.? A crop of books dubbed "hip-hop literature" is following the tradition of 1970s paperback blaxploitation writers Iceberg Slim and Donald Goines, whose books are filled with hustlers and strippers.

And someone birthed hip-hop, whose entire aesthetic—at least as promulgated on cable and radio—seems to be based on the world's oldest profession; all men are P-I-M-P-S and all the women are hos. As a whole, the Hip-Hop Generation has found prostitution to be an apt metaphor for American capitalism, which under our generation's watch has taken the literal and figurative pimping of black culture to new depths.

But Rock isn't just speaking in metaphors before the sold-out Constitution Hall audience. The grip that strippers hold over men is as real as it gets. It can be a force as strong as heroin, as the married Rock personally attests. "Someone has got to entertain the married men of America," he says. This is not to disparage the strippers, Rock says. He means them no offense, he says over and over again. "Somebody's got to do it," he says, shrugging.

So this is how a new standard for black fatherhood has been set; call it the "pole test." Judging by the number of times the line about keeping his daughter off the pole has been repeated, like most great comedy it taps into a deeper kind of truth. To us, it begs the question: But seriously, who *are* these men? Don't look to popular culture for answers. Strippers are almost never allotted a high degree of character development, whether before the camera or on the stage. To get answers, you've got to ask the strippers themselves.

We asked four strippers, all randomly selected through personal contacts—one on the East Coast, one on the West, and two in between—about their relationships with their dads. These are four women, four different paths. Our sampling, by the way, says nothing empirical about how contemporary black men father their girls. As a symbol of patriarchy, though, the stories of these women say a whole lot. We'll leave the psychoanalysis to the professionals. But listen closely and you'll hear the many ways that the porn industry, and the Married Men of America filling the audience, have fathered these women, providing a near lifetime of guidance, affirmation, and sustenance. Both biologically and figuratively, the answer to the question "Who's your daddy?" is complicated. These women are reluctant to assign blame. They protect their daddies, whether familiar, monstrous, or strange, as fiercely as they protect themselves.

Yasmine dances at a strip club on Michigan Avenue in Detroit. Men in athletic jerseys, men in suits inhale steak specials and topless women on poles. Women are not allowed inside unless they are employees or arrive with a male escort. Fluorescent lights flicker inside, and on the sunniest day the club is midnight-dark.

The bubblegum-pink dressing room is small. Mindless chatter bounces off the walls, the kind heard in a high school girls' locker room. The twentysomething dancers click-clack in the classic clear heels that Rock dubs the official "ho uniform." A television rests atop a vending machine peddling $8 cigarettes. In the background, sounds of suburban domesticity waft from an *Everybody Loves Raymond* episode, followed by the catfights on the catwalks on *America's Next Top Model.*

Inside, flesh is everywhere. Half-dressed dancers fasten each other's hooks and zippers, compare boob jobs, and flaunt goodies from their shopping excursions. The cell phones never seem to stop ringing. Hot curling irons line the horizontal mirror.

Yasmine enters. Cornrowed extensions fall down her back, fake hazel contacts stare at us from above exposed breasts. A tongue ring flashes when she speaks.

> *"Make the money, don't let it make you."*
> *"Closed legs don't get fed."*
> —FROM THE FILM *THE PLAYERS CLUB*

"I'm your daddy," said the tall, dark man with a receding hairline and thick Coke-bottle glasses pushed above his nose. Yasmine was 11 years old. All of her short life she thought her younger brother's father was hers. Plus, she had a stepfather at home. When her mother had a nervous breakdown, triggered by getting strung out on cocaine-laced weed, the five siblings were sent different ways. The summer day in 1991 when Yasmine moved in was the day she met the man.

She was not exactly impressed. Yasmine's mother had instructed her to refer to all her boyfriends as "Daddy."

Now Yasmine stared at the man claiming to be her biological father. "You and every other nigga," Yasmine recalls as her reply.

When she recounts this story, Yasmine is fresh from Cancún, her brown skin lightly sun-kissed. She has exchanged braids for a long, bouncy weave. She is still reeling from the news she learned earlier that day—that a childhood eye injury has grown into glaucoma. Before her steaming plate of lamb chops and buttery baked potato arrives, the bartender slides Yasmine a drink. A Purple Rain—a shot each of gin, rum, vodka, schnapps, Chambord, and triple sec—helps loosen her inhibitions and her tongue.

Yasmine struggled even before she moved into her father's house. As an 8-year-old, she assumed motherly duties, grocery shopping with $500 worth of food stamps lining her pockets. In sixth grade Yasmine would arrive at school hours before sunrise to escape her mentally unstable mother's home, often dressed in the same clothes as the day before. She had unbrushed teeth and rumpled hair. The child smelled ripe. Teachers never inquired about her problems, so Yasmine lost faith in them.

When Yasmine moved in with her biological father and his longtime girlfriend, their two daughters were part of the package. Her torture started soon afterward. Her father's girlfriend was happy to play the role of the evil stepmother, putting the tweener to work—and on birth control pills. Yasmine had developed a figure early, and her period debuted at age 9. Family gossip about a previous rape led them to believe that an early introduction to sex would surely lead to promiscuity.

One night before school resumed that fall, Yasmine sat on the floor, her back against her father's bed. His girlfriend snoozed under the covers. Her father forced his hand down Yasmine's shirt and massaged her 34C breasts. Then the rape started. It became a routine. After his girlfriend fell asleep he'd have sex with Yasmine, his eldest daughter.

"After a while I got used to it. I was used to disappointment. My mother let me down. Why did they send me to a father I didn't know? I didn't believe he was my fucking father."

If child protective services knocked on the door and questioned her about abuse, tipped off by the neighbors' suspicions, Yasmine lied. They said they wouldn't remove her from the home regardless of how she answered. "The system is a joke," Yasmine huffs.

Her dad fooled people by playing the role of an overprotective father. He insisted on attending her eighth-grade prom and would show up at school dances. When Yasmine resisted his sexual advances— he'd wake her up to meet him in the basement—a beatdown was as inevitable as getting raped the next day. She found an outlet in writing letters to herself describing the abuse. Why cry, Yasmine thought. Alas, her father's girlfriend discovered the letters and passed them around to other family members like embarrassing school notes as they drank cocktails and ate crab legs. No one believed Yasmine. And Yasmine was nothing but a nasty bitch anyway, her quasi stepmother would shriek. Yasmine saw a psychologist after her mother's breakdown. The psychologist reported back to her father and his girlfriend that the teen made up the story about her father's abuse.

"How can I have sex with a grown-ass man?" she asked.

Yasmine ran away several times. She tired of being raped three or four times a week and being treated like a backwoods stepchild, time and again receiving paltry Christmas presents while her younger sisters rejoiced in a Toys "R" Us windfall. At 15 she fled to stay with a good friend's aunt, who welcomed her. The woman moved to the South and longed to take Yasmine with her, but her father refused. Afterward, he and his live-in girlfriend broke up. Yasmine and her father moved into a new house. "I was hoping things would change. That's the worst thing that could've happened. It went from sugar to shit," she says.

His drinking escalated, and the two shared a bed. When she got pregnant, neighbors speculated that Yasmine carried his child. But this time no one intervened. And he could talk his way out of anything, often threatening to send her to a juvenile home. Thankfully, he was not the child's father. The sex finally stopped at age 18 when Yasmine got pregnant again by another guy. When her father crept toward her in a sexual advance, Yasmine hit him. He pulled a gun on her. She moved out, physically unscathed, and emancipated herself.

She had to find a way to support herself. Working at the fast-food chain White Castle wasn't cutting it. Yasmine's cousin and her friends always sported new clothes, hairdos, and immaculate makeup. They stripped for a living. "I wanted to live like them," she recalls. She had graduated from high school on the honor roll and got accepted into a community college, but her father had belittled that idea when she lived under his watch, insisting school wasn't a place for a girl with kids. Instead she prepared for life as a stripper.

Living on her own, Yasmine tried to make amends with her father. She wrote him a letter at age 21, as a birthday gift. No response. She heard crack cocaine gripped him. He lives perhaps three miles away, but Yasmine doesn't bump into him on the street, at the gas station, or in the corner grocery store. "I don't expect people to have sympathy for me. I don't complain. I make sure nothing happens to my kids."

But the demons are still there. During our interview, she vacillates between professing love and hate for her father. It's as if she is clasping a daisy and plucking the petals one by one, reciting, "He loves me, he loves me not." Yasmine doesn't blame her father for her strip-club career.

We sit at the bar for a couple of hours. At one point she pauses. "It's hard to talk about," she says, sipping her second Purple Rain. The relationship is complex as calculus. "You don't know what it's like to be abused. It's a connection you can't understand. We were one person. He had a stroke one night I spent the night out and I woke up that morning throwing up."

Moments later she says, "I can't see myself talking to him. I would kill him."

Recently her grandmother told Yasmine that her grandfather had sexually molested her father during childhood.

Like Pecola in Toni Morrison's *The Bluest Eye*, Yasmine has dreamed of being white because she hated what she saw in the mirror. Pecola and Yasmine might have been friends. Their abuse started at the same age. Both carried babies. Both dealt with drunkards as daddies. Both tried disappearing into their own misery. But only one knew her pregnancy wasn't the result of her father—and she found that out only after her labor.

Yasmine says she hated black men and never dated them until meeting her husband, a police officer. Her husband encourages her to seek therapy; she's resisting.

"My therapy is conquering the world. I want to get out of stripping. I'm tired," she says, explaining that her goal is to work with sexually abused children. But for several years stripping sustained her more than family and friends. Stripping gave her energy when she was emotionally sapped.

"Without this I wouldn't have nothing. When I dance I let my anger go. Just put it on stage. I let the anger flow."

I walked in a young lady and came out a woman.
                    —DIAMOND, IN *THE PLAYERS CLUB*

Sam's father stares at her from a frayed color photo. The photo captures a short, charming man wearing standard 1970s gear: butterfly collar, small Afro. She thinks he looks suave. Her father also lives in second- and thirdhand stories about a man from South Carolina, sweet as Godiva when sober, violent as a repeat offender when drunk.

Sam's parents didn't walk down the aisle, and her father deserted the family for good well before Sam's first birthday. She's been told he was a womanizer who beat her mother and destroyed Sam's baby clothes in one of his rageful fits. Put together, the information Sam knows about her father wouldn't fill a one-page letter. A last name didn't legally bind them. She doesn't know his birthday.

For years, she didn't think it mattered much. Growing up in a rough neighborhood in Maryland without a father was the norm. Her siblings and mother were a good support system. She said she never felt his absence. "I didn't want for school clothes. There were gifts under the Christmas tree. My mom sacrificed.... I never missed him."

Her mother frequently asked if she wanted to contact her father. Sam vaguely recalls going to a woman's house, probably his girl-friend's, and waiting outside for her father. He never came. As a teenager, Sam butted heads with her mother, who always worked more than one job and ran a tight ship. Sam rebelled against her mother's strictness by running away. After high school, she worked at Chuck E. Cheese's and enrolled in hairdressing school. Coerced by a friend to dance together on an amateur strip night, Sam got hooked. She could use the money. "I felt, hey, I have a nice body. The men can't touch me." Sam dropped out of hairdressing school. Dancing consumed her as she signed up for double shifts, hoarding up to $1,000 a night. She dressed in elaborate costumes dotted with sequins and ruffles.

"I became really, really good at it. I had a very small waist back then and a large rear end. I had to learn to use what I had. I could move it and shake it any kind of way." Her stage name was Pleazure, and she stripped to Sade and Prince, used slow music and feathers like Josephine Baker, earning titles such as "Miss Buns" and "Rumpshaker of D.C."

Sam's family hated it. Chris Rock would have been proud of her older brothers. They literally tried to haul her off the stage. Bouncers wouldn't let the brothers into clubs. The quick, easy money laced Sam in nice threads and furnished apartments. She recalls popping Ecstasy pills and drinking a lot to get through most nights.

Then she met her future husband. He was running around in the strip club he owned, smacking dancers on the rear. She'd told him she'd work a couple of nights at the club for extra money. Backstage, he laid his hand on her behind and Sam thought, I am the Rump-shaker of D.C., this is so beneath me. But she needed the money. Love grew, and she became his main girlfriend.

After a while, though, they both grew tired of the scene.

"I was so young, but I had already seen so much," she says. Dancers being stalked and killed. Girls getting locked up, raped, robbed, beaten. Alcoholism, drug abuse, degradation, the humiliation, the misery all had taken their toll. One Sunday, they went to a church service led by a minister who had been visiting them in one of her boyfriend's clubs. When the minister asked if anyone wanted to pledge their life to God, Sam felt her hand rising. She looked over, and her future husband's hand was already in the air. Two weeks later, they were baptized. A week after that, they had their marriage license. Soon, Sam retired her dancing boots. Her husband gave up his strip clubs and dancers. The pair married, and for a while they operated a go-go gospel dance club. They had a baby—a son.

Still, Sam wishes her toddler-aged son could know his grandfather. Questions about her father nag at her every day. "I still don't know how to love men. I'm not really content. I'm never fully happy," Sam says, admitting that her discontent includes her marriage. Today she recognizes the void her father left.

Years ago, when she encountered one of her half sisters in the mall and learned that their dad had died, Sam just blinked and kept stepping. But lately the questions have grown more insistent. How did he grow up? What was he like? Why did he leave? Does he love her? In late winter 2005, Sam was about to embark on a Down South pilgrimage to meet her father's people and place flowers on his grave.

Sam doesn't look to the man in the photograph for her choices. "I can honestly say the family filled that void to the best of their ability. I can't put that blame there."

She runs alone, and damn it's cold.
No love in her life
Precious eyes to behold.
> — "JACKIE" (UNPUBLISHED POEM)

Jackie (not her real name) has kept a journal since age 8, inspired by *The Diary of a Young Girl*, by Anne Frank. She is open about the poetry but is not ready to release the prose about her father. On the surface, her childhood looked as comfortable as fresh laundry. She was reared in an upper-middle-class Los Angeles family. Besides being given material goods, Jackie studied ballet, jazz, and tap dance. Her father was in politics, mother a school administrator.

But there were secrets.

When Jackie was 4, her step-grandfather masturbated while she sat on his lap eating ice cream. A male friend of the family performed oral sex on her as part of his babysitting duties. Her father pressed her hand on his erection and inappropriately touched her body. Her mother, who was bipolar, ignored Jackie's pleas.

Jackie is now in her mid-20s, and irrespective of the therapists who say a child can never be blamed for sexual abuse, she still blames herself. She describes the abuse as a power play, waffling about whether molestation is even the right word for what happened. "I remember turning it into a barter. You better buy me toys. Instead of [being] a shrinking violet and being the victim, I turned it into prostitution. Since you're going to do this, I realize I had power. I'm going to get toys out of it and I'm going to scream. I let myself get molested," she says. In her young mind she wielded power by accepting Barbie dolls, miniature fur coats, shiny bikes, and video games.

The abuse continued until she was about 12. The so-called family friend and the step-grandfather had abused other cousins and were punished though the court system. The law never caught up with her father. She had to put a stop to it herself. "I started getting really mean and crazy. I'd threaten him: 'You have to fucking stop doing this.' I'd cry and scream and get hysterical. I'd take his hand and shove his hand off of me. I made it so difficult. The last straw for me was when he asked to look at my breast. He was not mean about it. He was very polite and nice."

She lost her virginity at 12 "to some stupid-ass boy in junior high because I wanted to be popular." Jackie's teenage years were tumultuous in a different way; hormones kicked in and her youthfulness clouded her judgment. By then her parents had divorced, and she and her mother constantly fought. She had virtually no criteria for sex—he just had to have a penis. In high school she went piercing berserk, putting holes in her nose, tongue, nipples, and stomach.

Jackie enrolled at a local university, and she took up Ecstasy, cocaine, and weed. After more combustion with her mother, Jackie moved out, dropped out of school, and took refuge in a hotel. Stripping appeared to be the natural next move.

"I already knew the stripping game. I don't know how to be a waitress, struggle with plates. I was very cute. I had fake boobs already."

Jackie parlayed her years of dance lessons into elaborate stage shows, dancing naked in tennis shoes to Nelly or in stilettos to 112, earning up to $1,500 a night. "I actually gained self-esteem after I was a stripper. Prior, I'd fuck anybody. I realized I had worth. Without my personality, my body itself had some value. I started to think if my body had value then my mind has value and then the spirit has value," Jackie says.

"My dad knew I stripped. He acted like he wasn't happy. I said, 'What the fuck are you going to do, give me money?' What could he say? I wasn't really connected to family. I was in an abusive relationship. Had I not been molested, I might not have stripped."

Before Jackie's epiphany about her self-worth, she spiraled in myriad directions. Asked about her prostitution, she rejects the label and takes a conciliatory posture, as she did with her childhood sexual abuse. "I hesitate to call it 'turning tricks.' It was bartering for goods and services, an extension of what I've been doing my whole life. I don't like the connotation of prostitution and I don't know if society is progressive enough to know the difference. I cared for gentlemen friends. Sometimes I wouldn't have sex," she says.

An overdose changed Jackie's mind about stripping. She woke up one morning not knowing how she got home and feeling as though her life was withering away. After more than a year of stripping, Jackie stopped cold turkey. Soon she reached out to her parents, who initiated family therapy. She continues her counseling because she craves a healthy romantic relationship.

Her dad apologized but plays dumb about the molestation. Jackie harbors no resentment. They are at peace. She returned to college and is poised to graduate. Her dad pays her tuition and apartment rent. They are normal as they can be.

"My dad is my hero. I respect him as a man. I'll always, always love and respect my father. Now that there are boundaries, I can forgive. I understand his frailties."

How much money was enough? Or would it never be
enough? It was time to cut her losses and move on.
                              —SHANNON HOLMES, *BAD GIRLZ*

Rena, 25, a kindergarten teacher, thinks her daddy looks like Ron
O'Neal from *Superfly*, with his long muttonchop sideburns. He
transformed himself from a small-town Ohio boy into a big-city
Detroit music producer who dabbled in real estate. He always
smelled good: Obsession, Lagerfeld, and Fahrenheit, the colognes
lingered on his collar. And he had charisma for days. "People looked
up to him," Rena recalls. "He always had cronies or flunkies, people
who did things for him, have his back."

Her father and her mother, a backup singer, never married, but
they did cohabitate for a time, splitting up after Rena's tenth birthday. Her daddy showered her with love, advice, and presents. "I still
had strong morals and ethics. I didn't want for a whole lot," says Rena.

Growing up in Michigan, she basked in her father's attention.
When he introduced her to his friends and girlfriends, he'd brag, "This
is my number one girl." He told her she was a race apart from everyone else. "You're a thoroughbred," he'd say. And he encouraged her to
work like one, too. Be a hustler, he'd counsel. Have more than one job.

Rena took this advice to heart. By high school, she always held
down at least two jobs: paper routes, washing dishes. Flipping through
the television channels, Rena watched girls in strip club commercials
rocking coiffed weaves, long lashes, and a Jayne Kennedy aura. "I
thought I could look like that," Rena recalls. During her senior year
of high school, she and a friend caked on lipstick, mascara, and eye
shadow, arrived at a club, and lied to the doorman about their age.
Inside, Rena said she stared like a pervert at one of the dancers, mes-
merized by her body and stage presence. Noticing the teen's
infatuation, the dancer became her stripper fairy godmother, giving

a quick lesson on how to use the bottom of her feet to alter her body into a seductive force.

"I've always been that thick girl, big hips and big booty," Rena says. "I was always insecure but guys said it was hot." Rena vowed that when she turned 18, she'd do it for real. "I thought I could look like that. They were everything a man wanted." When it came time to pick a stage name, "Goldie" was the natural choice—the name of the lead character in the blaxploitation flick *The Mack*. Goldie demanded respect, just like her daddy. It's an unconscious occupational bond she has with her father.

Rena ventured away to a state school for college, and as she acclimated herself to studies and dorm life, she began plotting a side gig stripping. On a weekend trip home, she entered an amateur contest. She was nervous, but she recalled what her fairy godmother had taught her. *Your ass is your biggest asset.* It worked. Clients tossed money her way and she won the $250 contest. "Once you see that attention, it felt good." It opened up a lifestyle of Tiffany jewelry, holiday splurging, and shopping sprees.

Throughout the college years and beyond, Rena remained close to her father. When she felt like quitting school, he admonished her for crying too much about her difficulties. When she got pregnant by a professional athlete who insisted on an abortion, her father had a man-to-man talk with him. Rena herself decided not to have the baby. Once, when she was home from college, her dad discovered a shoebox full of singles stacked more than $500 high. "You aren't dancing on tables, are you?" he asked. She dodged the question, and he swiftly took her to the bank to open an account. But soon she was applying for a city-issued stripper dance card.

Rena used to marvel at Diamond, the heroine of the film *The Players Club*. But Rena has carved out her own place on the stripper stage as she transforms into her alter ego.

Toffee-colored Goldie disrobes at a club in the 'hood on Detroit's east side. Drug dealers and felons commune with each other, gawking at girls on stage. There's no visible champagne room, and the tiny space has the mores of a neighborhood bar. The DJ spins R. Kelly and the latest rap hits, weaving in Jill Scott and Goapele. Goldie looks bored on a random Friday night. While her G-string-wearing coworkers are carelessly whispering to customers between sets on stage, she parks at the bar, sipping water. When she does give a lap dance, Goldie appears aloof and faraway, her back toward the patron. Maybe she's thinking of her next lesson plan or out-of-state vacation. Her expression screams *Let me give this nigga a dance and keep it moving.*

She tries to keep reality and fantasy separate, at least somewhat.

Rena has never left the strip club with a customer for a midnight romp back at his place. But she hooks up with guys later. It's landed her free cruises and Las Vegas junkets. "If I know you like me, I will play you off. I'll play guys to get my hair done and bills paid. If I feel like sex, yes, but not as a barter.

"It's all a form of prostitution. Guys already have a perception. No one wants to hear how educated I am, that I'm a schoolteacher. You play them before they play you. They're already expecting a freak in bed. Treat them like a trick. No kisses. Oral is out. No affection."

Later, Goldie admits: "I wonder why I still do it. I make a good living [teaching]." She answers her own question. "It's the attention. It's a big part of why I like it. I was greedy. Enough was never enough." Sometimes she pulls in $500 a night for a few hours of work.

For five years Goldie has stripped at the same joint, where she is now probably the most senior dancer. Rena has never fully revealed the source of her moonlighting funds to her father.

When a friend of her father's saw her in the club and threatened to expose her, she issued a preemptive strike. She told her dad she'd been somewhere she shouldn't have. It's your business, he told her. End of discussion. "He raised me to take things to the grave. People don't have to know everything."

Goldie hasn't succumbed to drugs in her strip world. She does live a double life, waking up every morning to teach the alphabet to 5-year-olds. She's in counseling now, and something happened to her several years ago that makes her question how long she'll be able to stay in the game. An intruder broke into the home Rena and her mother lived in and brutally raped them both. The rapist ripped her skin, and afterward Rena had trouble sitting. Since then, she's tried to tuck away the incident. "It didn't affect me. Yes, physically. But I didn't want it to hold me back. It was just sex."

She didn't see the man's face, but she has a good idea where they may have been introduced. After the attack, he whispered "Goldie" in her ear.

Chapter 7

Babydaddy

Although Nia was a successful entrepreneur and a thoroughly modern woman, marriage and family were not part of the grand scheme for her life. She lived with her boyfriend Damon and also co-owned an event-planning company.

That's how she met Eric, a tall, sexy chef with a winsome smile. They became friends, which evolved into an occasional sexual rendezvous.

When Nia (names have been changed) got pregnant at age 30, she did not rush to the altar. But she thought that having a baby might even strengthen her on-and-off relationship with Damon, which suffered bouts of infidelity. She had the baby.

Meanwhile, Eric had moved across country and married. When he and his new wife came back to Washington, D.C., for a visit, they stayed at the house with Nia, Damon, and the child, a boy then ten months old. Seeing something familiar about the baby, Eric pulled Nia aside. "Are you sure it's Damon's?" he asked, inquiring about the baby's paternity. Nia emphatically shook her head no.

Eventually Damon, too, got suspicious. The baby boy was darker than Nia, and Damon is light-skinned. He insisted; she took a paternity test.

When the results came in the mail, which confirmed Eric as the father, Nia put Sade on the stereo, sat on the stairs with a bottle of wine, and cried. Next: expletive-filled shouting matches at her job. Being cut off from Damon and his family. Forgettable Father's Days. "Humiliating" visits to court to enforce child support. Eric would accuse her of conspiring with the white man to bring him down. Later, her baby's biological father divorced his wife and tried to hit her up for money. He also hasn't shown much more than a fleeting interest in his first born, who is now eight years old. She said she never wanted a relationship with Eric.

"I was hurt, embarrassed...you think it can't happen to you and that it only happens to a hoochie mama," Nia, who grew up middle class, says. "I didn't tell my family—no one—for a long time. I just lived with this guilt."

She never thought it could happen, but here it was. An innocent flirtation had turned into something eminently more complicated. Her life had devolved into a unique brand of theater as ubiquitous in real life as it is in popular culture: babymama drama.

Chances are, actress Shar Jackson will forever be known as Britney Spear's husband's kicked-to-the-curb, twice-over babymama. When the accomplished attorney Michelle Obama introduced her U.S. senator-elect husband, Barack, before his acceptance speech, she jokingly dubbed him—among other things—her babydaddy. At their co-ed roller-skating baby shower, engaged actors Boris Kodjoe and Nicole Ari Parker donned matching outfits labeled "Nicole's Baby Daddy" and "Boris' Baby Mama."[1] Even our esteemed leaders such as Jesse Jackson Sr. have turned out to be babbydaddies.

Once a badge of shame pinned on deadbeat parents, the terms *babydaddy* and *babymama* have become the favored shorthand for modern parenthood—not marriage. They also signify something larger at work in the Hip-Hop Generation: a metaphor for fragile romance and a commentary on our ambivalence toward conventional family structures. Seventy percent of black babies are born out of wedlock. As increasing numbers of black women don't marry, many of them become single mothers, or babymamas.

Far from being just a racial problem, this trend reflects a similar shift in the larger American landscape. Marriage is a complicated institution. It has changed over the past fifty years, as symbolized, for example, in the angst-ridden relationship between Ross and Rachel, two unmarried parents on NBC's *Friends*. Celebrity mothers like Jodie Foster have rebuked marriage as a prerequisite to having a baby. Across the board, cohabitation has been normalized, birth control has ushered in a sexual revolution, more women work outside the home, sex outside of marriage is destigmatized, and the divorce rate has soared.

For many of today's women of an array of social classes, getting pregnant raises the stakes in a relationship in ways that were less well appreciated in the past. It is not just the parents but the child who must live with the consequences of a potential bad marriage, be it physical abuse, emotional abuse, or neglect. A wrong choice becomes harder to reverse once it is codified into law. For the sake of their children and their sanity, women want it all: a marriage that maintains a healthy balance between satisfying emotional and economic needs. Too often we've seen past generations make that decision via shotgun, and women get the worst of the deal.

There are, of course, terrible consequences to the rise of the terms *babymama* and *babydaddy*. They feed into the worst stereotypes about black culture and they racialize dilemmas that have more institutional and societal causes. We all remember President Ronald Reagan painting the image of the black, gettin'-over welfare queen in the 1980s. Her habitat was the projects, her kids were abundant, and she hustled a yearly tax-free income while cruising in her Cadillac. In the late 1990s, *Sports Illustrated* famously detailed a stream of paternity suits facing black NBA players. The unmarried Shawn Kemp, who by age 28 had sired seven children, became the poster boy for irresponsible fatherhood.[2] Conservatives prattle about protecting the sacredness of marriage; meanwhile, half the marriages in this country are doomed to divorce.

But there is another way to look at the phenomenon. Far from being a cynical devaluation of the role of marriage, it sometimes signifies the opposite. The current generation of marriage-age singles witnessed divorce rates explode as children. In some ways our embrace of these terms is a throwback. Increasingly, today's parents are willing to accept the labels *babymama* and *babydaddy* while they hold out for something more important: a real-life fairy tale.

The terms *baby mother* and *baby father* may have drifted from the Caribbean to America centuries ago, according to John Rickford, a noted linguistics professor at Stanford University. The term *childfather* (usually pronounced "chile fadda") is sounded with a low tone followed by a high tone, with the stress on the second word. The words also could have developed along parallel lines in both cultures, where unmarried women maintain relationships with the fathers of their children, Rickford said.

Linguist Geneva Smitherman describes the American origins in *Black Talk: Words and Phrases from the Hood to the Amen Corner*:

> *Baby's daddy, that is, a child's father, generally one not married to the child's mother and considered insignificant. The phrase gained currency from the popular 1997 jam "My Baby Daddy".... Originally a DIS of the BROTHAS, the linguistic counterpart, baby momma, emerged as a label for*

*irresponsible mothers who are thus also insignificant.
Underlying both phrases is a sad SIGNIFYIN commentary
on the deteriorating state of male–female relationships in the
COMMUNITY and the negative impact of these relationships on Black children.*[3]

The terms have also had a lively romp through popular culture
and mass media. Among the first sightings was a late-1990s rap
song, "That's Just My Baby Daddy," by rappers B Rock and The
Bizz, which takes a humorous look at a jumbled mess of couples
lying and denying the babymama or babydaddy in their lives. R & B
singer Dave Hollister's girlfriend's babydaddy doesn't want to see
her happy and is always tripping, the singer wails in "Yo' Baby's
Daddy." Queen Pen raps in "Baby Daddy" that she regrets making
love to a guy, resulting in a fourth baby. Dave Chappelle struck
gold in a television comedy skit as Oprah's babydaddy. The universally panned film *My Baby's Daddy* followed three friends who got
three women pregnant at the same time. Virtually every daytime
television talk/carnival show has had a "Who is your baby daddy?"
segment.

In his song "Down Wit Da South," rapper Trick Daddy gives
one solution to the drama distinctive to the relationship between a
babydaddy and a babymama: "Shake that ass," he advises. "Shake
that ass, shake that ass and make your baby daddy mad."

In her book *Against Love*, social critic and Northwestern University
communications professor Laura Kipnis argues that prevailing attitudes toward marriage are a "popular uprising" against the "regimes
of contemporary coupledom." And, as she told a writer for
Northwestern's alumni magazine, "Adultery is a de facto referendum
on the sustainability of monogamy."[4]

Considering the disproportionate impact on black children who grow up outside two-parent homes, a fair question is whether the black community can afford to reject marriage and monogamy. Federal agencies say that children who grow up in two-parent families with healthy marriages do better on a host of outcomes than children who don't. Married couples build more wealth on average than singles, therefore decreasing the likelihood of poverty; children in the married household enjoy better physical health, and healthy marriages reduce the risk of adults and children either perpetrating or being victimized by crime. A 2003 *Crisis* magazine cover story rightly asked: How can the black family thrive when nearly 70 percent of black children are born out of wedlock, and 47 percent of black single-mother families have children in poverty?[5]

It's no laughing matter, Ebony Joy James, a PhD candidate in marriage and family therapy at Virginia Tech University, says. "Everyone won't have money like Puffy or Lil' John. Everybody's real quick to say babymama, and that's pure ghetto. It's not even hip-hop." James says it is almost easier for a woman to have a baby than stay in a relationship with a man in our times. A baby arrives regardless of whether the mother is ready. "You don't get that same innate feeling in a relationship all of a sudden. That's a big difference between having a baby and being in a relationship with a man."

Social scientists have found myriad reasons for the emergence of the babydaddy, everything from the storied black man shortage and dating patterns to, ironically, a renewed reverence for the institution of marriage. Black men at the top and the bottom, socioeconomically, appear to be most ambivalent about standing at the altar. Evidence points to men in the middle getting hitched.

Black views are changing along with the rest of contemporary society, according to social scientists. But white and Hispanic parents are 2.5 times more likely than black parents to formalize their romantic relationships through marriage, according to the 2004 "Fragile Families and Child Wellbeing" study by Princeton and Columbia universities, which followed nearly 5,000 children and 1,897 new unmarried parents in twenty U.S. cities.[6]

The shift has taken place over many years. In 1970, 10.7 percent of mothers of all races were unmarried; for white mothers it was 5.5 percent, and it was 37.5 percent for black mothers, according to the National Center for Health Statistics.[7] Over the years, that number has increased. In 2004, 35.7 percent of babies were born to unmarried women, according to a U.S. Department of Health and Human Services study. This rate for black mothers is 70 percent, compared with 24.5 percent for white mothers.[8]

One reason for relatively low marriage rates among blacks is a shortage of marriageable black males. Black mothers have stronger pro-marriage attitudes and value marriage more highly than white and Hispanic mothers. The policy implication, the fragile families brief concluded, is that urban labor markets must improve in order for black men to strengthen black families.

Other sociologists have looked at dating patterns to explain the disparity in marriage rates. *The Sexual Organization of the City*, edited by a group of sociologists headed by Ed Laumann, looks to sexual networks in Chicago to explain the racial gap in marriage. The whites they studied often use dating as a precursor to marriage; single black men often use a strategy of dating that makes marriage less likely. For instance, black men are more likely than white men to start a sexual relationship with a new woman while maintaining physical relationships with old girlfriends. More widespread dating polygamy in the black community leads to more out-of-wedlock births.[9]

Other researchers have examined how the mentality of unwed mothers contributes to the gap. For their book *Promises I Can Keep: Why Poor Women Choose Motherhood Over Marriage*, sociologists

Kathryn Edin and Maria Kefalas spent five years in poor Philadelphia neighborhoods interviewing single mothers living below the federal poverty line. The women interviewed—black, white, and Hispanic—did not link childrearing to walking down the aisle. In fact, they held marriage to a much higher standard, believing in the institution as sacred and refusing to make a lackluster choice of mate that could potentially lead to divorce. Several women had dealt with unfaithful, crime-prone, or jobless boyfriends. The mothers tied having children to their identity because children gave them structure and did not remove dreams and goals from their lives.

Edin and Kefalas also found that black women are the group least likely to wed, but the authors don't attribute that to race. Racial attitudes toward marriage among all of the low-income women were similar, making class the unifier among the 160 moms who were interviewed. "Poor women are not disinterested in marriage, quite the contrary," the authors write. "But many, like Michelle, the thirty-one-year-old African American mother of a seven-year-old and four-year-old twins, say, 'I'm not rushing into anything.' " Michelle's reasons: wanting to save money, own a home, and buy a car.[10]

Other black women expressed fears of a man owning them or being tied to someone who could be too controlling and irresponsible. Patricia, 31 years old and a mother of four, told the authors she mistrusted men. "They think they are supposed to have more than one girlfriend, making kids all over the place. It's hard to have someone be yours this day and age, just all yours...."[11]

Women like Dominique, a mother of three, told the researchers that men drift in and out of their children's lives, but a mother could never violate the natural order of things by abandoning her offspring. For the women, having a baby out of wedlock was not a mark of personal shame, but of valor, because a woman judges her success on how well she raises her children.[12]

The 2003 U.S. Census data show the patterns of marriage by race, income, and gender. A close examination reveals the following statistics.

Never-married black men:

67 percent in the 25–29 age bracket have never married

50 percent ages 30–34

38 percent ages 35–39

Meanwhile, 37 percent of black men (ages 15 and older) have a married spouse present. Only 28 percent of black females have a married spouse present.

Never-married black women:

63 percent ages 25–29 have never married

45 percent ages 30–34

32 percent ages 35–39

And it's not just poor people who aren't getting married. The figures suggest that low- and high-income men are least likely to partake in nuptials. Eighty-six percent of black males without an income, ages 25–29, have never been married; 79 percent for males 30–34. The percentages are high for incomes under $25,000. The percentages decrease in the $25,000-to-$75,000 category. But 76 percent of black males earning more than $100,000 have never married.

The percentages for black women don't fluctuate as much as those of their male counterparts. For example, low-income women (under $25,000) within the 25–34 age bracket who have never married hover in the 50-to-60-percent range. Figures for middle-income black women are similar.

In contrast, only 26 percent of white women have never been married; 29 percent of white men. For whites, income levels don't appear to be as big a factor when it comes to getting married.[13]

Sociologist Ed Laumann's research also confirms that black men at both ends of the education spectrum are less likely to marry. The most educated and the least educated men have lower marriage rates than those with moderate levels of education. The most educated men tend to have lower marriage rates because they are more likely to engage in long-term polygamous relationships.

Laumann's conclusion about what this sexual market offers black women is bleak. "We would particularly expect marriage to be an implausible option for African American women," he notes, "not only because so many of the partners available to them will be engaged in polygamous relationships, but also because they do not have the social resources (in terms of social networks) to guarantee that they have chosen the right partner."[14]

That's you baby's mama. Don't be late payin' your bills. It takes two to make a kid.
                                        —"Baby's Mama," Babyface featuring Snoop

In Aida's native Ethiopia, a pregnant woman is like an egg—don't disturb it. Her ex-boyfriend didn't adhere to the adage.

The couple had recently broken up when Aida, a photographer, realized she was pregnant in December 1998. Their relationship in Washington, D.C., had gone from exchanging corny jokes to taking walks in Malcolm X Park to living together to doing community service projects together to, finally, abuse. They began dating in their early twenties, and at first an easy rapport flowed between them. His charm intoxicated her. An intense love swelled, but the relationship turned tart.

"I've never been in a relationship where there was so much insecurity," Aida, 31, says. He was jealous and accusatory, pulling stunts like going through her phone book, memorizing numbers, and calling every guy to query him about his feelings for Aida. When nothing confirmed his suspicions, he had women plant calls to him to try to make her jealous.

"It became a cancer I couldn't recognize," she says of their relationship. "Because of not having a dad in my life, it's like shooting in the dark. I don't know what a man should be like. I didn't have a male role model in my life." By the time she was born, her father was readying to join the mass exodus of Ethiopia's upper class. He moved to the U.S. and they reconnected when she moved to D.C.

"With him [the boyfriend] I accepted everything. [I thought] maybe I'm the only one who's crazy.... It wasn't until it ended that I realized that it isn't a relationship I wanted to get into again," she says.

Aida had moved in with her boyfriend after the two dated for a couple of years, and the relationship dissolved from devotion to despair. He slapped her with an open hand a few times.

"I was so shocked," she says of the first time he hit her, after a visit to the Laundromat. Aida can't remember what the argument was about. But she is clear on the emotion that swept over her. "That was something very foreign to me. We went back to the apartment, and he was sobbing. In past relationships he'd been violent and never told me about it."

She urged him to seek therapy. At first she swallowed the abuse, thinking it came from his background, and she admits being young and naive back then. When nothing changed, Aida envisioned herself getting violent, too, so she told them their relationship was unhealthy and needed to end. Chagrined, he refused to let her come back to the apartment to pack her things, and he boxed Aida's belongings himself.

But when she told him she was pregnant, he thought maybe they could reconcile. Aida was not swayed by his overtures of flowers, pleading messages, and balloons. "I made it clear that I didn't want to be with him. To him, he thought there was a connection because I was keeping the child. I didn't want to have an abortion; that's what it basically came down to."

He broached the subject of marriage, but Aida balked. No. I'll
call you when Lamaze classes start, she told him. The hints didn't
work well, and his controlling nature resurfaced. He thought she was
going through "crazy hormones." Aida recalls, "In his mind, this
'crazy bitch' is going to come around. It came out in anger at the hospital a few hours after delivery. He starts talking about 'let's discuss
the baby.' And I can't walk. We had to get security to get him out
of the hospital. He was going crazy. My girlfriends, my mom were
fighting with him. The nurse called security."

The drama continued. They had the trifling court sagas that
lasted a year. He made her take a paternity test. Then he tried to get
full custody. Then he professed wanting to marry her—again. Then
he balked at paying the court-ordered child support of $600 a month
and spent three days in jail. Aida says, "I try to be a peaceful person.
I don't want drama in my life. I still try to believe that it was possible to have a civil relationship with your child's father. With him—it's
been a problem, challenging. At times it doesn't work."

A soccer mom and accomplished visual artist, Aida says her ex
called one time to tell her how lucky he was not to have a crazy babymama. He also declared that he was the only one of his friends who
still didn't get sex from his babymama. Disgusted, she told him to
stop talking to her inappropriately.

Aida married another man in New York City in 2003. He has
been more of a father to her "beautiful child," she says. She and her ex
live in separate cities on the East Coast, and he rarely sees his son. The
excuse is that he is working to become a millionaire and afterward will
spend time with his son. Aida has told him it's not about how much
money or material security he flings at them; children look at love.

"I think he's a lonely man. I feel sorry for him."

She also predicts another round in court. "I've tried to be a good
parent and involve him in the process without wanting anything for

myself," but the relationship is still strained. "There is a saying in my country—it's like a dog. If you play with it too much, if you have no control it will bite your hand. If I'm friendly he thinks he can get me back. I don't like being an asshole but that seems to work for us. He hasn't sent money in I don't know how long."

She says her son tells people he wants to be like his dad, with muscles and a shaved head. "He talks about him. I told him to write a letter [to his father]. Children, especially boys, hunger for their father. My son is in the stage where he knows his father is not around. He'll say, 'It's okay if you don't come see me. I know you have to make money.' A 5–year-old should not have that kind of mentality."

For Nia, the single mother in Washington, D.C., the worry is about her son's lack of a relationship with his father, and how her choices have contributed to that. "I'm truly blessed and fortunate not to rely on that [Eric's money] for our living condition. My family is supportive and I make enough money to survive. But I think it's important that the father contribute something," Nia says.

She says Eric doesn't call his son often and has had a peripheral relationship with him. Nia says she asks her son, now 8 years old, if he wants to call his dad. "He said no. I just don't want to," Nia recounts. "He said, 'Mommy, do you like my dad?' I said, 'I will always care about your dad but I don't dislike him and you should-n't either.' I never speak badly about him in front of [my son.] I feel badly Eric doesn't have a better relationship with his son. I feel I have to overcompensate for my mistakes."

There has been an ongoing movement to recognize, celebrate, and rejuvenate interest in black marriage while trying to whittle down the number of out-of-wedlock births. Right-wing conservatives have often led the charge; in the early 2000s, President George W. Bush promoted a so-called healthy marriage initiative for poor people, which included counseling, public advertising campaigns, and marriage mentoring in "at-risk" communities.

The push has also come from the black community itself. Nisa Islam Muhammad started "Black Marriage Day" to counter the low-marriage-rate and unwed-mother statistics. The website for the event, www.blackmarriageday.com, states, "Much of what we hear about marriage in the black community is a blues song about low rates, out-of-wedlock births, escalating divorces and how somebody done somebody wrong. We want to replace that blues song with a love song of joy." The idea is to honor married couples and fortify the existing unions. Across the country on Black Marriage Day, churches offer workshops and renewals of vows. One elementary school teacher sponsored a mock wedding in her class because none of the students had ever attended a real one.

Sheila Kendrick, executive director of Sisters Against Dead-Beat Parents in Detroit, has turned the need to defuse tense circumstances among babymamas and babydaddies into a thriving nonprofit organization.

Elsewhere on the Internet, communities have cropped up to debate babymamas and babydaddies. A blog for new fathers, www.daddytypes.com, discusses paternal roles and how to turn a child's room into a Pottery Barn display. A strain called Serious Baby Mama Drama dispenses advice. In one e-mail, a flustered father poured out his angst, wondering whether his live-in babymama cheated on him and how to provide for their growing brood.

Writer Maryann Reid is on a mission to turn babymamas into wives. Her novel *Marry Your Baby Daddy* is about three sisters and their complicated, unwedded relationships. Reid's research included interviews with hundreds of couples, crisscrossing class lines, from teens to professionals. She sought to find out why marriage didn't appeal to black men and women. The project led to "Marry Your Baby Daddy Day," a September 2005 mass wedding that recruited sponsors for in-kind contributions to pay matrimony costs for several couples.

Reid says the invitation to jump the broom stemmed from wanting to increase the percentage of two-parent homes in urban areas. "The stigma of out-of-wedlock birth isn't enough to get married," Reid tells us. "A lot of them have fantasies of what a wedding should be like, romanticized. A lot of them have fantasies—a palace, Brian McKnight singing, a $5,000 dress—lofty fantasies they feel they can't achieve. They don't want to do city hall. Several admitted no one in the family married. It's generational. The stigma of having a child [out of wedlock] is very comfortable, very acceptable. There were couples who had been through hell together, so city hall wasn't good enough."

India Williams met Ahmeid in college, bonding as displaced New Yorkers attending Grambling State University, in Louisiana. Their courtship was scripted out of a chick flick: weekly movies, football games, semiformal dances, and concerts. The next year, they moved in together. Senior year she got pregnant, but graduated on time, both families flying down for the commencement exercises and fawning over the new addition to the family.

Williams, now 27, remained in Louisiana for seven months while Ahmeid moved back to New York to find a job. They didn't want to move in with their parents, and the families didn't badger them to get married. Ahmeid had always been a good mate and father to their 5-year-old daughter and 23-month-old son. They initially didn't think they needed a formal ceremony to validate their bond. "Having a wedding and saying you're married doesn't define whether the relationship is healthy or prosperous. A ring doesn't make your husband committed," Williams says.

She figured, if she was going to march down the aisle, she wanted the frilly, conventional, high-priced fairy-tale wedding. For a while she was a stay-at-home mom, so rent and food took precedence over a $10,000-plus celebration.

The live-in couple received a domestic partnership certificate, a form that attested their committed relationship, in New York City in 2000. At city hall, Williams surveyed the kitschy plastic bouquets and wedding-cake dresses. She decided a quickie municipal wedding was out of the question. "It lacked that feeling of unity, the feeling of family. I didn't feel that when I went down there. When we get married, I want it to be how I dreamt," Williams says. Short of the dream, her attitude was: If it's not broke, why fix it? The couple had already been through many trials, including suffering through a miscarriage with twins and a complicated second pregnancy.

Williams's parents never married, and she never had a father figure in her life. She describes her mother as "a little fast, all over the place. She was always a hard worker. [But] she allowed street life to dictate her path. I was always a person who required stability. I didn't have that growing up so I created it for myself."

In 2005, the couple decided the time was right to make things official. Ahmeid saw a newspaper article about Marry Your Baby Daddy Day and handed it to Williams. "You should apply," he told her. After Maryann Reid picked them to partake in the sponsored mass wedding, Williams said there was a different air in the house; everyone was excited. Her daughter gushed about her own dress, chirping about the family being engaged. Williams always knew that Ahmeid was "the one." Now she was ready to show the world—which she did in high style, wearing an ivory mermaid dress with splashes of green.

In the period leading up to the mass wedding, people criticized Reid's endeavor and couples like Williams and Ahmeid. If you can't afford a wedding, you can't afford kids, they said. Others accused Reid of pulling people out of the projects to force them into marriage. But Williams says these critics seemed to miss the whole point of the exercise: to make the fairy tale come true. "The whole point [of the day] was to show the difference—there can be a difference in lifestyle," Williams says. "You choose your path. I never considered myself as a 'babymama' or him a 'babydaddy.' We are a committed relationship, raising our kids.

"He's genuine. I know what I'm getting. There's not too much room for surprise. He's such a family-oriented person. He puts his kids first. I'm happy to say I have a dual-parent household. He always wanted us to get married."

Chapter 8

Tyrone at Work

The phone rings in Spencer Leak Jr.'s office. The woman on the other end has just lost a loved one and is worried about how she is going to pay for the homegoing service.

"Yes, we have a payment plan," Spencer says. The 36-year-old vice president of A. R. Leak and Sons Funeral Home is accustomed to such questions. As he once explained, "We can't be in the heart of the black community"—Chicago's South Side—"and not have a payment plan."

"Two-thirds down?" the woman asks on speaker phone. Spencer explains her options and how the funeral home can work within her budget.

"That's very doable," she says, a lift in her voice. "Thank you, sweetheart."

"Take my cell phone number down," Spencer adds before hanging up. He always gives out his cell number.

An unbroken chain of Leaks has been doing this work since 1933: giving comfort and solace to Chicago's black families. Spencer's grandfather A. R. Leak founded Leak and Sons during the Depression with a $500 inheritance. Since the funeral parlor handled the viewing for singer Sam Cooke in 1964, Leak and Sons has been an institution in black Chicago. Spencer Leak Jr. knew in first grade that he wanted to be a funeral director—just like his daddy.

For decades, funeral homes have been one of the most stable businesses in black communities, a tried-and-true ticket to upper-middle-class wealth. But even this most traditional of black businesses needs an infusion of new ideas. Facilities fade, accounting systems become obsolete or ineffective. Leak and Sons almost went under in the early 1990s after the patriarch Leak's death.

Spencer also sometimes questions some of the ways of his father, Spencer Sr., who is the CEO. He gives away so much money and so many services for free. Spencer Jr. is told that one day he will understand. But he also realizes the mortuary trade relies on repeat business; personal relationships cultivated over the years have fostered Leak's reputation.

As Spencer Jr. forges his way as heir apparent of the family business, he thinks about all the people his dad has helped over the years, why his grandfather started Leak and Sons, and how he, the namesake, can carry out a legacy while being progressive, too.

He sometimes wonders what he might have learned from working in corporate America, and whether that experience would have helped him run the funeral parlor. Spencer also laments not having the same networking experience as his peers. "Just to see where the real money is," he says, "to meet the players in the moneymaking world."

This is the only workplace environment Spencer has ever known, a place where ministry and profits find a way to coexist sensitively. He's curious about the other side, black men who work in the capricious corporate world. But here, at Leak and Sons, Spencer enjoys a different kind of sanctuary.

"I like to be in control," he says. "I'm in control of the ship. If the ship goes down, at least I'm in control."

For men of the Hip-Hop Generation in search of solace, the job is usually the last place to look. Even as the doors have begun to open in corporate America, young black men increasingly seek to return to the kind of sanctuary Leak enjoys: a place to earn their bread while carrying on or creating legacies and institutions in their communities.

The current business landscape has unsettled workers regardless of race, gender, and class. Workers have never really controlled the ship, but at one time they seemed to know the general direction it was going. Across the board, corporate paternalism is dead. On a whim, jobs are downsized or sent overseas. And in our generation, no one expects to spend thirty years at a job anymore. No pensions, no retirement gold watch, no loyalty even from Uncle Sam; quite possibly no Social Security.

For black men trying to make a living, these dilemmas are stark. Providing for their families while preserving their dignity as men has been a challenge since the days of slavery. As legal barriers disappear, whatever male privilege they belatedly enjoy is often canceled out by racism. Media misrepresentations chase them to their jobs and their own businesses.

That the previous generation of climbers aren't exactly thrilled with their careers only fuels their cynicism. In his 1993 book *The Rage of a Privileged Class*, Ellis Cose points out that despite the material accoutrements and status achieved by black middle-class professionals of the civil rights generation, there is a "sadness born of the conviction that for black superachievers success not only came harder but almost invariably later and at a lower level than for comparable credentialed whites."[1]

These discoveries pass on to a generation that did not grow up with segregated water fountains or in an era of sit-ins and boycotts. This generation still know they must be twice as good. White peers are overly impressed by black men "speaking so well," enjoying pursuits like golf, skiing, and overseas travel, and presenting resumes that belie their assumed inner-city expectations.

To wit: our own fathers—one Caribbean-born, one Chicago-born—railed about the workplace, to a household of eye rollers, when we were growing up in the 1980s. Terrence and Joe lamented working for The Man, pontificating about how corporate America sucked. Neckties were like nooses. Bosses asked why Joe chose to live in the ghetto, when in actuality it was a stable black neighborhood. Supervisors acted as if Terrence was out of line when he offered opinions at meetings. We heard axioms such as: There is nothing. Harder. In this world. Than being a black man in corporate America. Own your own business. Be a dentist. Write your own ticket. There is nothing worse. Than going to a job. Everyday. That you hate. Our peers have listened. Young black men ages 25–44 are the group most likely to try to start their own businesses in this country, according to *The Entrepreneur Next Door*, a 2002 Kauffmann Foundation report on nascent business owners. While the start-ups may not always succeed, this group is more likely to give it a try. Approximately twenty-six of every 100 black men with graduate education experience report efforts to start a new business, compared to ten of every 100 white men.[2]

When Tim Bates, a professor at Detroit's Wayne State University, first researched the area of black-owned businesses in the late 1960s, he saw mostly black-owned, mom-and-pop, neighborhood-based businesses involved in revitalizing depressed city enclaves. Many first-wave entrepreneurs were first-generation college graduates or had schoolteacher parents with a small pool of intergenerational wealth to draw from, Bates says. And it was harder to get financing compared to their white counterparts.

Today, the field has grown much broader. The post-1995 generation of blacks coming in have sought to leave the corporate sector to get paid, Bates says. They have excellent CVs, they've earned MBAs, and they have investment banking backgrounds. They are starting their own venture capital funds. Bates also found that the majority of those storming the business world are men.

The Hip-Hop Generation expects to hit an unbreakable ceiling at some point, writer Cora Daniels notes in her book *Black Power Inc:* "Breaking through the ceiling is no longer the point. This is not a full-out dismissal of the established system the way a traditional Black Power movement would be. Instead this generation is doing what it does best: using the system to do whatever they want."[3]

Some foresee the ceiling and decide not to enter the building. Others absorb the corporate knowledge for its short-term benefits and use it later. Pimp the system before it pimps you.

The entrepreneurs of today owe a debt to the funeral home directors and insurance company founders of yesterday who established their businesses because whites didn't want to deal with black folk. Like Spencer Leak, several self-employed black men we interviewed see their business as part of a larger picture—a contribution to black life and the community, a way to invoke social change. We talked to young brothers working in investment banking, bookstores, public relations, federal contracting, and music. Many of these men try to remix legacies their fathers created. Others are making inroads in new areas like financial services and hip-hop management. Whether they are hanging up their shingle or cranking it out in the corporate meat grinder, black men struggle to balance self-awareness with a steady paycheck.

"This generation is aggressive, focused, impatient, unwavering, bold, and demanding when it comes to race. Black is first; black is what matters; black is important. They have managed to turn mainstream success into a kind of militancy that doesn't reject the system but uses the system for its own goals. That is new. That is powerful because the results should be longer lasting," Cora Daniels writes in *Black Power Inc.*[4]

There is a lot to like about corporate America. Plenty of experience, checks that don't bounce, and cash to stockpile to make dreams come true. So it has been for Cassius Priestly, a senior vice president of the SunTrust Bank business banking group in the Washington, D.C., area. He has taken advantage of diversity initiatives that help track minorities for upper management positions. In his mid-thirties, he is one of the youngest players at his level in the organization, which he joined after earning an accounting degree at Grambling State University.

"It starts with confidence, not worn on your shoulder or being arrogant, but internal confidence. You can be yourself and still climb," Priestly says. "I don't look at myself as an African American in corporate America; you can't live your life like that. I'm a guy in corporate America."

Colleagues have informed him of things said behind his back that are racially motivated. He wants to know what these people are saying so he can keep an eye on them. But ultimately he believes his race is an asset to the company. He is sensitive to the needs of people of color. Now that he has seniority, Priestly encourages diversity in hiring. He always remembers his father's old adage: "You may not be able to control the direction of the wind, but you can control the way you point your sails."

But occasionally, ignorance about black culture forces some to be a Carter G. Woodson, "father of black history," incarnate at work, educating white people about the ways and patterns of Negroes as if they exist in a museum case.

McClinton Jackson III counters stereotypes just by being himself: a thirtysomething black man with an MBA from the University of Virginia, and a corporate world veteran. He is a Morehouse alumnus who worked for America Online as a strategic manager in the digital services division before switching to a real estate firm. At work, though, he tries to skip the black history lesson. By talking openly about his life, he hopes to provide his white peers a window into a black world they are not used to seeing. "In a subtle way, I talk about who I am and the activities I engage in, and that indirectly gives them a better understanding of me—and maybe African Americans in general," Jackson says.

Sometimes, the challenges are more annoying than anything else, as when he sees white colleagues exchange stock tips and debate intellectual topics among themselves, but only talk to him about sports. "Indeed, I like sports. But that's not the extent of who I am."

At other times, colleagues comment excessively about his physique—he is broad-shouldered, at 6'1" and 220 pounds. Colleagues joke that his size means he can threaten others to get the job done. When a graduate school classmate commented gapingly on his dimensions, Jackson had to put him in check. "I understand you find my physique or stature impressive, but you're undermining my intelligence," Jackson recalls telling him. "The person said, 'I never thought about that.' "

However, there are times when people's misperceptions get in the way of Jackson's ability to do his job. At one job at a major corporation, a nosy coworker heard Jackson speaking in slang and misinformed Jackson's bosses that he was dealing drugs over the phone in his cubicle. "It's something I've accepted that's the cost of doing business," Jackson says. In the past, when people spouted ignorant comments, he kept quiet, fearing that he might show his hand and become emotional. Engaging in dialogue works better, and it's part of the game. He also believes people respond as they do from a lack of knowledge, not as a personal attack.

Vince, a pharmaceutical sales representative on the West Coast, can relate. Once, on an out-of-town business trip, a drunken white female colleague felt him up, calling him a "sexy bitch." Vince ignored her advances and didn't report her to management. When he makes sales calls in Arizona, white women clutch their purses upon seeing him. This, in an area sprinkled with methamphetamine labs and trailer homes; they are apparently unaware of the irony. Alternatively, Vince has had nurses of color in doctors' offices confess that he's a breath of fresh air—a minority who knows his material.

"You are what they think minorities can't be," Vince has been told. He is determined to crush the stereotype with each sales call. "I'm going to show you the exact opposite of what you anticipate seeing."

With each new job experience, McClinton Jackson, who has worked for various major companies, gains more insight into how the corporate game is played. The pressure to assimilate is subtle, but progressive. At first, many black men who are new to the workforce see the corporate game through an ethnic lens, and try to build alliances with black executives and company-sponsored black support groups. But eventually they see the limits to how far that will take them. The higher up the ladder, the more they are expected to produce, which determines bonuses and salary. Race becomes a secondary concern as it affects their livelihoods.

"Brother execs have to focus on building winning teams, and sometimes this focus can conflict with the desire to look out [for their own]," Jackson explains. "The reality for many young black businesspeople, myself included, is that they come to the table with less exposure to the corporate game than their majority counterparts."

This means senior black executives do not have the luxury of hiring according to a social agenda that corrects past inequalities, as it may compromise their professional goals. Because of this ongoing game of catch-up, thinking "black" in white corporate settings by default puts you at a disadvantage. But it doesn't stop Jackson from trying. "Balancing is not impossible," he says. "Brothers (and sistahs) are obligated to look out and be each other's keeper."

Jackson has concluded that the only logical way to balance these competing concerns is entrepreneurship. It offers the freedom to hire as one sees fit and to do the right thing. Down the road, Jackson plans to help start a private investment firm, combining his love for finance and entrepreneurship.

Tony Stovall's career path has been on Wall Street. "I was the 'Negro banker,'" he says of his first job. "There's always one at each firm." Discontented with the traditional corporate sphere, Stovall was motivated to look elsewhere after busting his ass for smaller rewards than his white colleagues.

Today, he makes a six-figure salary from his partnership at Rice Financial Products Company, a black-owned firm that invests money for city governments. Since its founding, Rice has managed more than $20 billion in transactions. When Stovall helped start Rice in the mid-1990s, the company had trouble recruiting clients for the first six months. Clients who found him perfectly capable as an employee in a white firm suddenly found his skills lacking. "When you start your own company, it's a different perspective clients have. [And] you just can't live off of black clients," Stovall says. Eventually the company raised its capital and credit rating, convincing potential clients it was capable of doing the job.

Stovall would like to retire by age 50. Until then, he's enjoying other fringe benefits, like writing company checks to black causes, no questions asked. "I'm more relaxed internally. The company itself is relaxed. I'm with other black folk. I can express myself freely and make the company grow."

Today's entrepreneurs are forging paths in areas where blacks have historically been less visible. Mentors and family connections help them attempt to build a legacy of wealth to pass down to the next generation.

Mossi Tull, 31, is the chief operating officer for Jackson and Tull, the civil engineering firm his father started in the late 1970s. He hopes to pass the business to his future children. "Being an entrepreneur is glamorized. [People say,] 'Oh, you own your own business and take two-and-a-half-hour lunch breaks' like it's a Puffy Combs video. It's not like that. It's a tremendous amount of responsibility," Tull says.

He began training early. At age 8, Tull tagged along with his father to the office. He'd sharpen pencils, spruce up the parking lot, and write the dates on checks. His father's dedication made a lasting impact. After earning a finance degree from Morehouse College, Tull joined his family's company, located in the Washington, D.C., area, full-time. Thirty years ago, Jackson and Tull provided civil engineering for small two-story structures and churches. Today, Tull has helped push the company into business development and governmental relations. "It can't be just the Halliburtons that get the contracts. We have to be able to compete. If we are 13 percent of the population, we can't get locked out of wealth building," Tull says.

Along the way, people have questioned how much Tull and Jackson can do as a black business, or how far it can go, even though it has major federal contracts with NASA (the Hubble Space Telescope) and the U.S. Air Force. The company employs 250 workers and generated $28.4 million in revenue in 2004.

Although white employees in an out-of-state satellite office mistake him for the hired help, Tull allows nothing to overshadow his vision. He quotes Winston Churchill and Booker T. Washington, and he admires the Joe Kennedy model of success—forging opportunities for offspring. Tull would also like to see progressive black institutions operate similarly to the Cato Institute or the Heritage Fund. He worries that black politicians are beholden to conflicting interests because they have limited access to cash. The NAACP or the Urban League should be able to turn to businesses like his company for donations—not to Wall Street.

"We have to own our own institutions, supported by us, in the right kind of way so they have only our interests at heart. I don't need to buy cars or $8,000 suits. I need to understand how to fund things that are in my interest as an African American. That's the real lick in being able to do something."

Black culture has always been a fertile source of creativity—and money. But this generation has strived to harness artistic and economic control over it, too. We have learned to take control of their own fate and start a business. And the yardstick of success isn't always sales, growth, and mainstream competitiveness.

Simba Sana, co-owner of the bookstore chain Karibu, has his regrets about leaving his job at a Big Six accounting firm. "There's a lot you can learn. I wish I could've stayed a couple of more years, saved money. There are a lot of benefits black men can get out of corporate life."

In 1990, he joined the accounting firm Ernst & Young right out of college. Two years later, he started moonlighting—selling oils, incense, and jewelry on busy Georgia Avenue in Washington, D.C., with partner Yao Ahoto. Sana's burgeoning Pan-African ideology nudged him like a petulant child, and he was willing to peddle any commodity to test black economic self-sufficiency.

When Sana left the accounting firm to pursue the bookselling business, his salary plummeted to less than half what he made before. It turned out to be a good risk, as today the onetime bookstore on wheels has matured into six stores between Baltimore and Washington,

D.C., and has become the country's largest black bookstore chain. Karibu (kah-REE-boo) means "welcome" in Swahili.

Sana hopes his company corrects the destruction caused by a generation of integrationist policies to black institutions and businesses. "There's a lot of benefits black men can get out of corporate life. The problem I see [in corporate life] is that we get hooked on that money and lifestyle so we have to make certain compromises. It's another form of slavery. Black folks in particular—middle-class blacks—they feel they need to treat themselves...[it's the feeling of] deserving that hinders you from following whatever dreams you have."

Bronx native Blue Williams ignored college professors who encouraged students to get jobs and be "good Negroes." He was, however, willing to forfeit his ego as he clawed his way up in the entertainment industry. He started as a roadie with R & B act Jodeci, and toured with Boyz II Men and M. C. Hammer, carrying the artists' luggage, driving buses, acting as security. Eventually, Williams parlayed a high-level job with Queen Latifah's Flava Unit into his own management company, Family Tree Entertainment, which has managed artists such as OutKast since 1997.

A mentor in the music industry told him he'd never get rich by working for someone else, so he started Family Tree. "How do I build a company that people respect?" he wondered. "Going to college gave me the ability to articulate myself. I can disarm [whites] and not threaten them because here comes a big black man.... All you have is your integrity. Do a good job so people don't mess with me. My reputation had to remain unquestionable." Williams feels confident that if he went into corporate America, he'd be successful, but it's not necessary. Corporate America comes to people like him because it sees the money to be made in hip-hop.

John Monopoly, 30, also couldn't picture himself holding court in a corner office. He inherited a legacy of entrepreneurship. His uncle was one of the founders of Johnson Products, the hair care company that brought black people Ultra Sheen, and his late father was in charge of marketing for the company. Monopoly plugged parties and hustled his share of odd jobs—coffee shop server, concert promoter, club manager—while he pursued his love of hip-hop. He also made a name for himself promoting teen parties in his native Chicago.

While making hip-hop beats, Monopoly met a young producer named Kanye West in the 1990s. He now runs West's record label and is helping to develop a clothing line. He hopes to own a multi-media company, dabbling in sports management, television, real estate, and radio. "I never thought nine-to-five. Most of it is my trying to think of ways to be a little more lazy," he jokes. Monopoly may have succeeded in another goal: impressing his uncle. "The whole concept of being able to work around something you love and make real good money at it, it's living a dream.... I remember being without, but you gotta do what you gotta do. I've been blessed."

Leak and Sons Funeral Home is filled with old-fashioned salon chairs, long hallways leading to somber viewing rooms and on-site chapels. In chairs lining both sides of the lobby, daughters, sons, in-laws, nieces, nephews, and grandchildren wait their turn to finalize arrangements. The hallway reeks of angst as people sniffle, tap their feet, stare despondently, and chat nervously on cell phones.

"Do you want to see the remains?" an employee asks a man who hasn't stopped chatting up his companion since plopping down in the lobby.

"Not me, naw!" the man says, fanning himself. He then wonders aloud whether the loved one was en route to hell.

Spencer Leak Jr. strolls the halls in his signature dark suit and gold tie. He nods to clients and shakes their hands as he walks past the peach-hued repast room. Some of his employees once changed his diapers as a baby. As a young boy, Spencer accompanied his grand father on errands. At 10, Spencer picked up trash around the building's block-long exterior. At 19, he was the youngest licensed mortician in the state of Illinois. Today, at 36, he has graduated from picking up bodies at hospitals to limo chauffeuring to preparing corpses to playing an integral part in the funeral home's future. He helps put some 2,000 black people to rest each year.

Death can bring out the worst in people, and the funeral industry requires composure and skill at offering consolation. Spencer has seen folks in his office bicker over how to spend Big Mama's insurance policy, and others try to squeeze a funeral discount from Leak and Sons before piling into their Mercedes-Benz and driving away.

When Spencer got on the management track a decade ago, he convinced his father to move the business forward. So Spencer found contractors to fix the building's butter cream exterior on the weekend. He used his excellent credit to buy new limos and hearses. He hired an in-house accountant and put advertisements on television. A second Leak and Sons has opened in the region.

Spencer has also dabbled in politics, hosting political fund-raisers for Democratic candidates. Jesse Jackson Sr. and Jesse Jr. are dear friends. So is Tennessee congressman Harold Ford Jr. Spencer is an up-and-comer in Chicago.

Like his father, Spencer attends many of the home's funerals, even after the bill has been paid. Like his father, Spencer works long hours and weekends. Spencer Leak Jr. may not have had experience in corporate America, but he has something that is arguably more important—name recognition. In the 1990s, he was a staple on the Chicago party-throwing circuit. He retired that gig, not wanting to be known as the funeral director who profits from parties.

People approach him with myriad business plans—from fast food ventures to cell phone companies. Whereas name recognition and branding work in tandem in gaining capital—especially in hip-hop—Spencer passes on most proposals. "I don't see myself being involved in those areas, because I don't have the time. I don't want people to use my name; I want to be involved," he says, as we ride in a black Cadillac hearse to a cemetery across town. A casket, with a body inside, shifts in the back. It brushes against our shoulders.

That is not to say he hasn't daydreamed about branching out. Who knows what is next? But whether it's a car wash or a casket production company, Spencer wants total involvement. He accepts that, for now, the funeral home comes first. But he is realistic. "I'm not going to make my fortune in the funeral business."

Chapter 9

Boy Born Friday

There wasn't a revolution after all. And that sucks.

In the mid-1990s, well after most of the beret-wearing shotgun wielders were dead, in jail, in academia, or gone corporate, Kofi "Debo" Ajabu still hadn't heard the news. In his hometown, Indianapolis, his fellow young black men were still being found hanging from trees. The Ku Klux Klan still marched in full regalia in the state of its birth, and race riots raged at his high school. And nobody told the news to Debo's father, a Vietnam vet who, when he wasn't working a day job as an electrical engineer, was leading the Black Panther Militia.

The revolution—that, Debo could imagine. He'd been trained for it since birth in 1973. Get up, boy! Running, push-ups, trips down to the shooting range, lessons in hand-to-hand combat. Have your water boiled and bottled. Furtive meetings, last-minute calls to arrive on the scene, bring your boys, make sure you're strapped. Debo fully expected that one day the old man would give the word and they would finally take down the city's power grid. Break out the guns and explosives and put the hammer in them for good.

When he did go out, Debo figured it would be in a blaze of glory, a small price paid for the liberation of all African peoples. That's what he *prepared* for. But there's a big difference between preparing for blood and carnage and seeing it up close.

It wasn't a revolution. Instead, he talks about his life in two distinct eras: "before the flick" that began March 16, 1994—"I was alive then"—and "later on in the flick"—a horror movie he's wandering through to this day.

It opens with Debo home from college, playing Fight Club with his roommate, getting as much ass as possible, toking all the weed his lungs can carry, playing video games, and reading books. That night, it was Stephen King's *The Dark Half*, about a crime novelist's hunt to kill off his evil alter ego. Debo thinks he's making a run with two friends to hang out, smoke some more weed, and check out a bike for sale. The next thing he knows, he's stranded in the richest and whitest of Indiana suburbs and the blood is flying, gushing, coagulating, making sounds, unimaginable sounds, like the creek by his house where he used to collect little critters.

At this final moment of carnage, all 21 years of his training fly out the window. It wasn't a revolution, and here right now, sitting in a visitor's room in the maximum-security prison in Pendleton, Indiana, serving year 11 of a 180-year prison sentence, this *really* sucks. Or, as Debo tells me, it's "the bootiest shit ever."

On March 19, 1994, the news spread across the front page of the *Indianapolis Star:* "The motive: robbery for rent."[1] There had been a triple murder in Carmel, Indiana, a wealthy Indianapolis suburb. The victims were bound and gagged and their throats sliced. They were two siblings, Nick and Lisa Allemenos, 17 and 13 years old, and their family friend, Chris James, a 23-year-old manager at their father's hardware store. The house was ransacked for electronic equipment and CDs, and two luxury cars were stolen. Two days later, police arrested Raymond Adams, 26, James Walls, 20, and Kofi

Modibo Ajabu, 21. All of the victims were white.

According to police interviews with witnesses, Adams had gone to the Carmel house the day before the murders to sell Nick Allemenos a quarter-ounce of weed. After leaving the house with two of Nick's teenage friends, the friends told Adams that the Allemenos family was worth millions and owned a hardware store. Adams called back the next day for the phone number to the Allemenos's home.

Both Adams, who is black and had an extensive criminal record, and his roommate Walls, who is white, were about to be evicted from their apartment on the city's North Side. Ajabu told the cops that he caught a ride with them to Carmel expecting to party at the Allemenos home and check out a bike that was for sale. He said Adams forced him at gunpoint to watch over the Allemenos family after he had bound and gagged them. Adams tortured the 23-year-old family friend, Chris James, until he gave up the combination to the safe at the family's hardware store. Before the three cleared out the loot from the house, Adams sliced their throats. Adams, Walls, and Ajabu drove the stolen cars to Chicago, where they ditched them and pawned some of the loot. When they arrived back in Indianapolis, police picked them up immediately.

Adams never admitted to committing the murders. While Walls was crying in the confession room[2] and Ajabu was giving a stream-of-consciousness narrative to the cops, Adams was asking for a lawyer.[3] But blood found on Adams, along with police statements from Walls and Ajabu and Adams's jailhouse confession to two cellmates,[4] all point to Adams as the mastermind and sole murderer. Somehow, when the charges finally went to trial, it became a death penalty case against Kofi Modibo Ajabu, with Adams as the prosecution's star witness. Adams and Walls pleaded guilty and are serving life sentences without the possibly of parole or appeal.

Debo was never offered a plea. He was barely spared a death sentence.[5] He's serving 180 years.

I (Natalie H.) knew Debo as the older brother of one of my best high school friends. We all attended Indianapolis's elite North Central High School, and we went to the Ajabu house for Kwanzaa celebrations. The Ajabus were the pulse of a fledgling Pan-African community in Indianapolis. Debo's dad, Mmoja Ajabu, was easily the most feared black man in the state—and he also made some FBI watch lists. He made it his business to give the white folks *the business*. As head of the Black Panther Militia, he was constantly in the news, organizing demonstrations, taking up arms to defend a black woman being threatened for moving into a white community, boycotting Korean grocers in the hood, protesting the death of a young black man who turned up dead in police custody; the list goes on and on. Debo's mom, Jane Hart-Ajabu, was a principal and later an administrator for the Indianapolis Public Schools. My friend, Nzinga Ajabu (later Harrison), went to Howard University with me, and later became a University of Pennsylvania–trained psychiatrist. The youngest sister, Binta, attended the Alvin Ailey dance school in New York. This was the kind of middle-class family who are never supposed to be the subjects of robbery and murder trials. For many of us in the black community of Indianapolis who knew Debo, his case has been an open wound that we've refused to look at. At the time, the murders were too heinous, and the reality of Debo's involvement too painful, even to follow the media circus that chronicled the trial of the "son of a Black Panther Militia leader." We never got over the shock of seeing Debo, 5'6" and 130 pounds, doing the perp walk on TV. Debo? A college student who always had his nose in some book. Debo, a martial artist, a chess player, who got average grades but spectacular SAT scores and was headed for his third year at Jackson State University, a historically black university.

Many of us averted our eyes, took an L, or filed the case away as a "loss"—the category disproportionately populated by black men in the U.S. prison system. I had left Debo there for years, until my own mother suggested I include him in this book. "Debo has just never left my heart," my mom said.

We lived in Indiana from the mid-1980s to the mid-1990s, and we still carry the psychological scars. The civil rights movement seemed to have skipped that place. I never forgot the fear, the threatening phone calls, humiliation, and intimidation by police, and, once, the wrongful arrest of my own brother, who is just a year older than Debo. Then there was Michael Blair, another middle-class brother who went to my high school. In 1994, he went missing and was found months later hanging from a tree—ruled a suicide.

Below our immediate consciousness, Debo has become a stock character, an implicit reminder of those who could have made it out, but never did. After spending many months researching his case, talking to family members, poring over court records, reviewing hundreds of newspaper articles, and spending six hours interviewing Debo in prison in July 2005, I've found plenty of places to point fingers. Obviously, start with Debo himself. Yet I can't help but see how he seemed compelled to arrive there, maybe not at that specific moment, but inevitably. Looking back on his life, I can see clearly how prosecutors, media, black patriarchy, the emasculating effects of racism, and violence conspired to put Debo's life on the line, and now hold it in suspension.

It was Indiana's Trial of the Century, overlapping and even eclipsing O. J. in the local parade of coverage on television, radio, and in the newspapers. At the time, the media treated Debo's case as both a Greek tragedy and a racial allegory. They were right—just not in the way that any of us imagined.

Months after we exchanged letters, Debo agreed to meet me in Indiana's Pendleton Correctional Facility in the summer of 2005. I'm surprised at how little he's changed. Debo's still the same, slight figure. He's got tattoos on both arms and his chest: a symbol for perseverance, his portrait, and a hyena. His hair has grown into locks hanging down to his waist, with a cowry shell attached to one of them. He could almost be a twin to his beautiful sister Nzinga, who, at the time was expecting her first son, Zahir, any day, looked like a black love poster. Debo has the same smooth ebony skin and angular features, but covered partly by a scruffy beard.

Debo wears a thin white T-shirt with his prison number on it, and khaki pants. He's 32 now, and he tells me in a husky, punchy midwestern twang that there are a few gray hairs in his mop of hair. I tease him about his advancing age with the viciousness of a woman vainly clutching to her 20s, but I honestly don't think he's aged much. A few crinkles around the eyes, maybe. But overall, his demeanor is surprisingly sunny. As Nzinga tells me, it's amazing how someone who's been locked up for eleven years could have preserved so much of his personality—and so many jokes. "You are what's called a *fetus*," Debo told his kicking nephew through her round belly. "That means you need to assume the *fetal* position."

The drama began at day one. His parents had chosen the name Kofi Modibo Ajabu, which was a mixture of African dialects. Kofi means "boy born on Friday," Modibo means "helper," and Ajabu means "one who gives and receives the prize." Hospital officials demanded that he be given his father's birth surname, the one Mmoja considered by then to be his slave name. They refused to issue a birth certificate; Mmoja Ajabu and Jane Hart-Ajabu took the infant home without it. Everybody called him "Debo."

Both Jane and Mmoja grew up as children of Baptist ministers. Mmoja grew up in Indianapolis and went to college on the GI Bill as a result of his service in Vietnam. Jane was a Purdue University graduate, a native of East Chicago, Indiana, who came to Indianapolis to take a teaching job. As Jane worked her way up the school system ranks, Mmoja worked as an electrical engineer for RCA, the U.S. Navy, and Public Service Indiana. The Ajabus tried to insulate Debo and the two sisters who followed from the toxic racial climate by enveloping them in a community of like-minded souls, committed to the liberation struggle of black people across the African Diaspora. In this community, they vacationed together, went to black cultural events, boycotted products doing business with South Africa, and taught their children Swahili.

Debo started reading at a young age, wandering around the house and consuming books from his parents' extensive collection. He scored well on aptitude tests, both in the school system and his parents' Afrocentric exams. His parents instilled in him a mistrust of the school system and essentially home-schooled him in addition to sending him to good suburban public schools. In grade school, the precocious Debo learned that challenging Eurocentric history didn't get him far with teachers, who marked him down for such blasphemy as pointing out that Columbus never "discovered" America.

Debo adored his mother and sisters. But he also had a life away from them. He was born not long after Mmoja Ajabu returned from Vietnam, so his dad shared with him most of what he learned there. Debo learned everything from hand-to-hand combat to how to use myriad weapons. To this day, it's Debo's habit to sleep maybe every other day. As a boy, dozing off at home, his dad might come by. "Get up, boy!" Then he'd fire questions at Debo. Or he might throw an object at him. "Reflex check!" Debo can remember being about three years old and going out with dad and two of his friends at dawn. They did breathing exercises, push-ups. It was boot camp.

One of his first opportunities to put those skills to use came in elementary school, when a white kid taunted him by saying that his grandparents owned Debo's grandparents and then spat on him. Debo fed the boy his metal Spider-Man lunch box. When Debo was spanked with a paddle by the principal, his father responded. "He rolled up his sleeves, and went and got a couple of his goons," Debo recalls. "Fellow goons that he's known forever. These are like, hard dudes. Like me even being in the penitentiary, there aren't many hard dudes left like that. I don't even consider myself to be a hard person. Not the hip-hop hard, I-got-big-gold and Run DMC leather. It's the hard, like, old man, cut-you-up-at-the-bar-type hard." They had a little chat with the principal. The principal walked on eggshells around Debo after that.

School bored Debo. He got into martial arts, and hip-hop, emceeing at age nine. He chose the rhyme name Hemlock, after the poison that Socrates used to commit honorable suicide following his trial for corrupting Athenian youth. Debo loved animals, giving them all "the runaway option." He liked playing video games and using computers. He once hacked into a phone records system using his friend's Commodore 64. Most of all, he'd retreat into his books and keep to himself.

Debo's parents' relationship was rocky. Keeping a job while being a full-time activist was a difficult balancing act. Mmoja Ajabu "was going through a whole lot of stuff," Jane Hart-Ajabu recalls. "Trying to figure out what manhood was, fending for your family. He said he was really angry because he wanted to be able to take care of his family." Jane was increasingly frustrated that Mmoja's activism took so much time away from the family. She wanted more of a partnership, instead of Mmoja ruling the house and everyone in it. A couple of times, an argument crossed the line. They separated several times in the 1980s, the first time when Debo was in eighth grade.

But as racial incidents in the state kept coming, Mmoja Ajabu felt compelled to leave the house to put out the fires. "Because we are so afraid of dying, we don't live this life," Mmoja explains to me. "We just exist in this life, afraid." So Mmoja saw it as his role to stand up. Problem with fires, though, there is always going to be another one.

Debo was in freshman English at North Central High School when he heard the melee. Some white kids from Ravenswood, a notoriously racist part of the city, had gotten into it with some equally quick-to-anger black students. It swiftly turned into a free-for-all, which culminated in a black student tossing a white student through a glass trophy case. When they learned that the black student was expelled, but none of the white kids, Debo's parents got involved with a black parents' group, which convened to examine the disciplinary disparities between black and white students. The group pressed for the removal of a white male principal, who was eventually replaced by a rising star educator, a black man named Dr. Eugene White, who went on to become the award-winning superintendent of the Indianapolis Public Schools.

Another racial incident rocked Indianapolis during Debo's freshman year. Michael Taylor, a 16-year-old whom Debo had known from church, died while handcuffed in the back of a police squad car. Police claimed Taylor had hidden a .32 caliber gun and shot himself in the head. The black community, fed up with being on the wrong side of questionable police tactics for decades, went into full protest mode.[6] The white supremacists marched on Martin Luther King Jr.'s birthday.

Mmoja Ajabu helped found the Black Panther Militia in Indianapolis in 1990. So, naturally, as his son, Debo had to be ready to serve on demand. He was expected to do recruitment. "You're a

young black man, you know other young black men, get me some
soldiers," Debo remembers his father telling him. Although his father
didn't mean it that way, Debo translated the command for his generation. "I was like, soldiers...gangbangers...same thing. You know.
Same thing," he says, laughing.

Once Debo joined the Vice Lords gang, he immediately was able
to command access to a built-in network of soldiers from all over the
country. His dad would take Debo and his recruits to training. There
were trips to the shooting range. They received lessons about how to
control entry and exit points in any situation, and how to take out
certain power grids in the city. Plus his dad was quick to get physical
with anyone who challenged him in the street. He threw a tire in the
face of one man, and kicked in someone's windshield. "Old man's very
serious," Debo says. "White people are afraid of him for a reason."

College was more of the same. Debo was admitted to Jackson
State in Jackson, Mississippi, on the strength of his test scores. His
dad dropped him off, and over Jane Hart-Ajabu's objections, left him
with a piece. In college, Debo had a ball. He communicated with one
science teacher in Swahili, and found for the first time a place where
his Pan-African upbringing was not out of place.

He also kept his foot in the gangster lifestyle. "You wouldn't
believe how many middle-class gangbangers there are," he says.
"And you know, it's like, for some reason, the middle class is like, the
worst of the worst. We gotta prove some shit."

On trips home, Debo never knew when he would get *the* call,
but he always knew he was essentially *on* call. Sometimes, it would
be to do backup security at a hip-hop conference in Milwaukee.
Usually he was in the mood to vent his frustrations. But sometimes,
Debo was just tired, like the time he'd been on a bus from Mississippi
for seventeen hours. At ten o'clock at night, Debo got the call saying
he needed to mobilize his soldiers. Debo grabbed a dozen of his boys

and went down to the Marion County administration building, to
help keep it hostage until the police produced a young black teenager
who'd gone "missing" from the squad car after a fight between
police and private security at a mosque.

Debo recalls that moment. Again, his dad called in the goons. "I
don't know where he found them. Real hard dudes. I don't even
know where he got them dudes from."

He's probably growing them in the backyard, I joke.

"Yeah," Debo agrees, "He's got a vat somewhere, where he's
feeding them salt and water. Real hard dudes. You could look at them
and it's like, 'I'm talking, but ain't nobody there.' I remember one
dude had on khakis and the big flannel shirts. He's like 'I'm just waiting on the word.' I'm strapped, and I know these fools are strapped."

Luckily, no blood was shed. In fact, the only time he remembers
actually getting to kick butt was at another incident that took place in
Ravenswood. A black woman had been run out of the white community. The Black Panther Militia assembled close to 100 members to
march through the neighborhood along with a minivan full of guns
and explosives. Debo remembers residents throwing rocks and sticks,
and firing shotguns in the air. "I had two or three kinds of knives. One
guy took a swing in the crowd. I was like, 'My guy, I've been waiting
on you. I'm glad you *shoowed* up.' I had my straight razor still then."

Looking back, he supposes his life as a vigilante, a roving freedom
fighter, was a bit romantic. Between the Panther work and running
with his gangster buddies, he considered himself part of a community
of renegades, outcasts living on the margins of society. Kicking butt
and making the world a better place for black people at the same
time. "But hell, really, when it comes down to it, it's just more con-
formity. But I was too young and stupid to know back then."

Between running with his dad, keeping his grades respectable,
and being in a four-year relationship with Sonya Hayes, a girl who

attended Howard University, Debo didn't have much time to think about a future. Nor did he have such an inclination. "The way I'd been taught, it was going to get ugly. And the survival thing was more about luck than skill. I had never been real big on depending on luck anyways. I fully expected to not make it more than anything. Anything I viewed probably was tainted by this perspective of, 'Hell, I probably won't be alive anyhow.' So I was kamikaze sometimes. I was probably kamikaze *most* times."

That doesn't leave much room for thought about what happens if you outlive the final, apocalyptic showdown. If you are confronted with a different kind of moment of truth, and you look at where you are stuck.

The summer after his sophomore year in college, one of Debo's middle-class gangbanger friends was killed. He explained his reaction in a letter to me: "Trip, rampage, population control, demolitions." He told his father about the situation, and that the police were probably not the only ones looking for him. His father suggested he lie low in Indianapolis for a while.

Debo was waiting for his enrollment forms to return to Jackson State for his junior year, in the fall of 1994. He was rooming with an old high school friend, D'Artagnan Partee, and working various jobs that included delivering pizzas. He was smoking a lot of marijuana, sparring with his friends, and he saw as many women as he could, even as he was trying to reconcile with his girlfriend Sonya. Partee called him one day from work to ask if he could help out a coworker at a restaurant where he waited tables. His name was Raymond Adams, a husky man of about 5'9", balding, with curly hair.

Debo agreed to give him a ride home from the restaurant. When they got to Adams's place, all his belongings were out on the porch. He had been living with a friend and his wife, but the wife said

Adams had to go. Debo took him to a hotel. The next day, Adams asked Partee if he could room with them at their three-bedroom townhouse. Debo agreed to let him stay and help with the rent.

As soon as soon as Adams came into Debo's life, the women in his life caught a bad feeling. Normally the alpha male of whatever group he was in, Debo seemed more submissive around Adams. Debo's sister Nzinga, then a high school senior, couldn't stand Raymond Adams, and told him so to his face when she found out Debo had lent Adams her car. She cussed him out. Debo's longtime girlfriend, Sonya Hayes, later told Debo's defense lawyers that she noticed Debo had less time for her and seemed controlled by Adams. When Adams came into the room, it seemed that Debo quickly got off the phone.

Once, when Jane Hart-Ajabu arrived at the door to the boys' townhouse, she overheard Adams shouting and cussing at everyone in the room, demanding to know who was coming to the door. When Adams saw her at the door, he changed his tune. She told Debo about her concerns and immediately told her husband that this guy was trouble. Throughout the police interviews and court transcripts, it's clear that everyone who had ever been in contact with Adams got the creeps.

Everyone, that is, except Debo. Debo knew about his extensive police record, and even about some current robberies of businesses that he was involved in. But Adams chipped in with the rent, and his marijuana sales were also helping to keep all of them high. Of his attraction to Raymond, Debo says now: "Some of it might have been vicarious living on my part. Curiosity can be some bullshit, straight-up.... Some of my interest was the fact that this was a whole different type of character.... I was curious. I never had the sense enough to get creeped out about anything."

Mmoja Ajabu responded to Jane's pleas by moving Debo and Partee out of the apartment and into his own three-bedroom house.

Mmoja stayed elsewhere but left his son to his own devices, as long as he kept up the bills to the house. At the time, he was dealing with his own problems with his job.

The transcripts of police interviews regarding the case provide a vivid picture of what life was like for Debo's circle of friends the day before the horrors unfolded. Fresh out of a place to stay, Adams started to spend a lot of time at the two-bedroom apartment of two young white men, Eric Johnson and James Walls. Johnson later told police that he didn't like Adams much either. First, he noticed that Adams had moved his belongings into his room. Next thing he knew, Adams's pictures were on the wall, and he was sleeping in the bed. Johnson said that since he was the only one in the house with a job, he decided to move out instead of continuing to pay the bills.[7]

That left Adams and Walls with the two-bedroom apartment to themselves, their phone cut off and facing an eviction. By the second week of March 1994, police found evidence that Adams and Walls had been driving around the city, looking for houses to rent. But if they didn't come up with some cash to rent a new place, Adams would once again be homeless.

On the morning of March 16, 1994, Walls and Adams went over to Debo's house to hang out. Both Debo and his roommate Partee had their cars in the shop. Both were hoping to catch a ride in Walls's tiny white Sentra. The roommates each told police they were catching a ride somewhere: Partee was going to work; Debo to a girl named Tonya's house. Partee told police that Adams bragged about his visit to the Allemenos house in Carmel the day before. He had driven to the house with two white teenagers—Nick's friend Peter Britt, a former coworker at a restaurant, and his friend Nathan Wright—and sold a quarter-pound of weed. Raymond ogled the house, the BMW, and Nick Allemenos's BMX bike, which was for sale. He smoked marijuana with them and played a game of Ping-

Pong. At one point Adams took out a sizable knife and laid it on the table, visibly unsettling everyone in the room. Riding back from Carmel, Britt, who had recently been fired from the Allemenos hardware store by his father, who was a manager there, told Adams the family was worth millions. He told them that the Allemenos's houseguest Chris James was an assistant manager at the store, and that their father was out of town on vacation. Telling the story later at Debo's house, Adams laughed at how scared Nick Allemenos seemed and remarked about how easy it would be to jack them.

Debo was napping nearby when Partee, as he told the police, overheard Raymond talking on the phone to someone about how easy it would be to "jack these white folks in Carmel." He told Adams to shut up. Robbing a house where people already know you was a plan too stupid to take seriously. He told Adams that joking about it on the phone was a bad idea. "We all know who Mr. Ajabu is," Partee told the police later. "I personally assumed his phone was tapped."[8]

Adams made several calls that day, so it is not clear who was on the other line when he talked about the robbery. Police confirmed that one of the calls was to Peter Britt, who gave Adams the phone number to the Allemenos house. Adams called Nick Allemenos, too, and asked how much he wanted for his BMX bike. When Nick said $75–$80, he told him he'd give him $130. Nick Allemenos told his girlfriend that he felt uneasy about Adams coming back to the house. Chris James, the family friend who'd been staying at their Carmel home following a divorce, told Nick not to worry, that he'd pack his gun, according to a statement to police given by Nick's girlfriend.[9]

The two sets of roommates got in Walls's white Sentra and dropped Partee off at his job at a gas station. Debo agreed to make another quick weed run at the Carmel house, and check out the bike. Afterward, he figured he'd go to see the girl named Tonya.

Turns out Adams had a different plan.

Got there and it was a jack. Fucked around, wound up being
a homicide.
—D'ARTAGNAN PARTEE, QUOTING KOFI MODIBO AJABU.[10]

As soon as they walked up to the door, Ajabu realized that things
were not going the way he'd planned. "He brings the kid around and
he's got a gun on him, right?" Ajabu told police in one of his marathon
statements. "So I'm like, damn, it's like, what the hell? I'm caught up
in some ugly shit."[11]

Pulling a gun on Ajabu, Adams barked at him to cooperate.
Inside the house, Ajabu said he heard Adams hollering at the siblings
and their houseguest to cooperate. "Don't be stupid, man!" He had
disarmed Chris James and tossed the gun to Debo. "Do you love
your sister?" Adams asked Nick Allemenos. "Do you love your
brother?" Adams demanded of 13-year-old Lisa Allemenos.[12]

Ajabu told the police that he didn't feel as if he knew Raymond at
that point, or what he was capable of. So he just cooperated and hoped
to avoid any bloodshed. "I don't want you all to get hurt. I don't want me
to get hurt. I was just like, give the man what he wants," he told police.

Ajabu did have the gun that Raymond had tossed him. And he
did have his considerable skills in martial arts. He had to make a
choice about how to approach the situation. He concluded it would
be safer for everyone involved if he didn't try to leave the house to
save his own ass, or to be a hero.

He told police that when one of the prisoners asked him to loosen
his tape, he told him no. "I'm about in the same predicament as you,
man...only I'm not tied up. Why don't you ask the man in charge
when he comes back,'" he recalled to police. Debo warned the prisoners that if Adams saw him helping them, he might get violent. "If
he kicks you or shoots me then, that would be my fault. I'd just as
soon save us a whole bunch of bullshit."[13]

When Debo overheard Raymond asking Chris James detailed questions about a safe at the hardware store, he was surprised. "I was like, safe? What safe?" he told the police. Even disarmed, Chris James continued to put up a fight. Adams and Walls took turns torturing him until he gave up the combination. They wrote the combination on a piece of paper and cleared the house of all electronics and CDs.

Ajabu and Walls told police that Adams strangled Chris James and then sliced his throat. He did the same to Nick and Lisa Allemenos. Blood was everywhere; you could hear the sound of the blood emptying out of their bodies. Debo walked outside for a moment, but not before stopping at the bathroom mirror. He wanted to make sure he was still there. He shook his head, and kept walking.

What followed the killing has to be a record for criminal incompetence. The perps left behind the piece of paper with the combination to the safe at the Allemenos's hardware store. Adams, Walls, and Ajabu each left the house driving a car, the Sentra they came in plus a BMW and an Audi. Ajabu was rattled while driving the Audi, fumbling with the lights and eventually ditching the car around the corner from the Tudor Lake apartment complex where Walls and Adams lived.

They reconvened at Walls and Adams's apartment. They left some of the loot in the place, threw some in the dumpster, and packed the rest of it in the BMW. They drove to Chicago to pawn the loot. In Chicago, more bungling. No one would buy their stuff. They started to sell the CDs at a used-music store, but couldn't wait for the manager to check each one for scratches. So they left the pile of CDs there. They couldn't find any takers for the BMW either, so they paid to park it and ditched it. There were able to pawn some of the electronics.

In total, the booty was about $200.

They spent the night at a cheap hotel, and took the bus back to Indianapolis, then a cab back to Walls and Adams's apartment. By then, the police had already been working for more than twenty-four hours—Nick Allemenos's girlfriend discovered the bodies when Nick didn't pick her up for school the next morning. When Ajabu, Walls, and Adams got out of the cab, the police were waiting.

The interrogation transcripts show police playing it cool. They separated the three suspects. The cops patiently let the three men describe the events of the previous week. Then they pointed out a few inconsistencies, bluffed on evidence they had, said the other two fingered each one as the mastermind. Lies, divide and conquer, basically everyday TV cop-show stuff. It worked on Walls, who dissolved into sobs. But it did not work on Adams, who asked for a lawyer as soon as things heated up.[14]

In interrogating Ajabu, the police had to employ even more of a bluff. They really had no motive, physical evidence, or proof of intent. But Ajabu still sang like Aretha. He talked incessantly, rambling on even as the police seemed to be trying to wrap up the sessions. He drew diagrams of the house. He even went back with police to the house to narrate a videotaped tour of the crime scene. Looking back now, he told me he realizes talking was a critical mistake that probably cost him his freedom.

"I was just completely out of sorts. Been off guard for a couple of days. I was on no sleep. I was there, glassy eyed, half crazy. I figured that if I told the truth, I wouldn't be all fucked in the game. It was like, 'I told you what happened, send me home.' Brains all scrambled. It wouldn't matter if a dog barked at me wrong, I would have been, like, 'Hey, wait a minute, I didn't do *that*.'"

But this was a scenario he'd been hearing about all his life, as a Panther. His father, and every B movie, had taught him: Never, ever talk to the police.

"Shocked, confusion, scared to death, and they tricked me....

Plus, how do I put this...preparing for blood and guts ain't the same as seeing blood and guts."

Later, Debo's roommate D'Artagnan Partee was jocular with police in the interrogation room. They bantered back and forth about the sheer stupidity of the robbery plan. Partee still didn't understand how his friend would ever be a part of it. Debo was not hard-up for a place to stay. And he was not stupid.

"They left the Batman clues," Partee told police, noting the obvious flaws in the plan. Everyone in the Allemenos house had seen Adams's face. Plus, at least two other people, the two teenagers Britt and Wright, knew Adams had been at the house the day before and that he was planning to return. Of course, once news of the murders hit the television, Partee told them, the two teenagers must have gone straight to police, leading to an easy arrest.

The detectives seemed to take offense at the notion that their job was easy. Wealthy Hamilton County, Indiana, isn't exactly a hotbed of crime, but the officers had had long experience at doing detective work. "That's not true," they corrected Partee, according to the transcript. The two white teenagers did not come forward. They were tracked down.

During the trial, Adams testified that Britt was in on the robbery plan, gave Adams information about the hardware store safe, and was to get one of the cars they'd stolen.[15] Adams was not a reliable source of information, but this testimony would explain why he so casually showed up at his Tudor Lake apartment after the Chicago trip, knowing that Britt had been there before and could point it out to police. Britt's dad had been a friend of George Allemenos and worked at his hardware store for years. Following Allemenos's wishes, prosecutors declined to press accessory charges against Britt and Wright.[16] A few years later, Wright turned up in the news again.

He had given an alibi to a robbery and shooting suspect at an Indiana hotel.[17]

In July 1994, three months after the murders, two fellow cellmates of Adams, Ricky Williams, and Aaron Allred, came forward to the police. Adams had bragged about killing all three people in the Carmel house, providing details about how he did it. He said he did it to avoid going back to prison. Adams asked Williams for the phone number and address where he would be staying after his release from jail the following week. Adams wanted his cellmate to go back to his apartment in Tudor Lake to retrieve a half-pound of marijuana that he'd hidden there.[18]

Crimes such as a triple murder rarely happen in the elite suburb of Carmel; the public demanded someone's head. The Hamilton County prosecutor's office, led by Steven R. Nation, who was campaigning for county judge, had everything he needed to deliver. Police interviews, blood found on clothes, other physical evidence and witness statements, along with a jailhouse confession, all pointed to one person: Raymond Adams. He had refused to cooperate with police, had a lengthy criminal record, and his statement about what happened did not jibe with what his two codefendants said, or what he told his cellmates.

Adams, it seemed, did not have a chance. But when it all shook out, prosecutors offered Adams a deal. They spared his life, offered him life in prison without parole in exchange for his testimony against Kofi Modibo Ajabu.[19] Adams broke his silence after negotiating through his lawyers to testify that he saw Walls kill Chris James, then watched Ajabu standing over 17-year-old Nick Allemenos with a knife. Adams said he thought the girl was still alive when they left the house. That's what he testified, and that's what prosecutors went with in the trial against Ajabu.

Prosecutors gave a similar deal to the third defendant, Walls. But they did not exercise their option to have him testify at Ajabu's trial.

As one prosecutor later explained to a *Star* reporter, his testimony would "confuse" rather than "clarify" the issue for jurors.[20]

The prosecutors appeared to have their weakest case against Ajabu. There was no motive, no proof of intent, no physical evidence, and no credible witnesses saying he committed the murders.[21] Both then and now, Debo said he knew nothing of the robbery plan and followed Adams to Chicago under duress and in fear for his life after witnessing the murder scene. But public sentiment demanded that prosecutors do everything they could to make sure Ajabu didn't walk. Unlike his codefendants, Ajabu was never offered a plea deal by prosecutors. They charged him with ten counts of first-degree murder, robbery, and kidnapping. He alone was going to trial, and they wanted the death penalty.

When county prosecutor Steven R. Nation initially announced he was seeking the death penalty against all three codefendants, Mmoja Ajabu spoke to reporters outside the courthouse. "I want to serve notice as a father: If my son is killed for something he did not do, other death sentences will be carried out." He repeated this phrase on various television and radio stations and newspapers. "A whole bunch of people will die," he said.[22]

Debo, for one, knew his father was dead serious. "They gon' really stretch my neck," Debo remembers thinking. "And then my old man is going to kill a bunch of people. And while I felt a little bit better that there would be some repercussions, if I got to see it, it would be from where dead people go."

As the court-ordered deadline for the defense and prosecutors to reach a plea deal approached, the *Star* published an article headlined "Ajabu urges his son to put faith in God, not plea deal." In it, Mmoja Ajabu is quoted as predicting a "monster" if his son is "assassinated."

"Ajabu's father speculated his son's execution would strike a chord in some people similar to one caused by the federal government's 1993 raid and ensuing deaths at the Branch Davidian compound near Waco, Texas. 'It would create more people who feel the government is out of control,' said Mmoja Ajabu, who faces intimidation charges for earlier comments he made about his son's case."[23]

Several articles published in the Star in the weeks leading up to the trial had to have raised the political stakes. Debo told me unequivocally that there was no plea deal offered to him, period. Yet virtually all of the *Indianapolis Star* stories covering the case thereafter were written with the stated assumption that Debo had refused a plea deal. This is an assumption that prosecutors did little to dispel. It helped to mask an otherwise illogical decision to pursue an expensive death penalty case against the one defendant with the least definitive evidence. The media falsely reported that prosecutors gave Debo a chance, and that he chose instead to take his chances before a jury. But even then, the newspaper still didn't fully explain why prosecutors would use the least credible defendant as their star witness and, more important, call for the execution of Debo while letting the other two codefendants live.

The media also followed the government's lead in leaving Raymond Adams alone in their coverage. In the dozens upon dozens of articles about the Ajabu case, I found only two that gave details about Adams, both published the day after the three suspects were arrested. One charted his arrest record since the age of 11 and noted that he'd been living on his own since he was a teenager.[24] A family member who declined to be identified said the family wasn't afraid of Adams, but didn't trust him after he stole some checks. A cop who had busted him several times before described Adams as a manipulator of people younger than him, and he was not surprised that

Adams was involved in the murders. Raymond Adams sounds like a pretty interesting character, but there were no follow-up stories about him. The media had bigger fish to fry.

Well before the Allemenos murders, I'm guessing Mmoja Ajabu had been giving the media wet dreams for years—just as he was giving the government headaches. To this day, he's such a passionate man. He makes for great copy. The murders came at the height of his activism. He was an enigmatic figure who spoke in hyperbole, sometimes delivered via a bullhorn, his nostrils flaring.[25] And for still and video photographers, he's irresistible in his kente cloth, all black, and sunglasses, with ankhs hanging around the neck. He cuts a dashing figure in his African clothing. He is bombastic, newsworthy, and, of course, eminently quotable.

Gallons of ink have been spilled about Mmoja's activism, starting with his work with the black parent's group at North Central High School; his increasingly militant activities during the early to-mid-1990s were covered on national network television and in a front-page story in the *Wall Street Journal*.[26] When the murders happened, the Ajabu saga assumed operatic proportions. The irony of the paramilitary Black Panther leader's son involved in a violent crime was the quintessential Angry Black Man's rhetoric come to life.

For the media and politicians playing to public appetites, a case with this kind of symbolism is manna from heaven. Only hotshot star reporters get assigned to the story; only top lawyers get to try the case. I don't even think the media and politicians are necessarily bloodthirsty or happy for the misfortune of others. At their essence, they are scavengers, feeding on drama and the competition for the juiciest slice of the story. That's how careers are made.

During Debo's trial, in 1995, the *Indianapolis Star*'s readers called in to the newsroom for recorded updates of the trial.

Disclaimers ran above stories: "Graphic details from testimony will offend some readers." On the advice of his lawyers, Debo showed no emotion throughout. His father, on the other hand, was a force stronger than nature, impossible to be contained. Every mood shift, sigh, eye roll was dutifully recorded by the cameras, or duly noted by the reporters. And of course, he summoned the goons. Dozens of them, wearing all black and carrying shotguns when they arrived at the courthouse in full force for the trial.

Debo had other worries during the trial. While waiting in jail in South Bend, Indiana, he watched a television report of a local Ku Klux Klan group visiting a school. When he realized the visit actually wasn't for his benefit, but just standard fare for South Bend, he was even more scared of his prospects before a jury. Aside from his father's goons, the courthouse was loaded with dozens of extra police officers for security. Much of the government security around him was actually for his own protection. "Same old street justice," Debo says. "I've never been opposed to the old street justice, but I was on the wrong side of it, most unappreciated."

The prosecution's case largely hinged on Debo's own statement to police and testimony from Raymond Adams. Prosecutors argued that even if Debo didn't commit the murders, he didn't stop it from happening. The defense argued that Debo had no knowledge of the robbery plan and feared for his own life after witnessing the aftermath of the murders.

The jury convicted Debo on all ten counts. Mmoja and Debo Ajabu raised their hands in exasperation at the same time.

Prosecutors' next move surprised many: They offered to allow the judge to do the sentencing as opposed to the jury, taking the death penalty off the table. Prosecutors said they were following the wishes of the victims' families.

During the sentencing hearing, Debo asked the judge to "cut him some slack." He said he'd never been in trouble before, and his mother was in the courtroom, in pain and hurting.[27] His father sat in the courtroom, wearing all black and holding a copy of Sun Tzu's *Art of War*.

For their closing statement, prosecutors had family members read statements as if from the victims. An 11-year-old cousin read one of them. "My name is Lisa Allemenos and I am 13 years old," she read. "I cannot be here to say these words because my life has been stolen away from me." George Allemenos read a statement as if from his son. "While Kofi Ajabu may or may not have killed me, one thing we do know is that he didn't save me that horrific night."[28]

The judge gave Debo three life sentences without parole.

The next morning's *Star* played the story on the front page— right below a story announcing that O. J. Simpson was acquitted of murdering his ex-wife and her friend.[29]

The people of Hamilton County elected former prosecutor Steven R. Nation, a Republican, to the Hamilton County Superior Court in January 1995. Until he was elected, he was the face of the prosecution in the Kofi Ajabu case. However, Nation later testified for the prosecution in the intimidation case against Mmoja Ajabu.

For Mmoja Ajabu, the years following the Allemenos murders were a maze of court dates and headlines. There was the lawsuit against his employer, who fired him for carrying a pistol on the job— which he successfully challenged in court.[30] Jane Hart-Ajabu filed for divorce in 1994. Then his house was firebombed while he was visiting Debo in prison. The insurance company eventually paid a claim, but not before accusing Mmoja Ajabu of burning his own house.[31] He spent six months in jail for intimidation tied to Debo's trial.[32] He made local history again by running for Congress while under house arrest.[33] He stepped down from the Panther Militia. He hosted a radio program called "Revolution is the Solution." And he was involved in another assault case.[34]

Based on the relentless stream of newspaper headlines, Mmoja Ajabu's life looked like a train running off the tracks. His next step, in the late 1990s, shocked most people, but in a way it took him to the only place left to go: Jesus. He scandalized black Indianapolis by joining Light of the World, one of the richest black churches in the city. He bonded with the congregation, and he later completed seminary in Atlanta. In recent years, you could find him quoted by the *New York Times* as a black clergy member criticizing the Bush Administration,[35] or pictured in a 2004 *Atlanta Journal-Constitution* photograph of an anti–Iraq war demonstration: an old lion, with salt-and-pepper hair, screaming into a bullhorn.[36] Now remarried, he is Minister Mmoja Ajabu. He's starting his own church in Georgia. When I asked him how he'd respond to all the folks who say he sold out, he gives me this reply: "I'm grown."

In the end, Debo was a red herring for both media and government. Some of it was the obvious, years of built-up animosity and fascination with his dad. But in an even worse injustice to the murder victims, the media and prosecutors missed out on one of the most compelling defendants and newsmakers in Indiana history: Raymond Adams. They also ignored the two white teenagers, Peter Britt and Nathan Wright, who played critical roles in setting up the robbery. Without them, Raymond Adams never would have known that the Allemenos kids' father was out of town, that Chris James was a manager at the hardware store with access to the safe, or that the family had money. They were the ones who gave Adams the phone number to the house, and they never went forward to police willingly. If you applied the prosecution's zero-tolerance standard to them, they would be at minimum accessories to robbery, and possibly even to murder. In the end, the prosecutors and the victims' families decided not to take their futures away by holding them responsible for the actions of a sociopath. So why would they hold Debo responsible for Adams's actions? It is a blaring double standard that falls predictably along racial lines.

Today, Mmoja Ajabu has no regrets. He figures his threats forced the prosecutors to back down. "I saved that boy's life," he tells me. One *Star* columnist perceptively compared the Ajabu saga to a Greek tragedy. But in constructing that tragedy, all the journalists missed the biggest irony of all: Debo had spent his whole life preparing for a bloody race war, a day of reckoning and judgment. In the end, the enemy was a member of his own race, and the people his combat training could have protected were white. When this grand moment finally arrived, he chose to ignore all the values he was raised with. First, he used nonviolent pacification against Raymond Adams. Second, he tried to help the police. Had he made a different choice in either case, he might be free today.

So, pick your fable: We are our own enemy, or Never trust The Man.

Within the first ten minutes Debo spent in his new home at the Pendleton Correctional Facility in November 1995, he had walked over to the biggest guy in the dorm, the perfect person to make an example of. Debo dropped to the floor, did splits on both sides, and then turned to face the man with his hands up. "Get up," he told the big guy, ready to deliver a beat-down as new prisoners often do to ward off future attacks. "Let's get this out of the way."

The man burst out laughing. "Nah nah, it ain't even like that no more."

"You sure?" Debo asked, and the man nodded.

"As a matter of fact...you play chess?"

"Yes, I do," Debo replied, and they've been friends ever since.

"This sucks, but I make a point to have like a grand old time every day," Debo says. "Don't get me wrong, this is like, the bootiest shit ever. Every day, I can just be myself and have a ball, because I like me just fine.... This sucks, but I'm not about to let [being in prison] determine who I am."

He says he continues to thank his mom and dad for raising him the way they did. The lessons they instilled in him about black history and an international perspective on black liberation have been invaluable in prison. Without that knowledge, he thinks he would have come to prison and died. "Maybe not physically, but I figure a damaged mind is a whole lot worse than being dead and socially dysfunctional. I got a solid foundation. I got something to work with. I sure do need it because there is nothing to stand on here. There is no base to operate from. Here it's all head games."

His walk has given him the knowledge and sense of self that allows him to transcend his environment, which he says is filled with "bottom feeders, the dregs of society." You can tell the time by his mother, Jane Hart-Ajabu, who visits him every other week for two hours. He catches his father on the phone from Georgia when he's sitting still. Around his prison dorms, Debo has found himself in the familiar position of being the best-read in the room. He finished his college degree through Ball State University's prison program, and earned a third-degree black belt in prison.

The brothers, especially the young dope boys, are drawn to him, look to him for guidance. A couple of them asked him to start a Kwanzaa community. So he formed a circle of about a dozen inmates, and had them write reports about each of the Kwanzaa principles. They practiced one of the Kwanzaa principles, cooperative economics, by collecting dues and establishing a co-op store. Together, they had a feast that fed the whole dorm. He has coached several young roughnecks into giving up drugs and finishing college. He also teaches martial arts.

Debo's case is still on appeal. In 1998, the Indiana Supreme Court threw out the triple life sentence. They remanded the case to the Circuit Court judge, who swiftly replaced his sentence with 180 years in prison. His newest legal strategy is to point out that the jury was told by the government to deliberate using the instructions for accessory to murder, but it convicted him of first-degree murder. He dreams of getting out and opening a martial arts school. He understands his appeal chances are clouded by Indiana's political and racial climate, but he refuses to give up hope. "This is not life. This is some strange other type stuff. This is completely not normal. I will never accept this. That's just the way I was brought up. Not necessarily the military aspect, but I was brought up to be free."

He realizes now that he spent a lot of his youth finding trouble. "Maybe if I had some idea of what I was looking forward to as a man, it would be different. But at the time, I didn't know it wasn't all about making other boys respect me as a man. If you are a man, you kind of don't need somebody to say, 'That's a man.' You take care of it. Preferably, peacefully."

I ask him what he thinks about the "revolutionary" approach to improving the lives of black people. He pauses a long time before answering. "I wouldn't take it back but I don't think that it's the only way. The whole freedom thing has been badly defined by our black scholars. I look at a lot of the stuff that my old man was into and a lot of that shit was straight-up reactionary. I've been doing martial arts long enough to know that if you are operating from pure reaction, more than likely you can't win. Your opponent just has to coach you into this direction...and it was a setup the whole time."

I ask him what he thought he was working all those years to accomplish, then. He pauses again, and laughs. "No nice way to say

this: Technically, I was just following orders," he says, laughing. "It's
funny now, because I'm old enough to find it funny. I never really
thought about it. This case forced me to be still. I still think there is
a need for revolution, but not the same kind of revolution. First of all,
we gotta have some definitions of stuff. What is freedom? What do
you want? Life is like a big quiz to me. There's bound to be an answer,
and I'm in."

Often other prisoners come to him and ask, What you on today,
Ajabu? He practices the Socratic method with them. For a year, he
walked around asking everyone the question: What does it mean to
be a man? "I would get all Chandragupta or whatever on them, or
some other yoga master. But I'd ask them, What exactly is a man?
'Well, a man is, uh—' they'd answer in manly voices. I told them
those deep voices don't work on me, man. What if something happens to your vocal cords? Are you a man? What if someone has a
deeper voice than you? Does that make them a more of a man than
you? That don't work. As my country friend says, that dog don't
hunt."

So I ask him for his definition of what it means to be a man. "It's
only partial. But you can get it. First off, being a man is really not
depending on what somebody else thinks of you. It's taking care of
your woman if she wants to be taken care of. Taking care of your
ankle-biters.... But it's definitely not just that. Being a man...well...
it's still a work in progress."

Chapter 10

Raising Tyrone

I walk into a Chinese restaurant for the reception welcoming my classmates and me back to graduate school. I (Natalie H.) am holding our ten-month-old daughter, Maven, on my left hip, while my right hand clasps the hand of our three-and-a-half-year-old son, Maverick. As soon as we enter the restaurant, Maverick spots Norm, a fortysomething white guy, a friend who is in my PhD cohort. Though my son has never seen this man in his life, Maverick runs toward him, arms outstretched, as if greeting a long-lost uncle. Norm stoops down to accept the hug, grinning back. While I'm being introduced to a few professors, I look up and someone is affixing a nametag to Maverick's button-down shirt. I blink again, and he's working the room like a gubernatorial candidate—"Hi. My name is Maverick, what's your name?"—and offering various students and administrators a tiny caramel hand. He had made it halfway around the room by the time I called him over to sit down.

The next afternoon in class, my classmates and our professor, a fiftyish white woman, remark about what a great kid Maverick is. "You have a fine boy there," Norm says, to murmurs of agreement throughout the room. My chest puffs up with motherly pride. My professor agrees, adding: "I just can't wait to watch him grow up, and see his wonderful career as a rap star."

Eeeeeeeuuuuuurrrrrk?

Stop the record. Stop the record. Rewind: "*Rap* star?" Did I miss something? Like Maverick break-dancing behind my back? No, that would come months later, thanks to the soon-regretted purchase of the DVD *You Got Served.* How about bursting into rhyme during dinner? Nope, Maverick had long since grown bored of his favorite rap song, a Black Eyed Peas hit he turned into a potty-training anthem.

So where, pray tell, would our professor get the idea that my son would have a future as a rap star? I don't know which increased my blood pressure more: the assumption that a rap career was an aspiration we'd dream for our son, or my own deep embarrassment for the comment, and the urge to shield my son from such a core part of my own identity as a member of the Hip-Hop Generation. It's a tricky paradox. As parents, we see it as our job to make sure our son doesn't live down to fake notions of black masculinity that too often are epitomized in rap music. But we find it equally important for him to be unapologetically proud of the ingenuity, strength, and vitality of black culture, which of course, includes hip-hop.

Our generation is filled with twenty- and thirtysomethings clinging to youth culture with an iron grip. Some of us loosen that grip and become a sanitized version of a "responsible adult" once we have children; others don't, instead allowing our culture to flavor our attitudes toward parenting. We integrate our kids into our everyday social lives as our own personal mascots or as really cute live accessories.

We are starting to see many of these parents—at their extreme—in pop culture. The singer Erykah Badu and rapper Andre Benjamin sport their young son with them on stage and at glitzy parties and awards shows. Rapper Game incongruously clutches his infant son while posing for his album cover and doing live performances. Rapper Snoop's sons appear in his video clad in braids and athletic gear.

At the 2005 BET Music Awards, cohosts rapper/movie star Will Smith and the actress and philanthropist Jada Pinkett-Smith showed their struggle to parent effectively and keep it real. In one of the skits, the Smith clan poses as you might expect multimillionaires to look, wearing Sunday-worthy suits and dresses. As soon as the cameras stop rolling, the oldest son starts complaining about the suit he had to wear. "Snoop's kids would never have to put up with this!" he huffs.

My husband, Rudy, and I were born in the mid-1970s and are part of this generation and aesthetic in our own middle-class, white-collar kind of way. To this day, Rudy is that 30-year-old who spends hours playing videogames, watching the Cartoon Network, and elbowing the teenagers in line each Tuesday for the latest hip-hop release. He's the lawyer going to work in jeans and a T-shirt, blasting hip-hop in his windowed office, who regularly gets mistaken for the office messenger. Me: I've built my career writing about black youth culture and music, and still take pride in getting my groove on at the club. Our kids go pretty much wherever we do, except the club, from the classroom where I teach college students, to my writing assignments, to Rudy's office, to Sunday football with Uncle Celo, fight parties, house warmings, and barbecues. They are used to being the only kids there.

Our kids' names are inspired by the African tradition of using nouns to reflect our aspirations for them. "Maverick" entered the American lexicon because of an early-nineteenth-century white Texas cowboy, attorney, and politician who refused to brand his cattle. He said if anyone found a cow without a brand that meant it was "Maverick." That's what I want for my son: to resist all the voices urging him to pick a brand—whether a brand of politics, of black masculinity, or of sneakers. I would be overjoyed if he grew up to be the same loving, intelligent, and devoted man that his father is. Ultimately, though, I want him to live up to his name and forge his own path—whether as a scientist, race car driver, or emcee. Any productive use of his talents works for me, so long as he doesn't let the door hit him on the way out of our house at 18.

To be fair, the professor who commented on Maverick's future turned out to be a favorite of mine, and someone who, I later learned, knew enough about hip-hop to understand that it can be an art and an honorable career path, despite the icky way the culture is depicted in mass media. But that still doesn't explain how she calculated Maverick's future prospects based on his behavior at that dinner. File it in under further confirmation of what author Jawanza Kunjufu calls a "conspiracy to destroy black boys."[1] That's the power of black masculinity, an already powerful force that is skewed and amplified before being broadcast by media. It's potent enough to cloud anyone's vision, even those who should know better. By our own self-imposed deadline, that meant we had another fourteen-and-a-half years to make sure Maverick knows better, too.

We are slackers, losers, selfish, alienated, disaffected, impatient, rootless, ambitious, hedonistic, nihilistic. In their fascinating book *Millennials Rising: The Next Great Generation*, authors Neil Howe and William Strauss use all of these qualities to describe the cohort known as Generation X.[2] Born between the early 1960s and the 1980s, this is perhaps a blander, paler version of what we and author Bakari Kitwana call the "Hip-Hop Generation."[3] Yet, oddly, Howe and Strauss also add a surprising trait to that list: devoted parents.

Much of this list reflects the reality of a generation dealing with the aftermath of the suspicions kicked up by the Civil Rights Generation (baby boomers) around institutions of government, democracy, and education as well as gender, sexuality, and culture. Our parents were busy "having it all" and establishing new paradigms. By the time the talk about "family-friendly" work policies came into vogue, we were already surly adolescents.

The boomers did, however, pass on their skepticism toward every major institution, right before taking over the helm of them—with stock options. For emerging adults of the Hip-Hop Generation, the best defense has been to erect an ironic shield, essentially a pose that prevents us from engaging in the world or believing in or working toward its redemption, except maybe joining the shameless march toward King Cash. This is a lazy cop-out that numbs our efficacy and stalls progress, as author Jedediah Purdy points out in his anti-irony treatise *For Common Things*.[4] Purdy is right; it is much easier to satirize the world than to stand up and take a chance on it. But that's essentially been our stance: Nothing ventured, nothing lost.

This dark pessimism seems to have had an inverse impact on our view of parenting. We are hopeful, devoted, anxious—neurotic even—about shielding our kids from the gloom that settles in when that kind of skepticism goes unchecked. We are wedded even less than our parents to the rat race, and instead put family and social life first. Howe and Strauss cite a 1974 survey in which 55 percent of college freshman said "raising family" was the essential goal of life. In 1998, that figure rose to 78 percent of college freshman. "For many Gen Xers, starting and maintaining a stable family can be a unique source of pride," Howe and Strauss write. "The pride you get for achieving something your parents did not."[5]

While the boomers put off childbirth, the age at which Gen Xers become parents has tilted downward. Other contemporary lifestyle trends reveal the change in attitudes toward family among the hip-hop generation, including the rise in home schooling, telecommuting, and young parents moving closer to their parents. From my own experience, I can add to that list co-ed baby showers, mandatory presence of dads in delivery rooms, and soccer fields flanked equally by moms and dads. Also, dads like Rudy, who has foregone more lucrative career paths to focus on family. Then there are friends like Derek and Kenyatta, two strong, college-educated brothers who have elected to stay home with the kids while their wives go to work.

And then we've seen stay-at-home moms make a serious comeback, as evidenced by the Mocha Mom craze, which started in Prince George's County, Maryland. Historically, staying home to rear children has been a luxury rarely afforded black parents. Not so for the Mocha Moms, an organization of black, mostly highly educated, stay-at-home mothers.

Even those of us who need the paycheck or are too self-absorbed to stay at home with children can't help but envy and admire those with the financial resources and temperament to devote their lives to raising their kids the right way. Sometimes, I fantasize about that lifestyle, a phenomenon my friend the author and journalist Lonnae O'Neal Parker calls the Donna Reed syndrome.[6] Once, my girlfriend Ginet and I schemed to crash a D.C. Mocha Moms meeting. We didn't actually qualify for membership; I was on maternity leave with my daughter and moonlighting teaching a university course, and Ginet was a lawyer in private practice with her husband. But our unique schedules allowed us some flexibility, so we planned to show up at a meeting and impersonate stay-at-home moms. Naturally, we never were able to coordinate our schedules to go through with it.

Research shows that, for black kids, the family structure is our best defense for blunting the economic impact of race. As Howe and Strauss note, among all families with children, black families earn only 52 percent as much income as white families. But among two-parent families, black kids are raised with 84 percent as much income. These days, your best bet in closing the socioeconomic and racial gaps is having strong two-parent families.

One of my favorite wedding pictures was taken during our civil wedding ceremony in a suburban Virginia park. A six-month-old Maverick, wearing a little seersucker tux with short pants, peeked over my mom's shoulder at the camera, pure mischief in his eyes.

He looked like the trickster then, and that seems to be his role. He came into this world with an agenda to set his parents straight. When Rudy and I learned we were expecting him in 2000, I was 23 and fresh out of grad school and in my first newspaper writing job; Rudy was 25 and fresh out of law school and in his first job. We had been dating off and on for five years, but we didn't think pregnancy was a good enough reason to rush to the altar. Could be that old cynicism, but we'd seen too many shotgun marriages turned shotgun divorces to put any urgency to checking off that box. Rudy seemed more relieved by the news that I was pregnant than anything. Between pregnancy and STDs, dating is like a game of musical chairs. He was just glad that he landed on me. He looked deep into my eyes, held my hand, and said, "Let's...buy a house!"

I was nearly nine months pregnant when we moved into a Victorian row house in a transitional neighborhood in Washington, D.C., an investment that soon became another testament to how perfectly Maverick timed his grand debut.

Unlike our parents, who intentionally chose suburban, mostly white school districts with top-notch school systems, we had different criteria for where we wanted to live. We wanted to live in a black community in the Chocolate City, in part to shield Maverick from the psychological trauma and alienation that we both knew from our own experiences growing up in white suburbia. We admittedly had a lot of romantic notions about being role models and helping a city rebound. Soon after we moved, we met some of the young black boys in the neighborhood. "You're a lawyer?" our sweet neighbor Brandon, about 8 at the time, asked Rudy. "Why would you want to live *here?*"

Other reasons for wanting to live in Washington had more to do with our own vanity. We weren't ready to give up our lifestyle yet. We wanted to stay in the mix, near all the clubs and restaurants, museums and theaters, our friends, and to feel the energy of the city that we'd missed growing up. Plus, to us, our idea of hell is a commute.

Some days, the choice feels a lot like class suicide. Both Rudy's and my parents hadn't fled poverty in the Caribbean, made it through college and the corporate world only to have their grandchildren dodging crumpled Red Bull cans and crack baggies on the sidewalk. Nor did they expect their grandkids would have to check the neighborhood toddler park for dirty syringes, condoms, and cigarette butts, or more often, be driven elsewhere to play outside.

Then, of course, there are the local public schools. I was taking the day off and pushing Maverick around the neighborhood in a stroller when I decided to pop in to check out the local elementary school. Rudy had volunteered at the school in college. And I had heard decent things about the school, which abuts the Howard University campus. I walked into the school and immediately asked for a tour from the school's vice principal.

She wearily led me around the school and answered my questions. No, she told me, there is no PTA, but if you're interested, we probably could use your help to get one started. She pointed out that I didn't have to enroll my son in the school just because it's in my neighborhood. In Washington, you can apply to go to any school in the city through a lottery. "Do your homework," she advised me. Look at test scores, and demographics of the schools. She gave me the names of a few schools with good reputations. She had just left a teaching job at a highly functioning school "across the park"—that's Washington's euphemism for the white part of town west of Rock Creek Park. The difference between the educational experiences was stunning. "These kids here have real problems," she told me.

When I shared the exchange with Rudy, he was apoplectic. Well, if they keep chasing off motivated parents, no wonder the school is in trouble! First thing we need to do is get rid of her ass, Rudy said. Right, I told him. We can get some of our neighbors together, write some grants, and push through a specialized Spanish bilingual program for at least one class. We don't have to chase the white folks to provide a good education for our son.

It would be another three years before we had to make a decision about where to enroll Maverick in school, and the reality of our own busy lives sank in. It would be a tough decision. When it comes to raising black boys, there really is no room for error.

The three of us were walking down the sidewalk late one night after having dinner at our favorite Thai restaurant in a busy retail strip on D.C.'s Connecticut Avenue. Maverick, not yet 2 years old at the time, was toddling along beneath the streetlights when we noticed his pace begin to slow. He stopped, sneaked a peek behind a shoulder, then snapped his attention forward and speeded up his pace. He repeated this several times: stopping and looking back, marching quickly forward. Finally, he looked behind him and a look of sheer terror spread across his face. His deepest fears had been confirmed: Someone *was* chasing him. He was about Maverick's height, dark, and following his every move. Maverick burst into tears.

Rudy and I struggled to console him—and get control of our laughter. "See, it's just a shadow," I told Maverick, pointing to my own shadow. "It's your friend!"

"Look," Rudy told him, plodding a foot down on the concrete sidewalk where the offending silhouette was cast. "You can stomp it! Arrrgh!"

I've always joked that that was the moment when the realization that he's a black man in America finally sank in for Maverick. He's a black man, and that means someone is always coming for his ass.

Most of the books and handbooks on raising black boys confirm our worst conspiracy fears about Maverick's future, which are unfortunately rooted in statistical truth. Educational consultant Jawanza Kunjufu wrote the first edition of his book *Countering the Conspiracy to Destroy Black Boys* in 1982. More than two decades and several editions later, over a million copies are in print. In it, he describes how institutions of government, the media, and the school system conspire to rob black boys of proper preparation for the workforce and a decent life expectancy, instead steering them straight to underemployment, the prison system, or untimely death. The book's 1995 edition quotes author Amos Wilson, in his book *Black-on-Black Violence*, lamenting the social statistics that show black men being cut down in their prime:

> The black man has packed all the guilt, failure, shame, fatalism, pain, hopelessness, and cynicism of a lifetime within a span of three decades. Somehow the cavalier optimism of youth and willful self-confidence of young manhood are dissipated at or before the point of actualization and assumptions of their powers to transform the world. Somehow, black youth and young adults are born into and come early to exist in a different ominous reality: one that was created for them; one under the control of others.[7]

Kunjufu recommends that parents start early in giving black boys responsibilities, resisting the urge to demand they do fewer chores than girls, a practice he believes contributes to the disparities in their school performance. Parents should also teach kids to save and invest money at an early age. Boys need more quiet time at home without music or television, so that they are not overstimulated when it's time to focus in the classroom. He also urges parents to keep their boys off behavioral drugs like Ritalin and out of special education, where they are dumped in part to increase budget allotments for schools. If they must do sports, let it be those where black boys are underrepresented, like tennis and swimming—not only to fight stereotypes, but to benefit from the shorter lines for college scholarships.

Kunjufu's book includes much useful information but, like most of the guides to raising black boys, leaves something to be desired. Some comments in the book about gays and lesbians reflect a homophobic strain in the black community that needs to be checked. Kunjufu says that parents and school systems must teach their black boys about their history in the world. If they don't, pop culture will quickly fill in the gaps, providing a distorted view of what being a black man is. Because blacks are both overrepresented and falsely represented in mass media, school systems and parents must constantly strive to provide boys with an accurate picture.

A variety of guides to raising children echo many of Kunjufu's suggestions. They also consistently describe hip-hop as some alien force that parents must first decode, and then denounce. Reading these books, I get the feeling that they aren't speaking to me, but to my parents. Keeping our babies away from commercial rap is common sense to many of us who grew up on hip-hop. By now, we're mostly alienated by the mainstream commercial rap that's coming down the pike and aimed at the emerging Millennial generation. Many of us are actually into that oxymoron "old-school hip-hop." But even our now "classic" artists, like Biggie and Tupac, NWA, Public Enemy, and the latest high-quality underground stuff that Rudy chases each week as if in an Easter Egg hunt, are too angry and militant and profane for young ears. Might give our babies nightmares.

Initially, I tried to engage some of these images. One of rapper 50 Cent's choruses was ubiquitous on radio airwaves for a while: "Shake, shake, shake that ass, girl," he rapped. When I heard Maverick singing the hook, I told him that it wasn't an appropriate way to speak to women. "That is what's called sexist," I told him. When he still seemed confused about why 50 would say that, I tried to explain. "Sometimes 50 Cent makes bad choices." Sometimes I get lucky and he misinterprets the lyrics. "What they gon' do? Shoot!" became "What they gon' do, shoe!" And that's how the Black Eye Peas song "Let's Get Retarded!" became "Let's Get the Toilet!" But eventually I just got tired of having to explain every rapper's bad choice. I gave up on commercial radio and bought an XM satellite radio, which has more choices and no commercials. The music video channels that I grew up watching are totally off limits.

There are people who clearly need to pick up these manuals, like the woman we saw in the movie theater bringing two prepubescent black boys to see the pimp narrative *Hustle & Flow*. Cosby would be going into fits! In *The Warrior Method: A Program for Rearing Healthy Black Boys*, the author Raymond A. Winbush explained why some black parents use poor judgment: "Black parents, in particular, have a meager supply of social and educational strategies to protect their sons from a society that has a love–hate relationship with them."[8]

That also includes parents with money. Black people as a group already know never to rest easy—how quickly, with one false move, our wealth can be snatched away. It is one of the great equalizers. No amount of money will insulate parents from the perils of black manhood in America, as the millionaire movie stars Will and Jada Smith can attest.

When I caught up with Winbush, on the phone from his Baltimore office, he explained how he founded an institute to raise healthy black boys. One of Jada's aunts was in a class taught by Winbush, a professor at Morgan State University in Baltimore. After her aunt gave Jada a copy of *The Warrior Method*, Jada liked it so much that she bought $2,000 worth of books on the author's reading list at a Los Angeles bookstore. Two weeks later, Winbush got a letter from the Will and Jada Smith Family Foundation. It contained a $50,000 check. He used it to set up the Warrior Institute, which runs rites of passage programs out of Baltimore.

His methods have caught on around the country, at public schools in Columbus, Ohio, and in Dallas, including the "Africentric" private school where Erykah Badu's child is enrolled. Winbush has two major criteria for those employing the Warrior Method: It has to begin at a young age and teachers have to have an understanding of how white supremacy works. Indeed, half a century after the landmark 1954 desegregation case *Brown v. Board of Education*, the socioeconomic status of black children has not improved.

First published in 2001, *The Warrior Method* is more progressive as a whole than Kunjufu's book when it comes to gender relations; it is well written and includes a good curriculum for parents filling in the gaps created by media and schools. The method is an application of a century-old rites of passage program in Ghana, where Winbush was studying when he wrote the book. Male rites of passage ceremonies are typically performed for boys at age 13 to mark their entry into manhood, a ritual that reinforces the expectations from their parents and society.

Rites of passage are good in theory, but I think parents should understand that they also inflame the Duboisian double consciousness—the inner war between those who are both black and American. Dipping a child in a traditional African ceremony loses effectiveness if it is negated by the child's everyday reality in school and at home.

Rites of passage, such as beautillions, that attempt to reconcile Western and traditional African styles have mixed results. In 2004, I wrote a *Washington Post* article about a beautillion taking place for 9-year-old boys at an Afrocentric Christian academy in D.C.[9] The kids wore white tuxedo tails and gloves and shiny red sashes, and waltzed across the room with their escorts. I was impressed by the boys' composure and self-assurance and the high expectations that the school and their parents had for them. But there were also definitely some elitist strains to the exercise. Any black tradition that both mimics old Southern gentry and excludes some black people is bound to include contradictions.

"It's almost like a Western schizophrenia of trying to blend two worlds," Paul Hill Jr., a Cleveland sociologist who has studied male rites of passage around the world, told me in a 2004 interview for the *Post* article. "The beautillion has to do with the regeneration and the perpetuation of that class from an elitist perspective. The question is how do you reconcile class and culture in a way that is in the best interest of the whole community?"

It's easy to see why Winbush's theories and methods are catching on. In a world filled with uncertainties, his tone is confident, assuring. Amid all these terrible statistics, he provides a sense of security: If you do X, Y, and then Z, you will raise a warrior. Most of Winbush's suggestions are good ones—even if some ideas seem a bit hokey and a throwback to 1970. You won't catch us pouring libations or having the whole family wear African clothes to school and work once a week. I tend to view these recommendations as I view church. I may not ascribe to all of it, but, on the whole, your life prospects tend to improve when you fall in line.

My biggest beef with Winbush is with the term *Warrior Method*. I question the choice of language at a time when violence is a leading killer of black males. Winbush disagrees. "I believe that black boys are at war," he tells me. "White society is at war with black males.... So, if you are at war, you have to have warriors."

He cites a recent incident in which police handcuffed and arrested a 5-year-old black girl in a Florida school, and the police murder of Amadou Diallo. He said warriors needn't be male, but they have to be willing to die for their culture. "We don't like to talk about armed blacks," Winbush says. "We don't like talking about black folks that retaliate. We don't like to talk about warriors in our community. We like to talk about the nonviolent stuff. I wanted us to consider Ida B. Wells, who in 1898 said in the home of every Negro should be a Winchester rifle. There are no consequences to killing us."

True enough. But consider the experience of Kofi Modibo Ajabu, my friend from Indianapolis profiled in chapter 9 of this book, "Boy Born on Friday." Debo read Kunjufu's book in its first release, when he was 11. His parents are both well-read cultural nationalists. His dad was a Black Panther who knows about armed struggle; in fact, he could have written his own manual called the *Soldier Method*.

Debo's sisters were spared the soldier treatment, and went on to excel. Debo, on the other hand, was raised as a soldier, and he did what came naturally, interpreting that language in a personal way to create his own version of a soldier—which, then and now, means being a gangbanger. Turning gang members into freedom fighters isn't necessarily a bad idea. But it can have many unforeseen consequences, as Debo, who is locked up for the rest of his life, learned the hard way. The reality is that for a minority group in America, armed struggle is the equivalent of armed suicide. Debo now considers armed strategies too reactionary. If you operate from a reactionary position, eventually you'll get trapped, he says.

Maybe it's time for us to try something else.

One of the nice things about our five-mile daily commute "across the park" to Maverick's school is the scenery. Although it's a D.C. public school, it doesn't feel as if it's in the city, with its sprawling green acres and adjoining recreation center, complete with a soccer field, tennis courts, and two playgrounds. Maverick can wander the woods at recess. There's even a mulberry tree bearing fruit.

"Where'd you get that from? The ground?" one of Maverick's prekindergarten classmates asked Rudy after school one day, pointing to the mulberry he'd popped in his mouth. The 4-year-old looked up at Rudy's 6'5" frame and eyed him suspiciously. "No," Rudy told him, not the ground, straight off the bush. "Did you wash it?" the boy wanted to know. When Rudy admitted that he hadn't, the boy shook his head. "You know that's nasty right? Eeww. You nasty."

What can we say? It's rough out there in the world of pre-K. Maverick had had his own run-in with the same kid a few weeks earlier. He had come home in tears after the kid teased him because he wasn't reading as fluently as the kid was. This, at age 4.

We did our part to prepare Maverick. We have read to him each night at bedtime since he was a baby. We took him out of the care of our wonderful nanny at age 1 to enroll him in a corporate day care chain. We wanted him to be around other kids and get the social skills he would need when he turned 2 and we applied to Howard University's Early Learning Program, which has been operating on the campus since the 1940s. In addition to requiring a twenty-plus-page application, Howard administrators observe whether prospective students "blend" well enough with the other children.

Maverick spent a year in Howard's preschool class, which we all loved. Then, with the arrival of his baby sister, Maven, we decided to save money by taking advantage of one of the city's better public elementary schools for pre-K. In the end, for all our right fist waving and our aspirations to change the world, I acted like a good buppie and followed, to the letter, the advice of that vice principal who discouraged us from attending the neighborhood school. I got on the Internet. Scoured test scores of all the schools. I searched for addresses that were west of Rock Creek Park—my former *Post* colleague, the columnist William Raspberry, had once told me that the quality of the elementary schools across this geographic boundary was universally comparable to the suburban schools. I looked for an enrollment with a relatively low free-lunch (read: poverty) rate, and at minimum, a sprinkling of white students, so Maverick would know what they look like.

The school we were admitted to via the D.C. public school lottery draws kids from all over the city to form a diverse student body that is almost 70 percent black, with the rest Latinos, whites, and Asians. Like all the elementary schools in the city's most affluent neighborhoods west of the park, scores are top-notch, and it is quasi-privatized by school PTAs that raise tens of thousands of dollars to hire art, music, dance, and science teachers and do school repairs—perks that are scarce in the rest of the traditional public school system. The day I went to meet the principal of the school, I saw two of Rudy's former law school classmates doing the same. We immediately agreed to try to get our sons into the pre-K class of Mr. Jenkins, a dynamic young brother who'd been highly recommended to me in one of my annoying-but-informational mommy listservs.

Being middle-class parents in a highly competitive place like D.C. often means that we treat our children like NFL free agents, constantly on the hunt for a better deal. Since it is a specialized early learning center that ends at third grade, Maverick's school gets treated like a farm team. Many parents leave before third grade to angle for the few slots in the bigger schools that go up to fifth grade. Those bigger schools often poach kids from Maverick's school, as they need to plug up their own enrollment shortfalls. I have my own worries about rolling the dice for the higher grades, but otherwise, the only real difference I can see in the bigger schools is that they are mostly white.

Despite all this hand-wringing, angst, and endless research, not a day goes by that I don't question the decisions we've made about Maverick and threaten to bolt in an entirely new direction. At this writing, I'm preparing to serve a term as secretary of the school PTA. I just got an e-mail announcing the resignation of our gung-ho PTA treasurer. He had big plans for his term as treasurer. But three weeks before school started, he and his wife defected to another one of the D.C. public schools, putting the rest of the PTA board in a bind.

Even though I was perfectly happy with Maverick's experience in his first year, this news immediately put me off balance, inflaming my insecurities about whether I was settling. I picked up the phone to check our own place on a waiting list for a Spanish bilingual public charter school on our side of the park that I also liked. This was a school I'd previously scratched off the list after concluding that since it was one of those newfangled charter schools with an evolving curriculum, I didn't want them "practicing" on my Maverick.

It took me just a few hours to come to my senses and stay put, honoring both the school's good work and my commitment to the PTA, but it just goes to show how the plethora of choices can drive you crazy. Am I neurotic? Totally. And all the conflicting advice about what is the right approach to educating black boys doesn't help.

Kunjufu praises the Montessori Method for allowing for differences in learning styles based on gender and race that can be tailored to fit black boys. But that runs counter to what both my old high school principal and Natalie M.'s mother, longtime Chicago educator Yvonne Moore, have told me about black boys and Montessori: It doesn't work for them because they need more structure.

The experts urge parents to prepare their kids for kindergarten, because this is where tracking tends to begin. Teachers often pick up clues in dress, grooming, and parental involvement to decide whether your kids are worth the effort. Everyone also agrees that having a black male teacher is a plus for black boys. However, Kunjufu points out that in his decades of school consulting he never met a black male kindergarten teacher; he cites a government statistic showing that black male teachers make up just 1.7 percent of elementary school teachers.

If you are not lucky enough to have a black male teacher, that's okay. The race and gender of the teacher are not as important as her expectations. "I reiterate that teacher expectations are the most important factor in academic achievement," Kunjufu writes. "You do not measure a school by its facilities, or the race of the student population, but on teachers' expectations. I believe that what teachers *see* in the child is what they will produce *out* of the child."

All the scholarship agrees, it is critical that black boys be engaged in school in the early years, starting in preschool and kindergarten, to avoid the Fourth Grade Failure Syndrome—the poor transition that black boys make between the primary and intermediate divisions. All the authors say that most black and white kids tend to do equally well until that point. Then the test scores of black males take a plunge.

There are purposeful and experimental all-black boys' schools. Natalie M.'s brother attended Hales Franciscan, an all-boys, mostly black, Catholic high school on Chicago's South Side. It had a reputation for nurturing students, and his parents wanted attention and small class sizes for Joey. His preference would have been a co-ed public school, but Joey, now 26, admits he would have gotten in lots of trouble in a less restrictive setting. Joey, who never really liked school, says school officials paid attention to him. "If you don't show up, they know you ditched. You can't get away with anything. The doors were always open if you had a problem."

Joey says gangbangers existed even in a school like Hales, but there was no pressure to join. Violence didn't happen in the hallways or on the premises; that didn't go down in Catholic school. He said the socialization included blacks across class lines. There was a sense of knowing where you came from. But ultimately, Joey feels being in a school environment that was diverse would have been more practical for learning how to function in the real world.

Many black parents of means and education think that by placing their black boys in high-achieving schools, they've done their jobs. But a study by the late Berkeley anthropologist John U. Ogbu showed the fallacy in that thinking. For his 2003 study and book *Black American Students in an Affluent Suburb: A Study of Academic Disengagement,* he spent months studying the elite public school system in Shaker Heights, Ohio, to find out why black children underperformed despite having socioeconomic backgrounds similar to their white classmates'.[10]

Ogbu found that many of the factors are cultural. Even controlling for socioeconomic status, he found that black parents were less active in going to school events like PTA and open houses. Also, they didn't come to school unless there was a problem. They saw their roles as intervening against oppression from the school, demanding that teachers do right by their kids. They weren't as concerned as white parents about issues dealing with curriculum or overseeing homework. They were more inclined to reward or punish kids for grades.

This approach is flawed on many levels, as Ogbu points out. Learning is cumulative, each day building on the day before. Black parents need to invest the time on a daily basis, by keeping in contact with the teachers and communicating with them as much as possible.

If you wait until the grades arrive to punish or reward your children, it's too late. They've already lost the opportunity to get the study tools needed on a daily basis to succeed.

Despite their affluence, many of the black Shaker Heights kids believed their roots were in the ghetto and ghetto culture. They emulated rappers, ballers, and entertainers rather than their well-to-do parents. They were drawing conclusions from the world around them: movies, music, and the five o'clock news, and the absence of other black cultural models in school.

The study shows the paradox of integration. By enrolling black children in overwhelmingly white environments, affluent black parents expect their kids to conform to the dominant culture. Those same parents come home sharing their racial struggles at work and in society, giving them a different message: Don't trust the system. In some ways, excelling in the insensitive dominant school systems socially and academically does force you to lose some of your identity. This is what I think black kids mean by "acting white." Those who cling to oppositional stances toward education are not necessarily criticizing the others for performing well, but for buying into mainstream hegemonic forces, the same ones their parents warned them against. Not "acting white" means being more skeptical about the whole enterprise to melt away differences in the melting pot. That is part of the reason Shaker Heights kids clung to black dialect.

We experienced a similar dilemma when Maverick started coming home splitting verbs, such as "I be walking." I usually correct him by explaining what the grammatical rule is. I tell him that there is nothing wrong with this dialect, but that I want him to know how to speak Standard English. One day, Rudy was driving him home from school. "Kids in my class use a *lot* of double negatives," Maverick said proudly, then reported that he had corrected one of them. Rudy was like, Shh, let's just keep those rules between us.

I would have liked to hear more from the parents of these black underachievers in Ogbu's fascinating study. From my own experience working full-time as a journalist, I was killing myself to work twice as hard for fewer rewards than my white counterparts. That eats away at a lot of family time. Later, between teaching and grad school, my life was so hectic in Maverick's first year that I had to stand up Mr. Jenkins, his pre-K teacher, on the one day I volunteered to spend in his class. So, in a way, I see how black families are at a disadvantage. There are a lot of stay-at-home mothers running elementary schools. It's been part of the major disconnect between black women and twentieth-century feminism. Black women have historically worked, and for a growing number of members of the middle class, that's changing.

For black parents, there is another dynamic that Ogbu failed to address: their own alienation and disaffection, which makes them avoid socializing in school environments that do not feel welcoming to them even as adults. I saw a lot of myself in the Shaker Heights kids and parents; they are dying for alternative educational paradigms.

During a visit to Indianapolis, I decided to stop by to see my old high school principal, Dr. Eugene White, a black man who has become an educational rock star in Indiana. He had since gone on to become an award-winning superintendent of the wealthy Washington Township suburban school district where my high school was located. A few weeks earlier, he had decided to take a job as superintendent of the Indianapolis Public Schools, and he had just published his first book, *Leadership Beyond Excuses*.[11] He had overseen unparalleled gains in black achievement in the district in Washington Township. Now, he said, he wanted to go to the larger, less affluent urban district "to help them out." One of his first acts was to promote Jane Hart-Ajabu (Debo's mother) as Chief of Human Resources.

I walked into his downtown corner office and folded myself into his 6-foot-4-inch-plus frame for a warm bear hug. I told him about Rudy's and my educational odyssey, and he told me about some of the innovative programs he was working on to fight the Fourth Grade Failure Syndrome for black boys. At the time we spoke, he and Ms. Hart-Ajabu had just sent out letters to the parents of low-achieving black boys who'd been plucked to be part of a specialized academy.

A few years back, Dr. White had made national news when he invited all 600-plus black boys enrolled at North Central High School for a come-to-Jesus convocation. Though they were among the highest achieving black boys in the state, he pushed them to close achievement gaps with their white, Asian, and female peers. He used statistics to show how those gaps were helping to feed them straight into the criminal justice system. Their little talk fueled a national controversy about whether he stigmatized them as a group. He had a follow-up dinner to recognize the black boys who showed the most improvement. As a group, the scores of black boys improved.

When we talked about my own experiences with Maverick, Dr. White could sense my wistfulness about not going through with the plan to stick with our neighborhood school. He quickly set me straight. "You never get a chance to do this but one time. This is your chance," he said. "You have the means to give him the best, whether that's in a school that is public or private. You've got to send him to a place that's ready for him. You've gotta find places that believe that he can be a Master of the Universe. If you are lucky enough to live in a community where you don't have to pay for that, good for you. If not, make that investment, it will pay you right back. You cannot feel guilty. You are not selling out. That's the American way."

Exactly. And that's also the American problem. Much of our life has been about remixing, restoring, renovating. We have an opportunity to do something that goes beyond our own children and our bragging rights. For the sake of all black boys floundering in public schools, I hope we can shed our own cynicism long enough to figure out a plan to rebuild.

Each day, our community looks more and more like a neighborhood our parents would want for their grandchildren. Our block has always been quiet, and we are extremely close with our neighbors, with a running club, a garden club, and barbecues. Each day, the streets get cleaner, crime decreases. White people are moving in, too, and paying increasingly exorbitant amounts of money to do so.

I'm still trying to decide whether to give in to my cynical impulses about gentrification in our neighborhood. I flip-flop on a day-to-day basis. We're happy living here, and we're definitely glad that our kids will be exposed to different cultures. I have to smile, seeing the thirtyish white guys walking down our block with their little ones. Pushing strollers or carrying their blue-eyed babies like really cool backpacks, they remind me of Rudy. Watching the exodus of poor black people from the city, though, I have to wonder if this is a new racial paradigm or another Trail of Tears.

The dilemma in raising our black son remains: What if our culture is the problem? It's like Mos Def says, We are hip-hop. It's our attitude. It's where we choose to live. It's the music we listen to, the values we raised ourselves on. Every day, we lament the current state of hip-hop, but even more, we lament the sad state of black reality that it caricatures and reflects, especially when it comes to black boys. I see hip-hop as a cry for help, for direction.

Maverick's spirit amazes me every day. He's the little man who has never met a stranger. Likes to sing hip-hop choruses during recess. He dotes on his little sister, and even taught her how to do a head spin. At our final parent–teacher conference wrapping up Maverick's pre-K year, Mr. Jenkins informed us that Maverick had the third-highest scores in the class, and he has shown improvement in every measure from the beginning of the school year, well meeting the goals to prepare him for the rigors of the next. As Mr. Jenkins likes to say, "kindergarten is no joke." The bad news: Maverick is constantly being dropped off late, causing him to arrive in class disoriented and confused about what part of the daily routine the class is in. So basically, his teacher was telling us that the child is doing fine; it's his parents who need to get their act together! Sorry, Mr. Jenkins. We'll try to do better in kindergarten.

We've also seen other evidence that the kid just might survive our culture after all. At Howard's preschool, all the kids and their parents gave presentations before a standing-room-only audience for Black History Month. Our friend Daniel Illori Cooper came to support Maverick as he gave his presentation, which he prepared with a *little* help from Rudy. Daniel published an entry about the speech on his Internet blog:[12]

> Last Thursday Maverick Michael Delano McGann, a three-year-old, stepped in front of his nursery school class at Howard University and gave a special Black History Month speech on his hero, Paul Robeson. During his presentation, complete with contact boards, illustrations, and audio aids, Maverick noted the achievement of the man known as a gentleman, scholar, athlete and "octopus." Although Maverick has trouble pronouncing the word "activist" his speech was very informative and many of the other students in the class were taken with his energetic style of instruction on the matter.
>
> Maverick showed all of his peers the brand new Paul Robeson stamp and...he provided his eager listeners with an

audiotape of Paul Robeson's rendition of the poem
"Freedom Train," by Langston Hughes. As a finale Maverick
announced that he was going to eat pizza, his favorite food,
to his jealous cohorts and thanked everyone for coming.

The director of the nursery school added that his speech
was wonderful in her closing remarks and proceeded to
retire his contact board for future school use.

When asked to comment on his recent success, Maverick
enthusiastically answered, "I win!" and then demanded that
I share some of my orange with him.

Chapter 11

Tyrones in Training

Boys play too much and try way too hard to be cool. Girls have to be strong to demand respect. The boy of their dreams is a cross between Omarion and Usher—but he's got to have a head on his shoulders. Boys could do a lot better in the hygiene department. As a whole, girls think cable music videos are giving boys and the world the wrong idea about who they are.

This is the news, among other revelations, delivered to us during two roundtable discussions with nine black girls, all ages 12 to 15, in two midwestern communities: one big-city urban, one semirural. They are typical teenagers, potato-chip-chomping, phone-gabbing, Top-40-loving. One of them wears a T-shirt that reads, "I Love Boys."

They are frank, sweet, they giggle often, and they are happy to give us their opinions on just about everything tangentially related to their relationships with boys their age—from best friends and boyfriends to popularity and success to sex and video hos. Most have cell phones that sporadically interrupt our conversation. Many of them have an innocence and strong sense of self that grown women could admire. But some of them still struggle with their self-esteem and with abuse from boys, even at their tender age.

These girls are on the front lines, shaping new paradigms in black gender relations as they struggle to negotiate their own space in the world. We agree with Beverly Guy-Sheftall, the founding director of Spelman College's Women's Research and Resource Center, who advocates more women's studies curriculum in K-12 schools. Boys and girls need to be armed with these tools to be able to cope with a variety of messages carried over the nonstop communications and mass media that rule their world.

They are getting some of those tools with the help of the girls' groups that have connected us with them. The group in St. Cloud, Minnesota, Today's Women/Sisters in Action, is run by Decontee Kofa. Its mentoring program aims to empower and train girls and women of color to be competent, work together, and develop supportive environments for themselves in the schools. Some of the girls' families moved to St. Cloud for safety and economic reasons; and the low cost of living is an improvement over the life in Minneapolis, about 70 miles away. Fewer than two dozen of 600 students in their school are black. They call their hometown "White Cloud."

The Chicago group—whose discussion we conducted in the high-rise apartment of its former mentor, Esther Jackson of U Go Girl!—is a similar program. Most of the Chicago girls are college-bound and live in working-class or middle-class neighborhoods.

Both groups have a macro understanding of how boys disrespect girls and how the culture of hip-hop videos influences their boy counterparts. Yet when it comes to their own relationships, some say it is "hard to let go." Or the relationships are long-term—in the angst of a junior-high life span: six months.

Five of the girls are from Chicago. Kiara is 15, lives with her grandmother, and her favorite musical artists are T.I., Destiny's Child, and Ciara. When she grows up, Kiara plans to be a fashion designer. She's a compact girl—probably a hair under five feet tall—with deep-set eyes framed by naturally curled eyelashes. On the day we spoke, she wore half her hair slicked back into a ponytail, and a red hoodie.

At age 12, Naomi uses SAT words and likes to point out the differences between rap and hip-hop. "Rap is too fast and it's irritating," she says. A cherubic seventh-grader who loves to draw, her dream is to be a veterinarian, working with wild animals and pets because she wants to be a "well-rounded animal lover."

At 14 years old, Joanna is six feet tall and plays on the basketball team, which helps her gets along well with boys. She has a big smile and long, dark, flat-ironed hair. She's an avid *Oprah* watcher and is already planning a career in pharmaceutical sales, following the footsteps of her big sister Esther.

Kim may be the boldest of the Chicago group, offering a lot to say about a lot of things. The 14-year-old says she can sing, and her voice is a deep husky alto. Kim likes to do hair and read books. She wants to read Sister Souljah's *The Coldest Winter Ever*. She plans to pursue a career as a surgeon.

Shajuanea, 14, has smooth, dark skin that is void of characteristic teenage blemishes. For at least a year, she's talked about being an entrepreneur. A gas station tops the list, "because that's where everybody spends their money." On weekends, she helps staff her father's booth at a local swap meet. "Anything you look for, we have."

The other four girls are from St. Cloud. Vivian, 13, listens to Beyoncé, Avril Lavigne, Ashlee Simpson, and Ashanti. Vivian's friends loathe her boyfriend. He's a player, disses her in the hallways, and is always hitting on other girls at school. She sticks with her boyfriend because he makes her laugh.

Michelle is wearing a heartthrob on her T-shirt along with the "I Love Boys" button. The seventh-grader has a lot of family problems and plans to become a psychologist so that when other people have troubles, they will have someone to talk to. The ponytail-wearing Michelle, 13, has a strong sense of self. She likes basketball, dancing, hip-hop, and R & B. She's looking forward to attending college and becoming a cosmetologist. She likes Ashanti, G-Unit, Nelly, 50 Cent, Lil' Romeo, and Usher.

Lisa's family is from Liberia. She is 13 and in seventh grade. She, too, likes Usher and Beyoncé, plus Linkin Park, LL Cool J, and basketball. Lisa gabs on the phone and loves talking to boys. A cascade of black and red braids tumble down her back.

Keshia, 14, is in eighth grade, enjoys doing hair, dancing, and running track. She listens to R. Kelly, Ludacris, 50 Cent, Aretha Franklin, Anita Baker, Luther Vandross, Al Green, Teddy Pendergrass, and Marvin Gaye. Keisha plans to be a massage therapist.

It's been more than fifteen years since we were at this critical, sometimes awkward age, and we're surprised at how little has changed. The girls watch BET as studiously as we did, even as the images have gotten increasingly grown-up. They are all too familiar, for their liking, with BET's raunchfest *Uncut*. The show comes on after hours, supposedly to shield the young. Duh, the girls say, eyes rolling, what kid has a bedtime on the weekends?

The girls have a refreshing self-awareness, candor, and charm, even as they face grown-up problems like infidelity, abuse, and low self-esteem, which chase some women their whole lives. The girls draw strength from advice given by their parents, siblings, and each other. They all seem to agree: Tyrone has a great sense of humor. He makes them laugh, even though he gets on their nerves.

...On the Perfect Boy

Keshia: It's this boy here named Royal, he is cute. He got all this stuff, but he is dumb.... I used to think he was cute, but everyone tells him that he is cute and he got conceited. Now he is, like, "I got all the girls. I know I am cute." Nobody tells him he is cute anymore, because he is so conceited.

Vivian: His skin is like honey/caramel, and he's real buff.

Lisa: He is like Omarion and Usher put together.

Vivian: He has, like, Indian hair. He has a mustache. He is fourteen.

Lisa: I don't know if he is coming from gym or something, but I guess because all those girls are walking with him, he takes his shirt off, and he is wearing a wifebeater.

Michelle: Or he be walking down the hallway with his pockets to his knees, like, what is that? Pull up your pants!

Lisa: Most girls do think that is hot, but he does it to get attention.

Keshia: He got all these features that make a girl think that, oh he is fine. But when it comes down to school work, he is dumb. We are on this new book called *The Giver*, and we was in the media [center] and the lady asked him his name and he was, like, "Royal. R-O-Y," and the lady was, like, "Is that it, 'Roy?' " and he said, "I forgot the 'oil.' " He forgot the *a* and the *l*. He wasn't doing it to be funny. He got the look but he don't have the brain.

Joanna: The perfect boy for me is somebody that really cares about me. They don't just like me for my looks. Handsome. He knows where he wants to go in life. Somebody that doesn't have a bad history. I guess it's somebody that I can bring home and wouldn't have to be ashamed.

Kim: Somebody who has something going for themselves. They have a nice personality. They know how to count their own money. You know, I don't want no dummy. A person that likes me for me. He has to be into some type of sports and he has to be intelligent.

Shajuanea: Somebody that is cool, a person that is clean.

...On Popularity

Joanna: Well this guy, his name is Torrence, and he's a senior. I guess he's very popular, because he is very handsome. He has a nice car and he knows a lot of people. He is one of the stars on the basketball team, and he's just hilarious. He is very funny.

Naomi: The most popular boy at my school would basically be Demonté. Why? Because he puts himself out there and he makes himself known. So, he's not shy. And he is popular in both good and bad ways. One reason is that he is a well-rounded guy. He has a lot of girlfriends. And another reason is like I said, because he puts himself out there and he convinces himself that he is a popular person.

Natalie Y. Moore: So what is the bad part?

Naomi: He has a lot of girlfriends. He has a lot of people that he goes with to boost his reputation, to be like his other brother that went to our school the previous year. And he tries to use his brother's name. He thinks that because Antonio was the stuff that he is the stuff too.

Natalie: Who would the most popular boy be, if you had to pick one boy, Kim?

Kim: It would be this boy named Marshall, and he a senior. He popular to me, because I went to school with him, and in school he is like a nerdy type and when I went to Dunbar, I seen him and he just look, I mean all the girls be on him and he can sing real good and he play basketball. I mean, he just cool with a lot of people. And then he with this little clique called ABC Boys; All 'Bout Cash, and they think they got money, so everybody just knows him. Everybody be reppin' they name.

Kiara: It's a lot of groups, like we got a group that's sophomores. They called R.A. DUB, they got they little goon squad.

Natalie: Is what boys have to do to be popular different from what girls have to do?

Kim: Girls do everything in the world to try to be popular.

Shajuanea: They go out with they big mouth and try to act like they hard, and tougher than everybody, and that's how some girls get known. Because for boys to be popular, all they gotta do is play sports.

Joanna: Basically sports and just what you wear, and who you hang out with, personality. Well at [our school] it's about sports, your looks, and at some schools it's, like, fights, the girls you with, but mainly sports.

Boys to Avoid at All Costs

Naomi: Well, what I mean by immature is that they play too much. There is a time to play and there is a time to be serious. Like if a teacher is giving a lesson, you don't scream and make noises. You don't laugh; I mean that's not what we're there for.

Natalie: Are these boys that are stuck on themselves, are they at least cute?

Kiara: Naw, that's what be making me mad, like, I be looking like, you is not all of that. I guess they say stuff like that to make them feel better. I don't like people like that, conceited people and stuck up people who think they are too good for everybody else.

Kim: My least favorite thing about a boy is when they show they money and brag about everything.

Natalie: How much money do they have?

Kim: They'll have, like, a ten-dollar bill, with, like, a million singles. And then when they are around a girl that they like they'll try to act weak to everybody else just to stunt.

Shajuanea: They said mostly everything except for the hygiene.

Natalie: What about the hygiene?

Shajuanea: Some boys are musty. They come to school with the same pair of pants on that they wore like three days ago.

Kiara: And their appearance. Like, if you gon' have a jersey and a white T-shirt on under it, make sure the T-shirt is clean, and white. Make sure your shirt is ironed and your pants got a crease in it. Make sure your hair is brushed, and if you got braids make sure your scalp is oiled.

Kim: They pants be sagging and they show their underwear.

Natalie: What is your least favorite thing about boys?

Keshia: Some of them, they are h-o-e-ish. Sometime how they be calling females out of they name. And when you walk past they try to hit you on your butt.

Michelle: Some dude had called me a bird before because I guess it's supposed to be something bad, but I didn't really make nothing out of it. I was just, like, "Oh I am? Thank you."

...On Boyfriends

Michelle: He is a good listener; he has a very nice personality. He respects me for who I am. He doesn't try to make me be somebody that I am not. I met him through one of my close guy friends.

Lisa: He is the type of person that you can talk to for a long time without any pauses, just an ongoing conversation. He can keep you laughing—he is very, very funny. We do have some problems. Some things that happened. Inviting him over and stuff. When I say no he does beg. He pressures me to come over. He will say, like, "I am bored. I want to come over." We hang out. He is 13. They sort of already were worked out. My parent and some family member got involved. They got the cops involved too. We just hang out in school.

Vivian: This boy I was going out with. Since I was going with him I guess he thought he could touch me. But I didn't really do anything about it because I was thinking that I guess since I go with him it is okay. He never did it in a disrespectful way. Sometimes I think, like, Why did I let him do that? Some days when I am not feeling like being bothered with people I will hit him back or something.

The other day, I don't know what he was doing, but he swung and he hit me in my eye. I don't know what he was thinking. I never asked him why. I don't think he would hit me in my eye on purpose. Because we always play-fight, I didn't really think nothing of it. It didn't even hurt, my eye was just watering or whatever. He makes me laugh a lot. He is 13. When we were, like, in the middle of our relationship, I don't know what happened, but we were, like, on a pause. Then all of a sudden one day we just started talking again. He don't know how to take things serious. When I tell him something he will listen and then after a while he will look at me and just start laughing. He is not the type of person that you tell stuff to.

Michelle: I don't like him. I can't stand [Vivian's] boyfriend, because I think he is a player and he mess around with other girls. Then when he is with his girlfriend he tries to act like everything is okay, but it's not. I tell her the things that he be doing and she understands and I guess she tells him to stop. But I guess he does stop sometimes and then later on it will happen again.

Keshia: I think he is a punk because he is on that "I want five and seven girlfriends at one time. I know I got a girl who really like me," and he think he is a so-called pimp. He is a punk because, don't try to be all, like, "I am a player and I can get this girl and I can get that girl and my girlfriend won't do anything about it."

Natalie: How does hearing all of this make you feel?

Vivian: Before I went with him I already knew what type of person he was and I don't know how to let go of him. I know how he do me because everybody tells me, but since we have been off of that break he has changed completely. I am trying to let him go.

Keshia: What I don't like about her boyfriend is the way he treat her, because there was this one time when we was on the bus and he called her a bird. I don't really conversate with them like that. I saw it on the bus and I wanted to say something but I found out after we got off, because they was on a different bus.

Getting R-E-S-P-E-C-T

Natalie: At school, do you think girls are respected?

Kim: No! But I am!

Naomi: Well some girls don't act like they want to be respected so they aren't respected. I mean they will let boys do anything they want to, like, hit them and wrestle with them.

Kim: Some girls get respect, like me. But the girls whose body been used up they get the least respect and some of them like it. They let them talk to them any kind of way.

Natalie: Even though there are girls who don't let boys abuse them any type of way, do you think that boys just in general do not respect girls?

Kim: It's about how you carry yourself. If you respect yourself, they will respect you.

Shajuanea: Some boys respect girls just to get what they want, and when they don't get what they want, they disrespect them. They try to call them names.

Natalie: Do you think that some girls deserve to get disrespected?

Kiara: I think that if you hear males talk about other females and then you think they are not going to talk about you, then you deserve to get disrespected. No one deserved to be called out of their name. If it ain't what your mama gave you, then don't call them that.

Kim: I've seen a boy spit in a girl's face before. She was looking stupid. She laughed. This boy tried to feel on my butt and I made him an example. I tripped him in front of everybody.

Natalie: Do you all think that you can do better?

Vivian: I think not me in particular, but other females that I know. They put themselves out there in a way that is nasty and they know they can do better, but when they get around certain people they get all ghetto and loud and stuff. I just think that they can carry themselves in a different way, because they make it look bad for all girls.

Keshia: Yeah, they could stop plucking eyebrows, getting piercings and getting tattoos, and wearing tight clothes. Just to get attention from somebody that probably goes with somebody else. They do all that just to get some guys that probably don't even want them. They can respect theyself and I think dudes would respect them because they respect theyself. That is what my mama told me.

Natalie: Overall, do you think that boys respect girls?

Keshia: That time when he had called me all type of B's and stuff I was walking down the street and he was, like, "Shorday!" and I rolled my eyes at him because he was yelling at me from down there and if you want to talk to me you need to come to my face and talk to me. I kept on walking and he was, like, "you B." I had to walk past him because I go home that way and he had hit me on my butt. My mama came outside and I told her what happened. She went out there with her ghetto self and she told him something. She was telling him, like, "This girl right here, you see her? She is fifteen, don't you ever put your hands on her." She was, like, she got cousins down there and she got aunties down there and they will beat your you-know-what.

Lisa: There is this one boy that will touch your butt or your boob, and they will just come up and grab you. Really, when they do it, I don't really do anything. I will just laugh and walk away. I confronted a counselor once. A counselor talked to the one boy, but it didn't really do anything.

Natalie: To go back to girls being disrespected, do you think that anyone stands up for girls?

Joanna: I think, like, your closest friends. If you don't want to say something, they will probably say it. It's three of us and a lot of people think that we are stuck up, and we're really not. A lot of guys, they don't mess with us, because they already know we are not like some of these girls. A lot of guys, they are so used to disrespecting girls, and one time this boy he walked up to me and he was, like, "Dang, what you doing? What that do?"

Natalie: What does that mean?

Joanna: It's so stupid, it's, like, What is your body doing to me? They say, "What that do?" That is so stupid. My friend was, like, "Excuse me, what did you just say to her?" Then he looked at her and was, like, "You a freshman talking like this?" I was, like, Yeah. Some of these girls, they just put themselves out there. I said to him, "Don't come up to me like that anymore, because I don't like that." I don't like to be disrespected.

Kiara: I pretty much agree with what she said, because sometimes you really have to put dudes in their place. You have to let them know that you are not about to be treated like that. So I will tell them, like, don't come at me like that.

...On Music Videos

Joanna: I see that girls are basically hos. Like they are just going to give it up because you have a lot of money. To me it's not really like that. Behind closed doors, they are probably some of the sweetest girls. A lot of the teenage boys, they pick up on that and so they try to treat the girls how they see them in the videos. That doesn't work with a girl who thinks real highly of themselves.

Kim: In the videos the girls be having on them little shorts, that be dancing with they butts be all out, I call them video hos. When a boy sees that, he gets addicted to what he sees, and they expect every girl to do that. Like in Lil Jon video, he is smacking a girl's butt, so the boys think they can do that, because they seen Lil Jon do it and the girl let him.

Shajuanea: What they be saying, like 50 Cent new song "Candy Shop," what they be saying to them females. Like they call them girls bitches and stuff. Like on that Ludacris video, he had half-naked females on there upside down and was talking about how he wants it and stuff like that.

Natalie: As a black girl who is going to grow up to be a black woman, how do those images for the world to see make you feel?

Kiara: I think that maybe the world is going to think that all black women are going to be like that. So young females should put themselves out there in their own way. Don't be one of them girls on the videos, don't be no gold digger.

Naomi: As a young lady growing, I believe that stuff on TV inappropriate and disrespectful to our group, because that is not all that we do. We have intelligence. We are not all sluts. We can do something. I would like to see a video where a woman is being respected and not being made.

Natalie: Are there any videos that make you really angry, or that you are really turned off by?

All: "Tip Drill."

Kim: Them girls just be playing themselves. Disrespecting themselves. Anytime you are making a video, and you are just straight-up naked, something has gotta be wrong. It's like them girls they just picked up out of the club or whatever and just put them in their video. That is disrespectful.

Shajuanea: I don't like the "Candy Shop" video. He is pouring chocolate syrup on young ladies to disguise what he is saying in his lyrics. We all know what he is talking about. He is talking about what he likes when he is having sex. What he wants them to do.

Natalie: So we have this image of black females in music videos. How do you think black males are portrayed?

Shajuanea: Our males don't look like they do on TV. On TV, they cover themselves up with jewelry, earrings, and money.

Kiara: Tornado, he is on the radio station, was telling us how some of the people on TV, that they rent their jewelry. They don't have as much money as they make it seem. They are miserable. What they gotta go through to be famous and how some people just think that the money they getting is a lot of money, but they can't spend it on themselves, because of some kind of contract they signed.

Kim: He explained to us that celebrity life is just a gimmick. Because they do got a lot of money. He said to think about it like this, if you were a celebrity, what you would do with all of that money. Like [MTV's] *Cribs*, he said that if you walked into one of their houses you would find a stove that is so new, it hasn't ever been cooked on. He was talking about money. Suge Knight took Tupac out of jail and just because he did him that favor, he made Tupac go to the studio, make him his money. Tupac was only getting, like, a little part of that.

Natalie: So what you're saying is that the guys on the videos are fake.

Joanna: I really think it is a big fake, because they are really making a big joke of themselves.

Natalie: How do those images make you feel?

Lisa: You have to look a certain way in order to be accepted.

Natalie: What is that certain way?

Lisa: Like you have to look like a supermodel or something. Like get plastic surgery just to make yourself look well, and if you don't, then you won't be accepted. I think that is how they put things out there.

Keshia: You gotta get plastic surgery, you have to have your shoes a certain way, with certain shoestrings, gotta have your pants a certain fit, and you gotta have your shirt up here, and showing all of that, knowing good and well your bra size is not the size you have on. I know this girl, she get a bigger bra. She is flat-chested and she gets a big bra and stuff tissue in it. Just to have these boys say, "Oh she got some big ol' titties." That's not necessary.

Natalie: What are some of the videos that you all think are really bad?

Keshia: There was this one video by the Ying Yang Twins, and she had her pants so low that her crack was showing. Her booty was just too big for the pants, and she was doing all kind of splits and stuff.

Vivian: I think Petey Pablo's video "Freak-a-Leak." All Lil' Kim's videos. When she blew up she said that she was going to be her and not change for anybody and I guess that's her. That's just nasty to me. How she just, in all her videos, she talks about what she is going to do with boys. Like "make a Sprite can disappear in her mouth." She buys different color wigs to match her outfits.

Natalie: Do you think that videos have a big impact on boys?

Vivian: That Snoop Dogg video where he says he is a "P-I-M-P." Stuff like that makes people think. Boys pick it up and they think, like, "I am a pimp and that's how I am going to act."

Lisa: I just think that boys watching all the music videos and seeing all the girls, and then they come back to school and then they are, like, "You don't look like this," and, "Oh, yeah, you got those big tits and you got that big booty." And if you got that then you're good and if you don't have that, then you are not accepted.

Natalie: Does that make you feel good?

Vivian: It makes me feel bad because a lot of boys say that my chest is big. And the way they put it just makes me feel bad. A lot of girls say that, too, like your chest is too big. What am I supposed to do about it?

Lisa: Just recently. This guy at the end of the day was asking me what size bra do you have and he was, like, "I know it's a C or a D."

Vivian: Most girls like that attention, that's why they stuff they bras and stuff, but I don't like it at all. They make me feel like I am not supposed to have a chest. I am glad I don't have no type of booty because when people be, like, "She ain't got no type of booty," I be, like, "Yes."

Natalie: When people say things about your chest, what do you say back to them?

Vivian: "Shut Up!" Most of the time in the past, when I was young and stupid, I got into fights, and I changed though. I would do bad stuff because people would say stuff about my chest—that was the most common reason why I would get suspended for getting into fights.

Lisa: I just be, like, "Are you jealous?"

Michelle: They say "junk in the trunk." They say I have a big ol' ghetto booty. Then they say it's like big ol' balloons. I get annoyed. No, most of the time I just ignore them.

Natalie: How do you think boys are portrayed in videos and music?

Lisa: You have to have this big eight-pack, you gotta have a baby face. You gotta be light-skinned. Cornrows. You gotta have the braids.

Michelle: And if you don't, then it's, like, "He's ugly."

...On Sex

Naomi: I don't believe in premarital sex.

Natalie: Well, I see some people may want to chime in on that one!

Kim: I am not going to give myself to anyone that doesn't deserve me. When I find someone that deserves me, then I will give it to them. But other than that, they don't deserve it.

Joanna: I believe that you should have sex only when you are married, because you might love this person and you have sex with them and they could be behind your back sleeping with someone else. Even though that can happen when you are married, but I don't want to give a gift that God gave me just to treat it any kind of way. That is just a big part of me and I don't care who it is. I am not going to have sex before I am married. That is behind the teachings of the Bible, and the girls I know, all the emotions they have from giving their virginity up, and I don't want to have to go through that.

Natalie: What kind of emotions are you seeing?

Joanna: Like I gave him this part of me and he doesn't even cherish this. He just used me for that and he don't even like me.

Kim: My mom always told me that when you have a boyfriend or whatever, that a boy can make you think so much that he is really into you. But when sex and kids come into it, the relationship is just gone. But you just gotta watch the boy that you giving yourself to, that he is committed.

Natalie: How prevalent is sex? Naomi, you're in seventh grade, and people have sex?

Naomi: Yes, in seventh grade. Most of the girls that I talk to, they haven't had sex. One girl that I know has come close to having sex. She said that 12 years old is too early to be losing your virginity. I know girls who have been pregnant but it didn't succeed. I know girls who have boyfriends who are 16 and have persuaded them to have sex. But those are eighth-graders so its seventh- and eighth-graders that's having sex, and some sixth-graders that go with seventh-graders.

Kiara: Some boys will lie and say that they did this and that to some girl. Some of them really do have sex, but then after they have sex, the boy will do them so wrong that they'll be crying and stuff, and I be, like, "You shouldn't have did it."

Kim: At our school, it's, like, kids who think the world is coming to an end so they are just going to have fun. Some girls will try to have sex with all the guys so they can be popular. But it doesn't make them popular, the boys will just call them a "busto" or a "throwback." There are freshman that's pregnant. Ninety percent of girls are having sex, and then, like, 50 or 40 percent of them are pregnant.

Natalie: Shajuanea, is there pressure that boys place on girls to have sex? Why do you think some girls fall for it?

Shajuanea: They will say, "Show me how much you love me." And they fall for it, because they think that they are so in love and they want to try to keep them, and so they will have sex to try to keep them. There is a girl that I used to talk to and she would tell me her problems, and then she asked me for my advice and she wouldn't take it. So I quit talking to her. She learned the hard way, and she is pregnant again and then she got something. She used to tell me she was allergic to condoms.

Natalie: Have you ever felt like a boy has pressured you into doing things that you may not want to do? Or that you may be seeking love that you may not be getting elsewhere?

Kim: For me it's like this: When I am cool with a boy, I let them know from the get what type of girl I am before they even get a chance, before it even gets that far. I am not like all them other girls that you mess with. "You ain't gon' get none. If you don't want the friendship you don't want nothing."

Natalie: Give me an example of what happened when you told a boy that.

Kim: One boy told me, "I don't want you, no way." So a lot of boys tell me I be playing hard-to-get and they call me stuck-up. They can think like that. That makes me feel good, because that makes me feel that I am the only girl that they have confronted that hasn't fell for their game.

Kiara: I tell them like Kim. I tell them, Don't treat me like all these other females that fell for you. Because I am not dumb. I will tell you something in a minute. If I feel like a boy has something on his mind, I tell him to tell me. Let me know, because that will just make my day. I mean, if you really like this person, they are going to respect what you say. So I tell them to tell me, because I can probably say something or do something that is going to make them feel better and that makes me feel good.

Natalie: How are you all so different from the people who you go to school with?

Shajuanea: I guess because we think different. I heard it all before. I sit back and watch my uncles and cousins spit the same game some boy done tried to say to me. I watch and see how they react after they done told some girl all that stuff.

Kim: I think I am different, because most girls will start having sex at the age of 12 or 13 and have abortions. It's not that many virgins [at my school].

...On Guidance

Vivian: My big sister does [give advice]. I learned not to do things that she did, because when she was my age she started having sex and stuff. She had eight kids and she is 25 right now. She lost, like, three of them and she just tells me what things I should and shouldn't do.

Natalie: What types of things does she tell you not to do?

Vivian: Don't have sex, and that is just plain and simple. She talks about the type of relationship I am in, and don't give in.

Michelle: I don't really get advice from anybody; I just decide on my own what's best for me. Well, my mom, she is always telling me don't do this and don't hang out with these people.

Lisa: My auntie, my mom, my dad, and sometimes my two counselors. They tell me what type of friends I should be looking for.

What type of boyfriend I should look for. Things that I do or things that I shouldn't do and things that I do do, how I should handle it. That is basically about it.

Keshia: No, because I just got in a relationship with my mom, I hated my mom, my mama hated me. So I didn't have nobody to tell me nothing. So I did stuff on my own, probably did stuff that I am going to regret for the rest of my life, but I just didn't have a bond with somebody to tell me what to look for.

Natalie: What do your brothers teach you about boys?

Joanna: Well, basically, they will tell me that I can't date until I am 30. I am not going to my prom. They haven't sat down and told me what they think, they just goof around a lot. They mainly say that I can't date or talk to any guys until I am 30.

Natalie: What advice do your parents give you about boys?

Kim: Well, you know how some teenage relationships—they call themselves being in love. Some females think that love is when a man hits them, because they think that means that they man cares about them and all that. But my mama tells me that love is, like, feminine, and it's, like, somebody that you can talk to that relate to you, and when he dislikes something about you he won't try to change you. He is just going to be himself and be nice towards you.

Joanna: My parents, well, they don't really talk to me about boys, because they don't believe in teenagers having relationships at my age. My parents are really religious. One of our bishop's grand-sons, we started talking and a lady from our church, she gave him my cell phone number, and I was, like, Let me tell my father. So I told my father and he was, like, "Why did she do that?" And he said, "Well, I am going to tell you this: You can't date him. Erase his number. I don't want you to talk to him, I don't want to hear anything else about you and this guy. You're not old enough."

Naomi: My mother mostly talks to me about things. She talks to me about teenage pregnancies, she talks to me about boys, and she tells me about protection, and boyfriends and stuff. One day she asked me what a sensible age to date was. I said, "About 16," and she said, "Yeah, that's sensible." She asked me, "What do you think is a sensible age to have sex?" and I said, "When I am married."

Joanna: I think I am different because I treasure my body. When somebody says, "Oh, that's Joanna," I want them to know that this girl hasn't been out there and she treats her body like a piece of jewelry. I have parents and sisters and brothers that demand so much, so I have to.

...On Success

Natalie: Tell me about the boy in your school who you think is going to be the most successful when you grow up.

Joanna: One of my friends, Malik. When he grows up, he wants to be a producer like Kanye West. Right now he is working with his father, and his father knows a lot of people out in the industry. Malik comes up with a lot of tracks, and a lot of rappers, like Diplomat, they rap off of Malik's tracks, so to me he is going to be the most successful, because he already looking ahead and he is already in that mind set. He got basically everything to be successful right now.

Kim: This boy named Jacquez. I think he is going to be successful because he has a shot, and he wants to be a surgery doctor too. He was picked to tell us about the shot because he is the smartest boy taking shot. He is real good, because you can ask him about something and he knows everything about the body.

Natalie: Kiara and Shajuanea, do you agree that Jacquez is going to be the most successful?

Shajuanea: He is a freshman, I don't really know much about him; I just know that he is ranked number one this year and he is real smart.

Kiara: It's this senior and he is real smart, like he wants to go to school and he is trying to do all of this stuff. He hangs with his friends, but most of his friends are stupid.

Lisa: Boys got problems, but I still love them.

Notes

Introduction

1. U.S. Census Bureau (2004), http://www.census.gov/popest/national/asrh/NC-EST2004/NC-EST2004-04-BA.xls.
2. Bakari Kitwana, *The Hip-Hop Generation: Young Blacks and the Crisis of African American Culture* (New York: Basic Civitas Books, 2003).
3. Calvin C. Hernton, *The Sexual Mountain and Black Women Writers: Adventures in Sex, Literature, and Real Life* (New York: Anchor Books, 1990), 39–40.
4. *The Quotations of Mayor Coleman A. Young,* new edition (Detroit: Wayne State University Press, 2005), 6.

Chapter 1: Boy Born Saturday

1. "Kilpatrick's Poor Judgment Invites Lurid Rumors Now Dogging Him," editorial, *Detroit News,* May 25, 2004; George Weeks, "Kilpatrick Joins Daley as Jeopardized Mayor," *Detroit News,* May 31, 2005; "Kilpatrick Takes Mayoral Campaign to Gutter," editorial, *Detroit News,* September 16, 2005; and letters to the editor, *Detroit Free Press,* May 15, 2003.

2. Cameron McWhirter, "Detroit Voters Wanted Change," *Detroit News*, November 7, 2001.

3. U.S. Census Bureau, "The White Population: 2000," Census 2000 Brief, August 2001, http://www.census.gov/prod/2001pubs/c2kbr01–4.pdf.

4. Natalie Y. Moore, "Mayor: Fix Detroit or Risk Takeover," *Detroit News*, January 13, 2005.

5. City of Detroit, "HUD Consolidated Plan," Detroit Planning and Development Department, June 2000, http://nytimes.com/2006/03/20/national/20blackmen.html?hp& ex=1142917200&en=6ca3ed1b3c6b74ca&ei=5094&partner= homepage.

6. Moore, *Detroit News*, January 13, 2005.

7. Ibid.

8. Moore, "Detroit Up Against More Layoffs," *Detroit News*, September 13, 2004.

9. *Black Enterprise*, June 2005.

10. *The Quotations of Mayor Coleman A. Young*, new edition (Detroit: Wayne State University Press, 2005), 13.

11. Moore, *Detroit News*, September 13, 2004.

12. Alexandra Marks, " 'Hip-Hop Mayor' Aims to Rev Motor City Engine," *Christian Science Monitor*, August 7, 2002.

13. Darci McConnell, "Kilpatrick Kin Land Key Jobs," *Detroit News*, April 28, 2003.

14. Matt Helms, "Desire for SUV Based on Image, Not Real Need," *Detroit Free Press*, January 27, 2005.

15. "Mayor's Expenses Approach $160,000," *Detroit News*, December 3, 2003.

16. Monica Davey, "Detroit Mayor Fights Accusations of Misdeeds," *New York Times*, May 24, 2003.

17. Walter Harris, deposition testimony, *Brown v. Oliver*, February 4, 2004.

18. Kwame Kilpatrick, deposition testimony, *Brown v. Oliver*, June 26, 2004.

19. Kwame Kilpatrick, deposition testimony, *Brown v. Oliver*, October 11, 2004.

20. Chris Singer, interview by Natalie Y. Moore, summer 2005.

21. Alison Bethel, "Kilpatrick's Star Rises in Boston," *Detroit News*, July 28, 2004.

22. David Runk, "Kilpatrick Wins Second Term in Detroit," Associated Press, November 9, 2005; Paul Clemens, "A Comeback Kid for a Dead-End Town," *New York Times*, November 14, 2005.

23. "Residential Construction in Southeast Michigan, 2003," Southeast Council of Michigan Governments Report, April 2004.

Chapter 2: Tyroninity

1. Kerner Commission, *Report of the National Advisory Commission on Civil Disorders* (Washington: U.S. Government Printing Office, 1968), http://historymatters.gmu.edu/d/6553/.

2. Tupac Shakur featuring Digital Underground, "I Get Around," *Strictly 4 My N.I.G.G.A.Z.* (Jive Records, 1993).

3. Thelma Golden, *Black Male: Representations of Masculinity in Contemporary American Art,* exh. cat. (New York: Harry N. Abrams, 1994).

4. Mel Tapley, " 'Black Male' Exhibit at the Whitney," *Amsterdam News* (New York), November 19, 1994.

5. Diane Haithman, *Los Angeles Times*, April 23, 1995.

6. Arthur Hirsch, "An Artist in Search of Himself—and Us," *Baltimore Sun*, June 8, 2001.

7. Golden, 19.
8. Golden, 23.
9. Haithman.
10. Michael Kimmelman, "Constructing Images of the Black Male," *New York Times*, November 11, 1994.
11. Clyde Taylor, "The Game," in *Black Male: Representations of Masculinity in Contemporary American Art,* exh. cat. (New York: Harry N. Abrams, 1994), 169.
12. S. Craig Watkins, "Framing Protest: News Media Frames of the Million Man March," in *Critical Studies in Media Communication* (March 2001), 83–101.
13. Kim Martin Sadler, ed., *Atonement: The Million Man March* (Cleveleand: The Pilgrim Press, 1996).
14. Michele Wallace, *Black Macho and the Myth of the Superwoman,* 2nd ed. (New York and London: Verso, 1999).
15. bell hooks, *Salvation, Black People and Love,* reprint (New York: HarperPerennial, 2001), 215.
16. bell hooks, "Feminist Inside: Toward a Black Body Politic," in *Black Male: Representations of Masculinity in Contemporary American Art,* exh. cat. (New York: Harry N. Abrams 1994).
17. Taylor.
18. Adrienne Maree Brown, "The Africana Q & A: Dave Chappelle," www.africana.com (January 24, 2003).
19. Ta-Nehisi Coates, "Keepin' It Unreal," *Village Voice*, June 10, 2003.
20. William E. Smith, *Hip-Hop as Performance Ritual: A Biographical and Ethnomusicological Construction of a Washington, D.C., Hip-Hop Artist Named Priest Da Nomad,* PhD diss. (University of Maryland, 2003).
21. Stephen J. Dubner and Steven D. Levitt, "Up in Smoke," *New York Times Magazine*, August 7, 2005.

22. Brown.

23. Ibid.

24. Geneva Smitherman, *Black Talk: Words and Phrases from the Hood to the Amen Corner* (New York: Houghton Mifflin Company, 1999), 147.

25. www.eurweb.com.

26. www.keithboykin.com.

27. Christopher John Farley, "On the Beach with Dave Chappelle," *Time*, May 15, 2005.

Chapter 3: Visible Tyrone

1. Vivien Burr, *Social Constructionism* (Routledge, 2003), 41.

2. Keith Boykin, *Beyond the Down Low: Sex, Lies, and Denial in Black America* (New York: Carroll & Graf, 2005), 5.

3. J. L. King, *On the Down Low: A Journey into the Lives of 'Straight' Black Men Who Sleep with Men* (New York: Broadway Books, 2004).

4. Natalie Hopkinson, "A Fashionista's Heavenly Hair Show," *Washington Post*, May 17, 2001.

5. Hilton Als, *The Women* (New York: Noonday Press, 1996), 30.

6. E. Lynn Harris, *Invisible Life* (New York: Anchor Books, 1991).

7. Harris, *What Becomes of the Brokenhearted: A Memoir* (New York: Doubleday, 2003).

8. Hopkinson, "Casting Light on a Hidden World," *Washington Post*, July 27, 2000.

9. Boykin, *One More River to Cross: Black & Gay in America* (New York: Anchor Books, 1997).

10. http://www.oprah.com/tows/pastshows/200404/tows_past_20040416.jhtml.

11. King, 26.

12. Ibid., 52.

13. Brenda Stone Browder, *On the Up and Up: A Survival Guide for Women Living with Men on the Down Low* (New York: Dafina Books, 2005).

14. King, *Coming up from the Down Low: The Journey to Acceptance, Healing, and Honest Love* (New York: Crown Books, 2005).

15. www.eurweb.com.

16. Hopkinson, "I Won't Let D.C. Lose Its Flavor," *Washington Post*, June 17, 2001.

Chapter 4: Thomas, 36

1. Etan Thomas, *More Than an Athlete: Poems by Etan Thomas* (Atlanta: Moore Black Press, 2005).

2. Dave Zirin, *What's My Name, Fool? Sports and Resistance in the United States* (Chicago: Haymarket Books, 2005), 69.

3. Ibid., 86.

4. Ibid., 100.

5. Michael Lee, "New Dress Code Draws a Few Threads of Protest," *Washington Post*, October 20, 2005.

6. Todd Boyd, *Young Black Rich & Famous: The Rise of the NBA, The Hip Hop Invasion and the Transformation of American Culture* (New York: Doubleday, 2003).

7. Zirin, 164.

8. Peter Vecsey, "Dress for Distress," *New York Post*, October 21, 2005.

9. Thomas, "Courting More Than Just Basketball," *Washington Post*, November 20, 2005.

10. Donna Ditota, "Former SU Star Focuses on the Court, and on His Causes When the Game Is Through," *Syracuse Post-Standard*, November 27, 2005.

11. Ivan Carter, "Wizards End Skid, Help Arenas Rest Assured," *Washington Post*, December 14, 2005.

12. Roscoe Nance, "Wizards Score One Without a Star," *USA Today*, December 14, 2005.

Chapter 5: Hip-Hop

1. Karrine Steffans, *Confessions of a Video Vixen* (New York: Amistad, 2005), xiv.
2. www.panachereport.com/website%20channel%20documents/ hip%20hop%20gallery/HipHopShortStories/Karrine%20(Supe rhead)%20Interview2.htm.
3. Gwendolyn D. Pough, *Check It While I Wreck It: Black Womanhood, Hip-Hop Culture, and the Public Sphere* (Boston: Northeastern University Press, 2004), 170–71.
4. *Essence*, January 2005.

Chapter 6: The Pole Test

1. Chris Rock, *Never Scared*, DVD (HBO Home Video, 2004).

Chapter 7: Babydaddy

1. *Jet,* February 28, 2005, 37.
2. Grant Wahl and Jon Wertheim, "Paternity Ward," *Sports Illustrated,* May 4, 1998.
3. Geneva Smitherman, *Black Talk: Words and Phrases from the Hood to the Amen Corner* (New York: Houghton Mifflin Company, 1999).
4. Martin Brady, "Agent Provocateur," *Northwestern*, Winter 2004, 30.
5. Leah Y. Latimer, "Not Married With Children," *Crisis*, September/ October 2003.
6. "Racial and Ethnic Differences in Marriage among New, Unwed Parents," Fragile Families Research Brief, Bendheim-Thoman Center for Research on Child Wellbeing, Princeton University; Social Indicators Survey Center, Columbia University, July 2004.

7. "Trends in nonmarital childbearing by race and Hispanic origin, 1970–2003," National Center for Health Statistics, www.cdc.gov/ nchs/data/hus/hus05.pdf#010.

8. "Preliminary Births for 2004," National Center for Health Statistics, www.cdc.gov/nchs/data/hestat/prelimbirth04_tables.pdf.

9. Edward O. Laumann, et al., eds, *The Sexual Organization of the City* (Chicago: University of Chicago Press, 2004), 178–179.

10. Kathryn Edin and Maria Kefalas, *Promises I Can Keep: Why Poor Women Choose Motherhood Over Marriage* (Berkeley and Los Angeles: University of California Press, 2005), 111.

11. Ibid., 127.

12. Ibid., 140.

13. U.S. Census Bureau, Current Population Survey, 2003 Annual Social and Economic Supplement.

14. Laumann, 187.

Chapter 8: Tyrone at Work

1. Ellis Cose, *The Rage of a Privileged Class* (New York: Harper-Collins, 1993), 74.

2. Ewing Marion Kauffman Foundation, *The Entrepreneur Next Door: Characteristics of Individuals Starting Companies in America* (Kansas City, MO.: Kaufmann Foundation, 2002).

3. Cora Daniels, *Black Power Inc. The New Voice of Success* (Hoboken, NJ: John Wiley & Sons, 2004), 161.

4. Ibid., 196.

Chapter 9: Boy Born Friday

1. Rob Schneider, et al., "The Motive: Robbery for Rent," *Indianapolis Star*, March 19, 1994.

2. Police transcript, Hamilton County Sheriff's Department, statement by James Walls to Officers Nickel and M. Russell, March 17, 1994.

3. Police transcript, Hamilton County Sheriff's Department, statement by Raymond Adams, March 17, 1994.

4. Police transcript, Hamilton County Sheriff's Department, statement by county jail inmates Larry Williams and Aaron Allred to Detective Jowitt, July 1994. Williams and Allred stated that their cellmate Raymond Adams admitted to the murders and asked Williams, who was being released, to return to the apartment to retrieve a stash of marijuana.

5. Rob Schneider and Karen Murphy, "Sudden Deal: Ajabu Won't Face Death," *Indianapolis Star*, August 31, 1995.

6. Rick Callahan, "Jury Rejects Police Claim Handcuffed Suspect Shot Himself," *Associated Press*, March 21, 1996.

7. Police transcript, Hamilton County Sheriff's Department, statement by Eric Johnson to police about his former roommate Raymond Adams.

8. Police transcript, Hamilton County Sheriff's Department, statement by D'Artagnan Partee, roommate of Kofi Ajabu, March 1994.

9. Police transcript, Hamilton County Sheriff's Department, statement by Karen Kennelly, girlfriend of victim Nick Allemenos, March 17, 1994.

10. Police statement by D'Artagnan Partee.

11. Police transcript, Hamilton County Sheriff's Department, statement by Kofi Modibo Ajabu, March 17, 1994.

12. Ibid.

13. Ibid.

14. Walls, statement to police. Walls was the codefendant who pointed to Raymond Adams as the murderer.

15. John Flora, "Walls May Drop 'Bombshell': Murder Defendant Points to Fourth Accomplice," *Indianapolis News*, August 30, 1995.

16. Ibid.

17. Kim L. Hooper, "Credibility of Alibi Witness in Hotel Shooting Challenged," *Indianapolis Star*, January 13, 2000.

18. Hamilton County Sheriff's Department.

19. Flora.

20. Schneider and Murphy.

21. Terry Horne, "Adams' Plea Deal Was a Gamble," *Indianapolis News*, August 26, 1995.

22. James L. Patterson, "Ajabu Makes More Threats; Prosecutors Look into Charges," *Indianapolis Star*, April 14, 1994.

23. Rob Schneider, "Ajabu Urges His Son to Put Faith in God, Not Plea Deal," *Indianapolis Star*, May 6, 1995.

24. Janet Williams, et al., "2 Suspects in Slayings Had Arrest Records," *Indianapolis Star*, March 19, 1994.

25. Andrea Neal, " 'I'm Just a Black Man In a Strange Land Trying to Take a Stand.' " *Indianapolis Star*, June 26, 1994.

26. Brett Pulley, "Urban Threat: In Indianapolis, 2 Men Tackle Plight of Blacks in Very Different Ways," *Wall Street Journal*, August 16, 1994.

27. Rob Schneider, "Ajabu Sentenced to Life Term," *Indianapolis Star*, October 4, 1995.

28. Ibid.

29. "Acquittal Draws Mix of Reactions," *Indianapolis Star*, October 4, 1995.

30. Neal.

31. Jenny Labalme, "Insurance Firm Challenges Mmoja Ajabu over House Fire Claim," *Indianapolis Star*, November 3, 1995; Ruth

Mullen, "Ajabu's Home on Northside Is Set Afire; No Suspects," *Indianapolis Star*, May 5, 1994.

32. John R. O'Neill, "Mmoja Ajabu Faces up to 6 Years for Intimidation," *Indianapolis News*, December 6, 1995; "Mmoja Ajabu Is Back in Jail," *Indianapolis News*, June 6, 1996.

33. Tom Chiat, "Judge Allows Ajabu to Campaign Without Monitoring Device," *Indianapolis Star*, March 15, 1996.

34. Joseph Gelarden and Rodger Birchfield, "Mmoja Ajabu Accused of Battery," *Indianapolis News*, November 22, 1995.

35. Jeffery Gettleman and Ariel Hart, "Bush Plan to Honor Dr. King Stirs Criticism," *New York Times*, January 15, 2004.

36. Craig Schneider, "Georgians Show Their Feelings about Iraq," *Atlanta Journal-Constitution*, March 21, 2004. The photo caption reads: "The Rev. Mmoja Ajabu of Providence Missionary Baptist Church in Atlanta leads demonstrators in chanting, 'Hey, hey, ho, ho, the occupation has got to go,' " in Piedmont Park."

Chapter 10: Raising Tyrone

1. Jawanza Kunjufu, *Countering the Conspiracy to Destroy Black Boys* (Chicago: African American Images, 1995).

2. Neil Howe and William Strauss, *Millennials Rising: The Next Great Generation* (New York: Vintage, 1995).

3. Bakari Kitwana, *The Hip-Hop Generation: Young Blacks and the Crisis of African American Culture* (New York: Basic Civitas Books, 2003).

4. Jedediah Purdy, *For Common Things: Irony, Trust and Commitment in America Today* (New York: Vintage, 2000).

5. Howe and Strauss, 56.

6. Lonnae O'Neal Parker, "The Donna Reed Syndrome: High Pressure, Demanding Bosses, Cutthroat Politics," *Washington Post*, May 12, 2002.
7. Amos N. Wilson, *Black-on-Black Violence* (New York: African World Info Systems, 1990), 49–169, quoted in Kunjufu (1995), 120.
8. Raymond A. Winbush, *The Warrior Method: A Parent's Guide to Rearing Healthy Black Boys* (New York: Amistad, 2002), 42.
9. Natalie Hopkinson, "Waltz of Passage: At the Beautillion, Boys Take a Bow as Gentlemen," *Washington Post*, May 30, 2004.
10. John U. Ogbu and Astrid Davis, *Black American Students in an Affluent Suburb: A Study of Academic Disengagement* (Mahwah, NJ, Lawrence Erlbaum Associates, 2003).
11. Eugene D. White, *Leadership Beyond Excuses: The Courage to Hold the Rope* (Indianapolis: Power Publishing, 2005).
12. Daniel Illori Cooper, http://groups.msn.com/DapeoplepassionsDanielICooper/.msnw?action=get_message&mview=0&ID_Message=156&LastModified=4675477558734547675.

About the Authors

NATALIE HOPKINSON is a staff writer at the *Washington Post* and a Scripps Howard doctoral fellow at the University of Maryland–College Park, where she is also a visiting professor of journalism. A graduate of Howard University, she lives in Washington, D.C., with her husband and two small children.

NATALIE Y. MOORE is a freelance journalist who has worked for the (St. Paul, Minn.) *Pioneer Press*, the *Detroit News*, and the Associated Press. Her work has appeared in the *Chicago Tribune*, the *Chicago Sun-Times*, the *Chicago Reporter*, *Bitch*, *HOUR Detroit*, *Black Enterprise*, npr.org, and *In These Times*. She is a graduate of Howard University and has a master's from Northwestern University's Medill School of Journalism. She lives in Chicago.